2: Barcelona – Betanzos
Bilbao
San Sebastián
Vitoria
Pamplona
Canfranc
Logroño
Huesca
Tudela
1: Canfranc – Montserrat
Burgos – Madrid
Zaragoza
Lérida
Montserrat
Barcelona
Medinaceli
8: Tortosa – Medinaceli
Tarragona
Tortosa
RID
Cuenca
I N
7: Cuenca – Valencia
Palma
Valencia
Albacete
Chinchilla
6: Guadix – Chinchilla
Alicante
Murcia
Lorca
Cartagena
dix
evada
Almería
Mediterranean Sea
LEGEND
7: Chapters
Tortosa Start or end of journey
Railway journey routes
Road route (where railway is in disuse)
Disused railway
City
Town/village

THE TRAIN IN SPAIN

The Train in Spain

CHRISTOPHER HOWSE

BLOOMSBURY
LONDON • NEW DELHI • NEW YORK • SYDNEY

First published in Great Britain 2013

A Continuum book

Bloomsbury Publishing Plc
50 Bedford Square
London WC1B 3DP

www.bloomsbury.com

Bloomsbury Publishing, London, New Delhi, New York and Sydney

A CIP record for this book is available from the British Library.

ISBN 978-1-4411-9805-1
10 9 8 7 6 5 4 3 2 1

Typeset by Fakenham Prepress Solutions, Fakenham, Norfolk NR21 8NN
Printed and bound in Great Britain by CPI Group (UK) Ltd, Croydon, CRO 4YY

Contents

Illustrations

Plate section

Canfranc
Jaca
Riglos
Huesca
Zaragoza
Lérida
Montserrat
Barcelona
N
50 miles
FRANCE
SPAIN
Pyrenees
ANDORRA
SPAIN
Mediterranean Sea

1

Sierra – Mountains

CANFRANC TO MONTSERRAT

Smoking in the Pyrenees – Noah's Ark aground – Altitude problems – Cowbells – Jaca's Juan and Juana – Under fingers of rock – Cable-car to Montserrat – The dragon's tail

Smoking in the Pyrenees

THIS IS a book about Spain, not about trains. 'Want a smoke?' the guard had asked. 'We're stopping here for five minutes.' That was at Sabiñánigo, in the foothills of the Pyrenees. The two or three other passengers in the single-carriage train had joined the driver, dressed in jeans and T-shirt, and the affable, portly guard in his grey uniform, for a cigarette and a chat. It was fresher out on the platform.

There was no smoking on board, but three hours of diesel fumes as the engine laboured uphill had made the back of the throat sore. The train had already climbed 2,000 feet from the heat and dust of Zaragoza in September, and had another 1,300 feet to conquer on the last leg of the journey up to Canfranc. Behind the train, strange cockscombs of rock ran across the sheep-bitten fields. Ahead, rose high, blue, geometrical peaks of broken cubes and pyramids.

Noah's Ark aground

LIKE A VAST Noah's Ark run aground, Canfranc station lay athwart a high pass of the Pyrenees. At 3,921 feet above sea level, this was no place for a station, especially such a station as this: 790 feet wide, wedged between peaks that send down avalanches from the French border.

The immensely wide façade of Canfranc station, 1924.

To build it meant planting 8 million trees, in order to stabilise the winter snows, and carving a deep, stone-lined channel for the torrent of the river Aragón. (When Hilaire Belloc saw the Aragón here in 1909 it was 'a torrent at the door', in the words of his *Tarantella*, the song beginning, 'Do you remember an inn, Miranda?'. He was unlikely to have admired its new ashlar straitjacket next to the station, as formal as a Versailles canal.)

At the opening of the line, in the heat of July 1928, the King of Spain (arriving in a train driven by the Duke of Zaragoza) joined the President of France to eat a lunch, sent up from Lhardy's in Madrid, of scrambled eggs with truffles, sirloin with buttered peas, capons with ham and a selection of pastries. They then took the train through the 8,600-yard tunnel into France and had another lunch. 'The Pyrenees no longer exist,' said King Alfonso XIII, daringly quoting Louis XIV's remark made under rather different circumstances.

But on Good Friday, 1970, only 42 years after the grand opening, the brakes of a goods train failed and it hurtled from the bridge at L'Estanguet, on the French side. Trains never crossed the border again.

A deep stretch of the tunnel has since been colonised by a laboratory of astrophysicists. Today, on the Spanish side, the 56-seater train chugs up from Zaragoza less frequently and slightly more slowly than when the line opened. The traveller gets out at a platform opposite the boarded-up hulk of the grounded Ark and walks out into the little town of 624 people amid the mountain maples and ash trees, where the screech of a jay tears through the clear air.

Altitude problems

IT WOULD, you would think, be downhill all the way from Canfranc. But there is a higher station in Spain, in the middle of the Iberian plateau, rather surprisingly on the local line through the suburbs of Madrid up into the Sierra de Guadarrama. There, the station at Cotos is at an altitude of 5,968 feet.

All Spain is raised up and walled in by mountains. 'The Tibet of Europe,' José Ortega y Gasset called it in 1906, thinking no doubt of its separateness as much as its topography. The highest peak in the Pyrenees, Aneto, at 11,168 feet, is outdone by distant Mulhacén, beyond Granada in the Sierra Nevada, another 245 feet higher. Between the two, sierras rise in corrugations running east to west.

Every station in Spain has a plaque of cast iron fixed to the wall, giving its height above sea level. The solidity of these ovals of iron is almost as comforting as the rainbow that guaranteed to Noah that the waters should no more become a flood to destroy all flesh. The wording is as familiar as the label of a sauce bottle.

'Dirección General del Instituto Geográfico y Estadístico' say the capital letters round the outside of the oval. At the centre is the height in Arabic numerals, in large type, breaking the exact line that indicates 'Altura sobre nivel medio del Mediterráneo en Alicante' – the height above the mean level of the Mediterranean at Alicante.

Why at Alicante? Because it was there, it seems, that the project to construct a national topographical map began. For a whole year, beginning in June 1871, the height of the sea at Alicante was taken at hourly intervals.

The spot from which the geodesists then set about triangulating their way towards Madrid was taken as the left-hand side of the first step of the slightly cracked red marble staircase in the lobby of the eighteenth-century Alicante Town Hall, on the newel post of which a brass plate records the honour. Compared with the sea, the step was found to be at a height of 3.4095 metres.

But its glory has departed, for this network of heights was made utterly obsolete by a survey covering the whole peninsula conducted between 2001 and 2007. Satellites have demolished the honour of the staircase of Alicante Town Hall.

Cowbells

AT CANFRANC there was no bus waiting. No one else had got off the train. No one was in the street. No cars passed. Birds chirped. It would be half an hour's walk uphill to the solid stone shelter of the lonely hotel at Santa Cristina, on a still wild edge of the gorge of the river Aragón.

There was a moment to look back at the dreamlike bulk of Canfranc station. On each side of the fat, French-looking, slate-roofed tower, two wings reached out, built of three storeys. Thirty dormer windows to the left, 30 to the right. Below each dormer, a pair of windows looked out from the first floor, above a continuous canopy. For each pair of windows a French window opened on the ground floor.

It was easy to start calculating, just as visitors started counting the windows of Philip II's monastery-palace at the Escorial, and multiplied for each façade and each courtyard within, till the total ran from hundreds into thousands.

Here at Canfranc, the ridge of the roof had a spiky ironwork spine. An emblem, looking like a fossilised leaf, was repeated endlessly: five panels with a black-silhouetted emblem for each stretch of roof above a dormer window. So that made 150, each side. And above each emblem, the same fossilised frond motif was cut out in reverse on the bar that topped the panel: three cut-out fronds for each of the 150 panels on either wing. So that's 900 of those. But wait. Hidden from sight is a parallel roof-ridge at the rear of the long building. So double the number of cut-out fronds to 1,800.

Canfranc 'international' station – this multiplication table in architectural form – took to itself the motto of the Emperor Charles V, 'Plus ultra', and translated it into the machine age. It was time to start walking.

Not a moment too soon. Cloud condensed in a rolling white wave as the wind drove over the mountains to the west, then was caught in a boiling updraft and thickened to grey as it streamed over the mountains to the east. The rain appeared in the distance, above the horizon down the valley, as a brown curtain against the evening sky.

When the rain arrived, the edge of the falling torrents, seen from the sheltering wide eaves of the hotel, was like the curtain of metal beads that many Spanish shops in the countryside have over their doorways to keep flies out. The rain was heavy in two senses: the drops were big and they were close together. It was an onslaught.

When the rain had gone, the ash trees and spruces looked heavy with their burden of water, their foliage combed down by the cloudburst. It had washed the heat from the air, but the martins were soon busy again catching insects in the air and blue tits pecked at shoots. A red squirrel bounced across the path. A cowbell rang from the other side of the valley. Canfranc had an Alpine feel, and in the town were posted up signs warning motorists not to park below the steep slate roofs in winter, lest the snow fall, in a domestic avalanche, and smash in the top of the car.

The vegetation along the boulder-edged Aragón was like that of a Surrey lane but lusher: hazel and box, bramble and clumps of clover, but with rock roses, too, and Mediterranean lavender. This was a different world from the familiar dusty, bleached, broken straw of the endless baked Castilian plateau of autumn.

Jaca's Juan and Juana

THE STATION CAT at Jaca made a decision about each piece of ballast that its paw should alight on next, as it made its way with care across the track. From the bright rail it suddenly leapt on to the platform. Above it, the name of the station in big, blue capital letters without serifs stood out on a framed panel made up of twenty-one ceramic tiles, seven across, three down.

The little city, only half an hour downhill from Canfranc by train, retained the air of an old-fashioned summer resort, with its horse chestnut trees, refreshing glasses of chalky *horchata* and little rock sparrows hopping about the mown grass around Philip II's pentagonal fort.

Jaca sits above the wide valley of the Aragón (where it turns abruptly right, westward), and below a bull-nosed mountain, the Peña Oroel. The stout city walls, on which the scientist Santiago Cajal played as a boy, were demolished as late as 1915.

The well-knit little cathedral, from the eleventh century, struck John Harvey, the historian of the Gothic, as 'restful and pleasing'. Its columns are pre-Gothic, and their round Romanesque bases prove convenient repositories for umbrellas and walking sticks for local people attending Mass.

Some of the C-scroll wrought-iron here is said to be of the very same workmanship as the gates now in the south aisle at Winchester cathedral and as the ironwork fitted by the Crusaders in the early twelfth century at the Dome of the Rock in Jerusalem. One Norman blacksmith made his mark on three martial kingdoms.

That is an historical curiosity, but a surprising architectural blessing at Jaca is one of the earliest examples of high Renaissance building in Spain: the chapel of St Michael, in the south aisle. A.D. M.D.XXIII says the label carved over the arch: 1523. The surprise is how well the Renaissance work complements the Romanesque around it.

Beside Romanesque capitals of writhing stems, like something in the Lindisfarne Gospels, the Renaissance chapel places grotesques and tritons, masks and foliage, harpies and gryphons, salamanders, cornucopias and pink-tinged putti. Above the entire splendid creation, two kneeling angels with gilt and feathery wings hold between them a stone panel that gives the clue to the meaning of the whole thing.

AD·CRISTV PERGVNT·
QVOS·IVXERAT·AVLA·VI
CISIM·CVM·CRISTO·IVNT
OS·CONTINET·AVLA·SVOS:

The abbreviated Latin inscription expands into an elegaic couplet:

> AD CHRISTVM PERGVNT QVOS IVNXERAT AVLA VICISSIM: CVM CHRISTO IVNCTOS CONTINET AVLA SVOS

Or, as it might have been put into English of that time:

> To Christe proceyde they whome the Chyrch hath splic'd:
> In turne the Chyrch its owne keepeth join'd with Christe.

As the classicist, Dr Peter Jones, has observed, the pleasant Latin verses would suit a marriage chapel, and so it turns out to be, in a way. The chapel was paid for by a prosperous Jaca citizen, Juan de la Sala, and his wife Juana Bonet. If it was meant as a funerary chapel for them, their tombs are not marked. Just outside the cathedral in the market square, No 3 is the house where the couple lived. Two portrait medallions on the wall still show the features of the husband and wife.

The iconography in their chapel suggests the parallel between marriage and the union of Christ and his Church, for the arch is flanked by the ecclesiastical founding Apostles, St Peter and St Paul, and the four Evangelists appear in roundels above. Two popular helper saints offer their intercession: St Roche, pointing to the plague sore on his thigh and accompanied by his faithful dog, and St Christopher, carrying the Christ Child over the river. For all its thoroughly academic Neoclassicism, as an exercise in Renaissance art (built by a Florentine, Giovanni de Moreto), this is a touching expression of marital love and Christian devotion.

Under fingers of rock

GREAT FINGERS of orange stone towered 800 feet sheer above the train as it followed the river Gallego through the empty landscape of Aragon. These were the Mallos, the string of tall, upright rocks running eastward across the path of the Gallego, in the direction of the mountain-top castle of Loarre.

It was the most spectacular sight on the journey from Canfranc to the coast, indeed among the most exhilarating stretches of railway in Spain. In the valley of the river Aragón from Canfranc to Jaca, the view had often been blinkered by the surrounding trees. But here the line, elevated above the valley floor, hugged the vertical columns as it passed the little village of Riglos, built up the slope formed from fragments that long ago fell from the heights. The Romanesque chapel of San Martín at the top of the village seemed to sit feet away from the blade of rock called El Cuchillo, 'The Knife'.

The train curved along beneath the fat plug of rock called El Pisón, 'The Rammer', and the needle that rises from its side, El Puro, 'The Cigar' (called in former times El Huso, 'The Distaff'), then over a viaduct and through a tunnel. The Mallos (perhaps from the Latin *malleus*, 'a hammer', perhaps from a Basque element, *mal-* meaning 'a height') look grey against the sky in the morning light, but grow yellow, then golden, then orange as the afternoon sun strikes against them.

These extraordinary rock pinnacles are composed of conglomerate, a sort of natural concrete of surprising toughness, weathered over aeons along vertical faults, until thin columns are left teetering at the valley edge. It is the same hard rock that provides a vast overhanging shelter for the mountain monastery of San Juan de la Peña in the sierra which the train had just circumnavigated in its journey from Jaca.

The railway has to make one diversion of several miles eastward round the Sierra de San Juan de la Peña, then another westward along the river Gallego in order to find its way through the sierras on the way to Huesca. The bus from Jaca to Huesca would take 75 minutes; the train takes 2 hours and 10 minutes.

As the train followed the contours, west along the Gallego, then south, then east, it opened up new views of the mountains and the valleys where cherries, almonds, figs and olives grow between little fields below pasture fragrant with thyme. And from every direction, the shadowed fingers of the Mallos broke the horizon.

Once the agreeable, dirty cathedral city of Huesca was reached, the journey to the Catalan metropolis of Barcelona took only as long as the journey had from Canfranc down to Huesca.

It was on the stretch from Huesca to Tardienta that, in 1865, as a boy of 13, Santiago Ramón y Cajal made his first, terrifying, railway journey. He had heard how, a few months earlier, the opening of the line had been marked by an accident that had left many killed or injured. Now before him advanced 'a huge and hideous black mass of connecting-rods, levers, gears, wheels and cylinders. It seemed like an apocalyptic animal, a kind of colossal whale constructed of metal and coal. Its titanic lungs belched fire; its flanks emitted jets of boiling water.' The firemen on the footplate looked like demons, and the flimsy and rusted rails trembled beneath the weight of metal as it passed.

Thrown into a carriage by his determined grandfather, he found his nostrils assailed by 'a smell of uncleanly and malodorous flesh'. Once the train got under way, the future scientist, fascinated by the sights from the window, regained his composure before the next station.

The last 200 miles of the present-day journey to Barcelona, in the Ave train from Zaragoza, went in a blur of an hour and a half. Ave notionally stands for Alta Velocidad Española, but it is also an ordinary word for 'bird'. It flies. The first Ave ran from Madrid to Seville in 1992. In the next two decades the high-speed lines spread to cover more than 1,600 miles, and other made-up names – Avant, Alaris – were coined for the trains that ran on them.

The high-speed network shrinks and stretches distances in Spain. The Ave from Zaragoza to Barcelona in 90 minutes cost €67 in 2013; by 'Express' the same journey took 5 hours and 26 minutes, for €27. The journey from London to York, a similar distance, would take two hours and cost from £29 (or £124.50 first class, compared with €100.40 *preferente* to Barcelona). High-speed trains invite higher fares.

Cable-car to Montserrat

FROM THE CABLE-CAR, the monastic buildings of Montserrat swung into view, clinging to the sheer mountain-side. It was impossible not to think of Shangri-La. Eighteen hundred feet below, a little train hurried from the north to the station on the green bend of the river Llobregat.

Montserrat Aeri is a station on the FGC, the railway line operated by the government of Barcelona. Next to the platform, at the entrance to the cable-car, a metal plaque gave the comfortingly German credentials of the machinery that holds passengers suspended in the air: Adolf Bleichert. Leipzig. 17. 05. 1930.

Suspended from the cable, the steel-floored cabin heaved upwards towards the saw-tooth ridge that ran for six or seven miles beside the river. The vista widened, but as the cabin drew nearer the rock-face its apparent speed increased, and it seemed certain to smash into the side of the mountain. Then, with a rumble, the cable pulled it over the rollers of a concrete stanchion and it began a new and steeper ascent. The pebbles of the geological conglomerate – for this was the same kind of resistant rock as the Mallos – looked like nuts in chocolate. Sinewy box bushes held fast on to narrow rock ledges.

The passengers' ears popped with the change of altitude. The air, when they disembarked at the top with shaky legs, was fresher than down by the river. A little further in from the edge was the church where the ancient image, the Black Virgin of Montserrat, emblem and patron of Catalonia, sat placidly amid the waxy warmth of a thousand lit candles.

Like many other relics and images in Spain, the three-foot statue of Our Lady of Montserrat was said to have been discovered, or recovered, after the Moors had been repulsed, this one in a cave by shepherd children in the year 880.

The long-featured, Romanesque, poplar-wood carving was probably made in the twelfth century. Its black colour is not the result of centuries of devotional smoke.

The Virgin sits on a formal throne, a faldstool, holding an orb in her right hand, with her left hand on the shoulder of her son, who sits on her lap, his right hand raised in blessing and his left hand holding a rounded fruit like a pine cone.

Pilgrims queued to do her homage, slightly quietened by the notices demanding silence. As they reached the top of the steps going up behind the high altar, they could see that she was protected by a plastic shield, like a display of wax fruit in a Victorian dome. Only her long fingers holding the orb were exposed for a kiss, which the pilgrims gave, then sauntered off to the echoey *cafetería* for a Fanta and triangle of tortilla.

Here in 1522 St Ignatius Loyola had laid his sword after a night's vigil, when he turned his back on soldiering to found the Jesuits. Here in 1599, Philip III had set the statue in place with his own hands in a new chapel.

Repeatedly in the nineteenth century the monastery was laid to ruin. In 1811 and 1812 the invading French carted away valuables, smashed statues, even pulled away marble and ironwork with hammers, before setting off explosives as they left. The 13 hermitages scattered over the expanse of the mountain ridge were left burnt and blackened.

An attempt at reconstruction was interrupted in 1822 by the arrest of six monks accused of opposing the constitutional government, and the next year the monastic community was again dispersed. They returned later that decade, and Richard Ford, the English traveller and doyen of Hispanophiles, was cheered by their hospitality, just before the First Carlist War brought further military depredations.

In 1835 the *desamortización*, Spain's own dissolution of the monasteries, brought about by the supposedly liberal minister of finance, Juan Alvarez Mendizábal, left the cloisters to nettles and ruin. The monks returned in 1844 and once again set about rebuilding the church and monastery.

In the twentieth century, although relations were good between the monastery of Montserrat and the government of Catalonia during the Republic declared in 1931, the monastery was closed down during the Civil War of 1936–9. The monks sought refuge in friendly private houses or monasteries in neighbouring countries. Yet 21 of them were killed – not in combat, merely for being monks.

So when visitors to the monastery see architecture, some of indifferent appeal, from the nineteenth and twentieth centuries, where they might expect something medieval, they should remember that it is not attributable to carelessness by the monastic community towards its historic legacy.

The dragon's tail

THE SUMMIT OF the saw-backed ridge above the monastery seemed the very top of the world. Nowhere else in this region of Catalonia near the sea comes close to its eminence. The summit here is a little disconcertingly called Pla de les Taràntules in Catalan – 'Tarantula Plain'. Sandy paths ran among the heath, a Mediterranean shrubland like the French *maquis*, with small evergreen oaks, flowering rosemary, heather, honeysuckle, box, gorse, dwarf pines, myrtle and thyme. Eighteen years earlier, all this had been a blackened wasteland from wildfires.

Now, the sun in the clear air shone hot, but a downdraught of air kept the morning shadows chill. The sound of very distant traffic in the valley below was less loud than a passing bee. Anchored to some stems were specimens of a little off-white snail, *Xerocrassa montserratensis*, which only lives above 2,000 feet. Its ribbed whorl of shell is like a tightly coiled ram's horn. The snail is endangered, finding it hard to outrun wildfires.

A gigantic ridge of rock, ribbed a little like the snail, supporting trees in bands, descended like a dragon's tail towards the distant river. Although, from the monastery, the summit had seemed only a few times higher than the building, the ridge is really another 1,600 feet higher up, but easily reached by a funicular railway.

Montserrat has more than its share of mountain railways. An alternative to the cable-car from the valley below is the *cremallera*, the rack-railway looping round the face of the mountain to the village of Monistrol. The funicular to the summit brings to Montserrat an air of Bournemouth or Torbay, but, especially before the day-pilgrims arrive, the heights of the serrated mountain are empty, fresh and peaceful.

Richard Ford was struck by 'the cones, pyramids, buttresses, ninepins, sugar-loaves, which are here jumbled by nature in a sportive mood', and it is often said that Richard Wagner visited the strange mountain, having it in mind as the Montsalvat of his opera *Parsifal*. In fact Wagner never visited Spain, but the Romantic notion of Montserrat had been handed on earlier by Goethe, who in 1800 was sent a stirring description of the magic mountain by Wilhelm von Humboldt.

In the long years after the Civil War when Catalan was suppressed in public use, Montserrat remained faithful to the ancient language. As early as 1947 it was using Catalan in public worship and in its own publications.

On the easy path that winds downhill to the monastery, an unknown hand had recently sprayed in English the words: 'Catalunya is not Spain.' Many other places in the peninsula would say the same, as the journey ahead was to show.

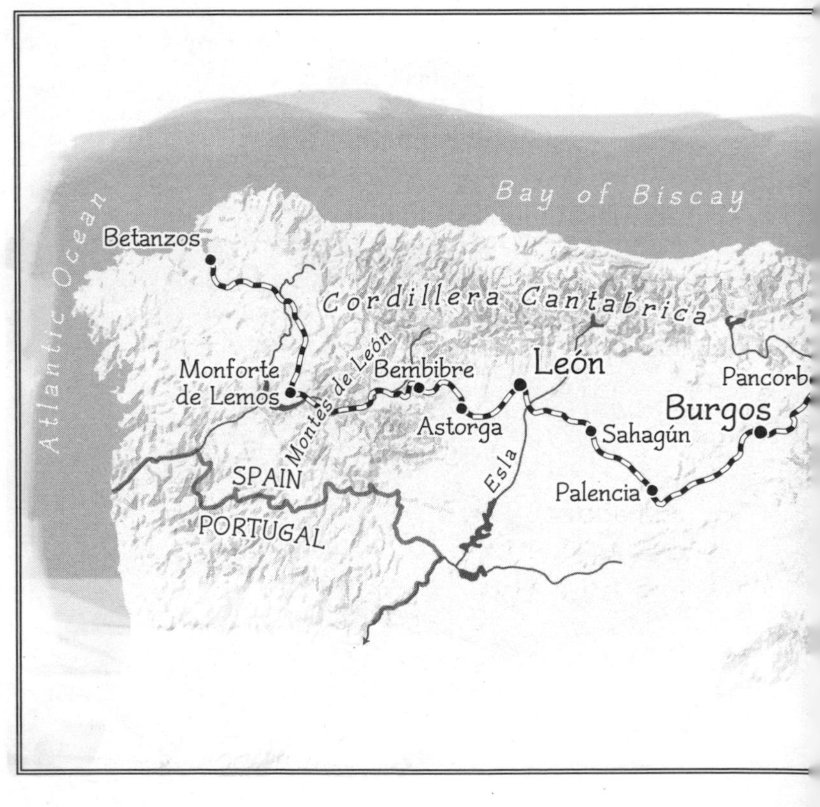
Bay of Biscay
Atlantic Ocean
Betanzos
Cordillera Cantabrica
Monforte
de Lemos
Montes de León
Bembibre
León
Astorga
Sahagún
Burgos
Pancorb
Esla
Palencia
SPAIN
PORTUGAL

N
50 miles
SPAIN
FRANCE
SPAIN
Pamplona
Pyrenees
ANDORRA
Zaragoza
Barcelona
Mediterranean Sea

2

Tierra – Land

BARCELONA TO BETANZOS

The sound of storks' bills – Dancing as civic cement – The wrong side of Tudela – 'I am a little black man' – Dancing by other means – The Son on the Father's lap – 'One of the best churches in Europe' – Horror of every kind – Faithfulness in effigy – Explosion of the highest Baroque – An angel propelled on a tightrope – Mountain pass to the meseta – The shepherd of Sahagún – A thunder of falling bricks – Thirty-four minutes – Mary Tudor's wedding guest – The incorrigible Duchess of Alba – The street of disillusionment – Turnip seed and birdseed

The sound of storks' bills

THE STORKS BEGAN at Tudela. There had been none at Barcelona, two and a half hours earlier. But here, inside the cathedral, they could be heard on the bell-tower outside, clacking their long bills.

The ancient Greeks said that Antigone (not the daughter of Oedipus that Sophocles wrote a play about, but the sister of King Priam of Troy) pitted her beauty against Hera's and was turned into a stork in punishment of her pride. Ovid in his *Metamorphoses* says that she 'with white pinions rais'd, / Is ever by her creaking bill selfe-prais'd'. That is how George Sandys put it in his translation – made in 1621, impressively enough 'amongst the roreing of the seas, the rustling of the Shrowdes, and Clamour of Saylers' on a voyage to America.

But the notion of the stork clacking in self-praise is hardly convincing, for the bird does not otherwise display the vice of vanity, being indifferent to its own ungainliness in carefully stepping on to its nest, piled higher, year by year, on the rooftops.

The clatter of the stork's bill was expressed by the Greeks in a word that covered a range of sounds: the applause of the hands, the beat of the dancing foot, the noise of a rattle, the clack of a castanet. There is to us something of the old-fashioned football rattle in the sound, and its tempo and pitch change like those of a ping-pong ball bouncing on a hard floor.

Among the human settlements, then, over which these dignified birds of good omen preside, is the little city of Tudela de Navarra, which has the same population as Bury St Edmunds in Suffolk.

Tudela, 250 miles from Barcelona, was the first place at which to stop overnight and explore on the long train journey from the Mediterranean to the Atlantic shore. It proved worth the break of journey. The whole trajectory, from coast to coast, could be done in 14 hours, from the orange groves of the Levante to the wet turnip fields of Galicia. (It's the green tops of the turnip, *grelos*, that they like to eat there.)

If anything, the train goes too fast, especially on the high-speed line between Barcelona and Zaragoza. The newly engineered route avoids towns and villages, leaves the fields a blur and makes birds invisible. But even the new high-speed railway follows the same gap in the coastal mountains that the Roman road took to make its way up the Ebro valley.

It turns inland from Tarragona, the Roman Tarraco, where the ruined amphitheatre is washed by the waves, westward via Zaragoza (Caesaraugusta) to Tudela (Latin: *Tutela*, 'protection').

So too, at the distant western end of this journey, the railway breaks through the Montes de León where the Roman road from Astorga (Latin: Asturica) followed the valley of the river Sil into Galicia, and so to Betanzos (Latin: Brigantium) and its Atlantic harbour.

Dancing as civic cement

IN BARCELONA, the day before, it had been a Roman gateway between stout turrets that led into the Plaça Nova next to the cathedral. This was not Antoni Gaudí's fantasy, the basilica of the Sagrada Familia, but the medieval cathedral of Santa Eulalia, with its white geese in their Gothic goose-house in the cloisters and a memorable view from the roof over the city.

Barcelona is a very familiar city to many Europeans: easy to reach, stylish, lively, sociable, Mediterranean, historic, with good wine, good food, old-fashioned confectionery, liberal manners and an element of tawdriness. It is not at all Spanish.

The night before the train left, as the people came out from Mass, a variety of beggars sat before the cathedral door: more than one old woman in black clothes half-sitting on the ground, a couple of limbless men in wheelchairs.

In the square, different groups danced the *sardana*, that round-dance that can be done by old men and children, by sporty types bouncing on their toes, or by old ladies stepping carefully with feet stretched out. It makes the heaviest light. A small band played. The people joined hands. The *sardana* is not put on for the sake of the tourists. It is a means of being civil, as citizens of an independent city. Above the spires of the cathedral, as the dance went on, hung a gibbous moon and the heavy red fire of Mars.

Next morning, the sun shone encouragingly for the newspaper-readers and dog-walkers in the Plaça de Sant Pere on the way to Barcelona Sants station. This was now March, and the plane trees in the street had, in this climate, kept untidy browning leaves on all winter.

Into the triangular square debouched three parallel narrow streets of old buildings with shops at the bottom and floors of flats above: the Carrer de Sant Pere més Alt, Carrer de Sant Pere Mitjà and Carrer de Sant Pere més Baix. One side of the square was sealed by the high, flat wall of the church of St Peter, a former convent of Benedictine nuns destroyed in 985, 1835, 1909 and 1939.

The eight café tables outside the Bar la Candela were being looked after by a figure in tights and pelmet skirt, bright lipstick, heavy eyelashes and braided dreadlocks beneath a tilted cap – a man. This was Barcelona after all.

The wrong side of Tudela

AT TUDELA, the road from the station was not a good introduction, for the straight Avenida de Zaragoza was a canyon of modern flats each side of busy traffic that had left the walls stained with grey dust. Every town has its dull, sad street to the station.

Nor would the heart soar, though, if Tudela were approached from the other side of the wide Ebro. From the bridge, the view upriver proved, in the noon sun of March, a strikingly bleached grey and yellow curtain of poplars coming into bud. Tudela from the far bank appeared low and mud coloured, the old castle hill above the bridge eroded into gulleys and topped by a statue of the Sacred Heart of no obvious artistic value. Below the bridge the highest point of the skyline was the stumpy, eighteenth-century tower of the cathedral, an octagon perched on a square, built in brick, to foreign eyes even ugly, like a water tower.

The 17 arches of the old bridge across the green-blue-brown river were good in their way, though only visible from the riverbank once they had been crossed. Between each arch of the bridge, the road was flanked by a pair of lamp posts, which *said* '1832' and bore a crown over the Roman numeral VII, for Ferdinand VII. But, whatever they said, they were modern reproductions, in '*estilo dos*' – style number two, according to the maker's mark. Richard Ford in the 1830s found Tudela 'a tidy town but dull', though he praised the 'pleasant walks near the river'. These are now cut off from the city by the railway embankment.

The roadway from the bridge ran straight on under the embankment into the quarter where the Christians once lived in the centuries of Moorish rule. Here the Romanesque church of St Mary Magdalen still survives. The streets around were old, narrow, crooked and shabby. One cul-de-sac in the Old Jewry, the Calle Dombriz, displayed a modest row of medieval jettied houses.

Once down the wide street called Muro (named after the walls that were pulled down after Navarre was absorbed into the kingdom of Castile in 1515), things cheered up, for here was the Plaza de los Fueros, which acts as the living heart of Tudela. The Fueros in question were the laws and privileges of the city, by which the Tudelans set great store.

In the middle of the square stood a fanciful bandstand or *quiosco,* like something plundered from a seaside pier. Beneath its octagonal roof hung four busts in pressed metal notionally representing Art in the widest sense, and, alternating with them, on metallic scrollwork, the names of four musical sons of Navarre – Gaztambide, Sarasate, Gayarre and Eslava. Of those Joaquín Gaztambide was born in Tudela itself, in 1822.

'I am a little black man'

THE BANDSTAND proudly bore the date 1921, but the square had been built in the 1690s, to replace the cramped old square north of the cathedral as a venue for civic events and bull-running. At 6.30 on a March evening it was full of the noise of hundreds of voices from the tables in ranks outside the cafés on the right-hand side, to the north.

A little group of eight-year-olds were playing football on the far side of the bandstand. A blind lottery-seller stood talking on the corner of Calle Muro. Someone had temporarily laid his jacket on the bed of cyclamens in a giant pot beneath an evergreen magnolia. Nine of these trees, not yet in flower, stood in a row down one side of the square. At the far end, the illuminated clock-face, high on the roof of the Casa del Reloj, in the middle of the west range, kept the minutes, its bell marking the quarters.

The strangely named Strauss Concept Café in the north-west corner was busy serving small groups occupying the woven plastic chairs at every table outside: a *café solo* here, a *caña* (pale draught beer) there, a whisky and Coca Cola, a Bitter Kas, a white wine and soda, a Nestea, bottles of Mahou beer, a Nordic Mist tonic, Cola Cao chocolate drink.

Cola Cao is a drink that, like Ovaltine, was once made only in the home, from powder. Now it is also sold ready-made in little plastic bottles, which cafés serve, in varieties such as Energy, Light, Complet or Con Galleta María (with Marie biscuits, the kind that have traditionally been dunked in the beverage).

In the 1950s, Cola-Cao, which then boasted a hyphen and a label of black men bearing baskets full of cocoa pods on their heads, entered the Spanish consciousness through the radio and a catchy song:

Yo soy aquel negrito
Del Africa tropical,
Que cultivando cantaba
La canción del Cola-Cao.

I am a little black man
In Africa, all day long
Working away and singing
The Cola-Cao song.

When Cola-Cao was first sold, Spain was still in the hungry Forties. The drink was marketed as full of vitamins, useful to cyclists or boxers in training, and likely to make children stronger and, so it was said, prettier. It was ideal for breakfast or for *merienda*, that meal with which Spaniards fill in the gap between lunch and dinner, especially for women at home and children.

Breakfast had traditionally, for those who could afford it, been of chocolate so thick that a fried extruded *churro* batter-stick could stand up in it. Cola-Cao was lighter. It prospered in an era of austerity and repression, before the coming of democracy and television. As the self-image of Spain has changed, so has that of Cola Cao. But people can still sing the song by heart.

Dancing by other means

DIAGONALLY OPPOSITE the Strauss Concept Café, the setting sun caught the warm brick of the Renaissance church of Santa María, its broad eaves so heavily embellished in fancy brickwork they resembled geometrically braided ribbon.

A group of four women at a café table joined in a complicated interplay of conversation, one speaking to another, another now speaking to a pair, all the time adding spontaneous gestures to the words: a shaking of the head, a movement of the hand, a shrug, a grimace, the twitch of a nose. At another table a mother played with her baby. Beyond, a young man talked with two girls.

A mother carrying a toddler on her hip pushed a buggy past with a baby installed, and talked to a seven-year-old girl in school uniform. Two young teenagers pedalled by on fat-tyred bikes. A man in his twenties with sunglasses on the top of his head swaggered off with a woman with a scarf knotted over her head like a sweatband. An old man in a jersey and grey flannel trousers, with a neatly trimmed beard, paused to draw in breath, his hands mottled and ruddy. Pigeons flapped up on to gables.

The waiter brought a round tray of drinks, his electronic bill-maker tucked into a holster at his waist. Two North African Muslim women, the shape of Russian dolls in their scarves, went by with three or four children. A bull terrier pulled at the lead held by a middle-aged man. A woman in thick spectacles, with a mauve jersey and mauve-striped trousers, looked vaguely for her husband. A man made silly faces at a baby in a pram.

A fat granny led a three-year-old girl by the hand. A little girl on a pink scooter followed an unshaven man with dread-locks and a bandana. A ten-year-old boy showed the uses of the diabolo to his little brother with uncertain success – the thing rolled along its string and flew into the air all right, but it refused to be caught again.

The waiter moved with insect rapidity from one to another of the 16 tables he tended, and all along that side of the square, the waiters of the Diamante ('since 1955') and of the Café Aragón did the same.

The hour of the daily *paseo* is the *sardana* by different means. At 7.15 p.m. the bell rang out from its curlicued iron frame above the clock, and the street lights in the square came on. High in the sky Venus burnt brightly in the solidifying sky, with Jupiter courting her closely.

The Son on the Father's lap

BY DAY, THE Calle Doña María Ugarte had an unhappy air. The street ran from a corner of the Plaza de los Fueros, away from the old town, towards the Misericordia hospital. Many shops had closed down: an electronic office equipment outlet; Las Chicas del Hilo, clothes menders; even the Salón Slot amusement arcade.

In the sunshine at the far end, two black African men stood silently outside the migrant advice centre run by the communist CCOO union. A generator made its constant fairground noise where a man was demolishing the inside of a shop. *Paz, amor y cócteles Molotov* – Peace, love and Molotov cocktails – someone had sprayed on a wall, carefully following the strict grammatical rule requiring an accent, and then signing off the slogan with the anarchist sign of an A in a circle.

The down-at-heel demeanour of the street was not Doña María Ugarte's fault. She had died in 2011, having spent the last 71 years of her literary life in the Dominican Republic. She was just the sort of person to name a street after. But for those in search of Tudela's past centuries, the streets to wander were those named not after prominent people of recent decades but after the ancient trades of the city: Herrerías (blacksmiths), Yeseros (plasterers), Caldereros (tinsmiths), Carnicerías (butchers), Chapinerías (pattenmakers), Cuchillos (knives), Zurradores (tanners).

These old streets were still inhabited, the big houses of the gentry having long since been divided into flats. The Plaza Mercadal was, it proved, no more than a wide thoroughfare, having on one side the back of the Palacio Marqués de Huarte (now a public library), and on the other the high stone walls of the church built by the Jesuits, who were expelled from Spain in 1767 (now a cultural centre). Slowly rotating steel mobiles had been set up on its highest ledges, apparently to dissuade storks from nesting.

An old fountain splattered at the top of the Plaza Mercadal, where it turned into Chapinerías. The streets were paved with setts. Most of the old buildings were built of long, thin bricks and were difficult to read for a foreigner, since brick in England, despite isolated patches from the Roman occupation, is seldom associated with ancient survivals, for which stone or timber frames are the norm. To a stranger's eye the old streets of Tudela appeared grubby, cracked and crumbling. Walls bulged. Some houses were in ruins.

Nowhere was the skyline more jagged with wide eaves than in the old curving street called the Rua, from which all the bustle of a high street had departed. There was something strange to be seen at the end of the Rua: the carving over the doorway of the church of St Nicholas. It dated from the twelfth century, a well-designed tympanum with a semi-circular border of deep-cut vegetation.

The whole thing was beautifully executed. Some have attributed it to Master Matthew, the sculptor of the Pórtico de la Gloria at Santiago de Compostela. It has in common with that masterpiece the representation of the Holy Trinity, here framed by an oval mandorla, as a crowned Father holding his young Son in his lap, the Holy Spirit taking the form of a dove above them. The sculptor here at Tudela has surrounded the Trinity with the four beasts of the Apocalypse, symbols of the four Evangelists.

This convention of depicting God the Father with the Son in his bosom (as it is expressed in the prologue of the Gospel according to St John) or on his lap is also followed in Romanesque stone carvings at Soria, at Santo Domingo de Silos and at Santo Domingo de la Calzada, as well as at Santiago. It has been called an Hispanic iconographical pattern, but some historians of art have pointed out that the model was first used in England, as in the full-page illumination in a manuscript book of Psalms known as Harley 603, made at Christ Church monastery, Canterbury, in the 1020s, and now in the British Library.

There, on the first page, God the Father is enthroned in a green mandorla, holding the Son close to him, their cheeks pressed together in a tender manner, as with the later Virgin of Vladimir, where Mary the Mother of Jesus is depicted in this pose. In the Harley Psalter, the Son holds an orb the size of a football, which may be taken to stand for the created cosmos. The manuscript shows the bird representing the Holy Spirit with its beak overlapping the face of the Father and resembling an eagle more than a dove.

For creative power, the tympanum at St Nicholas, Tudela, comes up to the level of this remarkable work of art. But if this was an unusual way of depicting the Trinity, there was something even stranger in the cathedral here.

'One of the best churches in Europe'

ON THE WAY to the cathedral there was a charming, old-fashioned draper, Tejidos Castillo, looking just the way a draper should look, with a wooden floor and bolts of cloth sitting on wooden shelves all up the wall. In the window was a blown-up postcard of the shop as it was in the last years of the nineteenth century, with the iron balconies outside hung with woven blankets of a heavy shagginess one could almost feel.

The fascia has retained to this day the boldly stylised, Art Nouveau, vitreous lettering of gold on black that must have been proudly fitted not so long after the photograph on the old postcard was taken. TEJIDOS it declared, PAÑERIA, NOVEDADES, and, in its mannered script, the V in NOVEDADES had the form of a harp of gold.

From there, the street ran uphill a little, past the covered market, where local artichokes, so fresh that they might have been carved in wood and painted, nestled beside cardoons straight from a seventeenth-century still life, and the kind of fat, blanched asparagus that looks like cigars raised in the dark.

Then the Calle Juicio, a narrow medieval street, ended abruptly at the doorway of the cathedral. Much may be said for such suddenness – a distant view can isolate a cathedral, making it look as though it has been washed up on a deserted shore.

The cathedral is by far the most remarkable building in Tudela. There is some point spending a little time examining it, for it is hardly known in comparison with the great cathedrals of Spain such as Burgos or Toledo, and it represents a type of building that there will be no space to discuss in detail later in this book.

'I may with safety,' wrote G. E. Street in his influential *Gothic Architecture in Spain* (1865), 'class this small church at Tudela among the very best it has been my good fortune to visit in any part of Europe.' Street, who arrived here on the brand-new railway, declared the cathedral 'quite worthy in itself of a long pilgrimage'. Perhaps he was a hostage of train times, for he regretted in his book the lack of opportunity to describe the wonderful Romanesque sculpture of the cloister, which in any case lay in a jumble of dilapidation in those days.

The historian of the Gothic, John Harvey, praised Tudela for being 'unusually light and elegant for its time', and today, from a bench inside the cathedral, the atmosphere felt tranquil and poised, with that twelfth-century restraint associated with the Cistercians. The bare stone walls had a light brown-grey colour, their smooth surface only interrupted by a narrow string-course of rectangular billet moulding, like sugar cubes stuck on.

The columns soared to meet uncomplicated vaulting. Clear noon light entered from the plain glass of the clerestory and from oculi – round windows, not rose windows – flanking the chancel. Street exclaimed here at 'the great power which the medieval architects undoubtedly possessed, of giving an impression of vastness even with very moderate dimensions'.

He attributed its architectural character to the proximity of French influences. He called the building small, but it is large enough for a collegiate church (administered by a chapter of clergy), as it remained for centuries, before acquiring the status of cathedral in 1783.

Its immediate inspiration may have been the Cistercian monastery of La Oliva, 25 miles away at Carcastillo in Navarre. But there were other influences at work. Some historians have looked to the Seo, the old cathedral at Zaragoza, further down the Ebro. Others have mentioned the former Romanesque cathedral at Pamplona.

Half of the site at Tudela had previously been occupied by the main mosque, some corbels from which, carved with acanthus or geometric designs, have been found in archaeological digs. Extra land had been acquired for the church in the 1150s, three decades after the town's recapture from the Moors. The new church was consecrated in 1188 and the vaulting of the chancel completed by 1228. The whole thing stands on the cusp between the Romanesque and the Gothic, for the pointed arches rest on capitals that feature stylised acanthus, gryphons, centaurs and, unusually, mules (meant here as heraldic emblems).

None of this was visible on first entering the west door, for, as in most Spanish cathedrals, the body of the nave was blocked off by the high-walled choir. This was the work of Pedro de Villalón, the splendid Dean of Tudela from 1513 to 1538, years during which Catherine of Aragon, the daughter of the

'Catholic Kings' of Castile and Aragon, became the occasion of Henry VIII of England's alienation from the papacy.

In the centuries before this church of Santa María became a cathedral, the dean here was as powerful as many a bishop. Dean Villalón was a protégé of the great Renaissance pope, Julius the Terrible, whose arms are carved in stone with Villalón's on the deanery, or as the Spanish more grandly think of it, the decanal palace, which he built.

He experienced his own tussle between Pope and Crown when he came to take possession of his living, for as he prepared to sing his first High Mass, the Mayor of Tudela and his men dragged him by the arm from the choir, appealing to the authority of the King. The next day the Dean excommunicated the Mayor, and in due course obtained a bull from the Pope confirming his prerogative to take the highest seat in the choir, though the Bishop of Tarazona himself should be present.

Horror of every kind

IN THE QUIET town today, the lovely window of the deanery, framed like the frontispiece of a book by a Neoclassical humanist, looks down upon the street from one side of the Gothic west doorway. And what a doorway it is!

Eight concentric pointed archways span the door, carved in deep relief with a total of 116 scenes from the Bible, heaven and, forcefully, hell. It is known as the Puerta del Juicio, the door of judgement, but as Street pointed out, it lacks a representation of Christ in Judgement, which would be expected in the centre, where the tympanum is blank.

Street was struck by the 'terror and horror of every kind' depicted in the scenes of hell, contrasting them favourably with 'our sculptors and carvers at the present day, who seem to believe in no Last Judgment, no masculine saints and nothing but female angels'.

Even so, the unknown sculptor of Tudela possessed a diabolical invention not nearly so common in medieval Judgement scenes as is often supposed, for many such scenes elsewhere possess a certain light-heartedness in their depiction of devils and the punishment of vices.

This sculptor's big-headed, big-mouthed, big-eared devils, though, punish the sins of the damned with much use of flames, pincers and ropes. One man is doubled up and hammered on an anvil, another cut into by a turning wheel, and two adulterers are carried by a demon on a yoke, suspended by their genitals. This last is said by historians to parallel a punishment in hell seen in legend by Mohammed on his Night Journey, though the resemblance may be coincidental. All in all, the images of the Puerta del Juicio are weighted towards violence more than piety.

On coming into the cathedral, which, unusually, meant going down, not up, steps, the first thing to meet the eyes was a large, double, painted panel of the Resurrection of the Dead and the Last Judgement, in quite a different style, inspired by Michelangelo and dating from about 1600. This is entirely uncharacteristic of the rest of the cathedral, dominated as it is by its Gothic form but enlivened by two further wonders: the tomb of a fifteenth-century chancellor of Navarre and the Baroque chapel of the Holy Spirit.

The tomb took a little seeking out, for it occupies an alcove in one of the chapels of the south transept. The cathedral is built in the form of a Latin cross, and on the upper side, as it were, of each arm (the eastern side) two chapels open out. (It is as though a regular three-apsed Romanesque church had another two flanking apse-chapels added.)

The tomb alcove takes up one side of a chapel closed off by a most beautiful *reja* or grille. Street paid it no attention, dismissing the 'metal screens' with the rest of the furnishings as 'not interesting'. Or perhaps he ran out of daylight, for he noted, of the glorious Gothic tomb that we are about to enter, that 'it was too dark to see what all the subjects were'.

The 10-foot high *reja*, which must be fifteenth-century, is of 59 bars of iron, each hammered into an octagonal shape, passing through a single, long cross-bar halfway up. Each pair of bars is joined at the top by a little shouldered arch, each with a further lobe of light let into the wrought iron at the centre.

Along the top of the railings, plain spikes, like those that held church candles at the time when the blacksmith made this work, alternate with others sheathed in turned-over leaves, like those of tulips, hammered in iron.

Walk through the fold-back gates beneath an ogee arch, and straight ahead is a painted medieval altarpiece 20 feet wide and higher in proportion, divided into five columns of pictures showing scenes from the Gospels: the Annunciation, Nativity, Resurrection, Ascension and Pentecost, with the Dormition of the Virgin Mary and incidents from saints' lives. Look at it by all means, but then turn to the left and examine a coloured tomb beneath a stone-traceried ogee arch.

Faithfulness in effigy

HERE, AS IN LARKIN'S Arundel tomb, lie Mosén Francés de Villaespesa, who died in 1423, and his wife Doña Isabel, who had died in 1418. Mosén was not his Christian name, but an honorific, the equivalent in the Aragonese language of *señor* or *monsieur*, for Francés de Villaespesa was the Chancellor of Navarre under its king Carlos III.

Man and wife lie side by side, his feet supported by a lion, hers by a pair of dogs. As they lie, their heads on tasselled cushions are canopied from one side by Gothic stonework, which points horizontally, hanging downwards only notionally, in relation to the crowns of their heads as they lie. He wears a round brimless academic hat of fur, she a bonnet trimmed with gold braid. She wears a coral necklace that might be a rosary, and holds it between her ringed fingers; he holds with his left hand a book closed with clasps, and with his right hand touches his sheathed sword. Everything is subtly coloured in red, green, gold, black and grey. Their poor noses have been broken by the ages.

This couple, touchingly portrayed, would be enough, but above them on the walls of the alcove, if you lean in under the tracery, the people of earth and heaven are rendered in brightly coloured carving against a dark violet ground.

At the lowest level, on earth, stand bishops, mitred abbots, clerics, acolytes. Above, runs a level where heaven meets earth, for on the left the priest saying Mass elevates the consecrated Body of Christ, while a thurifer billows incense, a server bears aloft a torch and a kneeling figure holds his hands up in a gesture we might take for surprise but in the convention of the day was an expression of worship. On the right, Mosén Francés and Doña Isabel kneel as in life, following the Mass, their 12 children and grandchildren on their knees behind them.

Between these representations of the Eucharistic liturgy is carved a most remarkable depiction of the subject of that liturgy. Mary and John are placed on each side sorrowing (as they were generally depicted beside the Crucifix in churches), but here the central figure is Christ not on the Cross but standing in his tomb.

He is not yet risen, for his eyes are closed. He is the Man of Sorrows, his head bloodied from the crown of thorns, his hands crossed at the wrists, with blood flowing from them, and issuing from the wound in his side. This 'image of pity' was popular throughout Europe. A similar painting, from 1532, survives on the screen of the little flint church of St Andrew at Wellingham in Norfolk.

Such a devotional representation of Christ's Passion is related to the legend of St Gregory, who, while saying Mass, saw Jesus become visibly present. Engravings of the Mass of St Gregory, with Jesus surrounded by the instruments of the Passion, were included in printed primers from the late fifteenth century, or sold separately.

Here at Tudela, the instruments of the Passion are represented around Jesus, but in a more striking way than as an array of dead objects. From a beam, the beam of the cross, hang pincers, hammer, scourge, lantern; on it rest the nails and the cock crowing at the ear of Peter. But where Jesus is spat upon, the head of the spitter is depicted. Where Jesus is blindfolded, his whole head is shown in relief against the background. A mocking bystander sticks out his tongue and gives the fig with his thumb. A soldier's hand casts the dice for his cloak. Only the restful tomb itself is shown in dignity, its side ornamented with four green marble trefoils enclosed by interlinking circles.

This is not quite the end of the surprises of this extraordinary burial alcove, for at the apex is heaven itself, with a flock of four-winged red seraphim above two angels censing God himself. Where, in the tympanum outside the church of St Nicholas, God the Blessed Trinity was represented by Father, Son and the dove of the Holy Spirit, here, more disconcertingly,

God is shown as three figures in one: three bodies pressed together, with three heads in gilt beards.

In the centre stands God the Father in a mitre or tiara. To the right stands God the Son, holding the Cross. To the left is the Holy Spirit, holding a dove. The composition is hardly satisfactory, but what could the artist do?

Explosion of the highest Baroque

THE FINAL WONDER of Tudela cathedral is one that G. E. Street and John Harvey do not mention: an explosion of the highest Baroque. The large chapel of the Holy Spirit was built between 1737 and 1744, as a home for the parish that the collegiate church administered and as a centre for devotion to the Holy Eucharist.

But even by Street's day, the astonishingly energetic figures that enliven it had been whitewashed over, to cover decades of candle soot, and by the time Harvey arrived here, those figures that were painted had been redone in the nineteenth century with solid oil colours, obliterating the skin tones and the polychromatic arabesques of their drapery.

After years of restoration in the early twenty-first century we can now see something like the fantasia in coloured plasterwork that the architects intended to ornament the Neoclassical outline of the chapel. Thirty years before its construction there had been a rehearsal on the other side of the nave, with the Baroque decoration of the chapel of St Ann, the patron of the city. Very fine it is, but not so unrestrained an exercise as the new chapel of the Holy Spirit, constructed when George II was on the throne of England.

Its fundamental shape is simple: an aisleless nave with shallow transepts either side of a dome, with a lantern above admitting light. The dominant figures are of the Apostles, more than lifesize. Other saints and sturdy-limbed angels have their place, with dispersed crowds of putti, and, between the figures, swages of vegetation, flowers, scrolls, curtains, ropes, cartouches, clouds, volutes, trumpets, feathers, palms, obelisks and scalloped fringes. All these gaieties are applied to wall surfaces of white, emphasising their rich colours.

To say, for example, that in the pendentives below the dome are placed the figures of the four Latin Doctors of the Church (Saints Augustine, Ambrose, Gregory and Jerome) gives no hint of the exuberance of St Jerome, suspended in space and positioned like a careless mountaineer, with one leg raised to find a footing on a plaster cloud, the other stretched down, the foot grasped by an obliging cherub, while the saint holds his left hand aloft and a book closed with clasps is insecurely supported by the fingers of his bent right hand emerging from the folds of his flowered silken cotta and damasked red silk cardinal's shoulder cape, hung with a golden tassel, no doubt keeping his broad scarlet hat from tumbling down on the upturned faces of the worshippers below. He looks down with a kindly and surprisingly composed expression.

On the wall behind his shoulders, unknown forms like the inside of a giant scallop shell gush upwards, pushing at flowers, scrolls and acanthus curls nudging over the stepped lower border of the dome. Multiply that by a dozen or 20, and the populated feel of the chapel, like a celestial dovecote, may be imagined.

Before ever walking in to the chapel, beneath its triumphal entrance arch, worshippers are greeted by four Apostles – St Judas Thaddeus (Jude), St Matthew, St Simon and St Matthias (who had been chosen as a replacement for Judas Iscariot). They burst out into the bare Gothic space of the south aisle like barkers at a fairground sideshow.

Not that the decorative programme of the chapel is without catechetical intent. Each of the Apostles has a clause of the Creed held up by a putto at his feet. This had long been a convention in church furnishing. Eamon Duffy in *The Stripping of the Altars*, his classic survey of English religious practice on the eve of the Reformation, mentions the common fifteenth-century portrayal, on the dados of wooden screens separating off the chancels of parish churches, of Apostles bearing scrolls each inscribed with an article of the Apostles' Creed.

St Peter held *Credo in Deum*, Andrew *et in Iesum Christum*, and so on. The conventional allocation of the clauses is given in the guide *Suffolk and Norfolk* by M. R. James, the historian better known today as the author of ghost stories. Such screens survive in Norfolk at Goodnerstone, Ringland, Mattishall, Thetford and Weston Longville, the last of these being, for the last quarter of the eighteenth century, the living of Parson James Woodforde. That great diarist did not mention the medieval paintings, which were in his day, as the figures at Tudela were to be, concealed by whitewash.

At Tudela, the clauses given to each Apostle differ from those allocated to them by St Augustine (as tradition claimed), although, as always, St Peter has the first clause and St Matthias the last. Notably they are rendered in Spanish at Tudela, written on parchment glued to the cartouches at head height, a helpful aid for those able to read who didn't know Latin.

Thus St James the Less, who (with St Thomas opposite) enjoys the most elbow-room in the assembly of Apostles, declares: '*Creo que subió a los cielos y está sentado a la diestra de Dios Padre todopoderoso*' – I believe that he ascended into heaven and is seated at the right hand of God the Father almighty.

Perhaps if some of the Apostles, since their recent restoration, now seem to stare rather wildly, that is a price to pay for their reclothing in gilt and polychromy.

An angel propelled on a tightrope

IT IS IMPORTANT to be aware that these decorations were not static exhibits in an ecclesiastical museum. The chapel of the Holy Spirit was a busy place. We must think of it as full of voices, of people saying their prayers, of the clergy reading in Latin, of the sound of chanting from the nearby choir performing day by day the liturgy of the hours.

Added to the voices was music, as Baroque in character as the architecture. In 1759, a great new organ was jammed high up beneath an arch of the nave, with its own gilt framework and sprouting trumpet pipes. From 1773 to 1807, the master of music here was the Tudela-born José Castel, who simultaneously achieved celebrity with his musical comedies in Madrid. Specially for the elevation of the collegiate church to the status of a cathedral (coming into effect in 1784, when the new cathedral chapter also directed that celebrations were to be held for the peace with England, by which Minorca was returned to Spain and the Bahamas to England), Castel wrote Vespers, a *Te Deum* and a new *Mass for Eight Voices, Violins, Oboes, Flutes, Horns and Bugles*.

In the streets outside, bulls were run, and triumphal chariots proceeded beneath garlanded arches while 48 dancers performed measured corybantic passes of an allegorical and, perhaps, anagogical nature.

The regular worship of the chapel of the Holy Spirit was centred on the main altar, an impressive example of its kind, with a retable dominated by a canvas of the descent of the Holy Spirit at Pentecost, and, above it, the Crucifixion. The anatomy of this retable rests on two firm pairs of gilt Solomonic pillars – columns with a barley-sugar twist – hung with giant bunches of grapes and surmounted by broken pediments with boldly striated volutes framing obelisks topped with spheres supporting sharp finials.

If that sounds busy, it is merely a frame for the visual centre of the structure, the tabernacle where the Blessed Sacrament is reserved and above which it was occasionally enthroned in a monstrance for public worship. This was the social as well as the visual focus of the chapel, for this place formed the home of a guild that embodied the life of the whole town, the Confraternity of the Most Blessed Sacrament.

Flanking the altar where the Blessed Sacrament was exposed for worship there are, against the end walls of the shallow transepts, two concentrated exercises in Baroque devotion. One is a retable framing a dark canvas of the Virgin Mary and St John beside Christ on the Cross, whose body is rendered in relief, projecting from the flat canvas. This retable is distinguished by burning gilt Corinthian pillars and scrollwork against a black background.

Opposite is the retable of the altar of the Immaculate Conception, with a statue of the Virgin Mary at its centre. Here the theme is encrusted giltwork around wreathed, gilt Corinthian columns, the whole having a bright background of small red, blue and green blotches, like some Florentine sweetmeat, perhaps imitating marble, but achieving an effect at a distance of undefined richness.

It might sound strange that the Confraternity of the Most Blessed Sacrament should have at its cultic heart a statue of the Virgin Mary. But the statue played and still plays its part in Tudela's remarkable annual public display of Eucharistic devotion. On Easter Sunday morning, the Blessed Sacrament is carried in procession through the streets, with this statue of the Virgin Mary carried before it, still veiled in black for sorrow at the death of her Son.

When the procession reaches the Plaza de los Fueros (or until 1851, the Plaza Vieja outside the cathedral), a child dressed as an angel is propelled by a pulley along a high tightrope (on the same principle as the *volo dell'angelo* from the campanile of St Mark's during the Venice carnival), to remove the mourning veil of the Virgin and announce: 'Rejoice, Mary for your Son has risen again'.

Mountain pass to the meseta

IT IS 175 miles from Tudela to Sahagún as the stork flies. The train had taken five hours, preferring to keep to the river valleys, and zig-zagging between cities as they were originally linked up by rail in the nineteenth century.

It went as far north as Pamplona in Navarre and Vitoria in the Basque Country, then south-west, out of the Ebro valley into the wide basin of the Duero, to Burgos and further south to Palencia, before heading north-west towards León, stopping here at Sahagún on the way. It was a different world from the territory of Tudela that had half looked towards Zaragoza and beyond it to the almond groves of the Levante.

Pamplona, with its signs in Basque (*irteera* for *salida*, 'exit'; *kafetegia* for *cafetería*) was a milestone of change, for it stood among rounded hills covered in green grass, unlike the barren shelves of land, the *páramos* above the Ebro, where any grass is dry and white in March, growing in tufts separated by bare land eaten into by infrequent rains and constant wind.

Here at Pamplona, the houses were topped with pitched roofs of red tile. There had been green wheat shooting near Tudela, with vines and fruit trees near the river, but an hour away to the north, deciduous trees were thriving even on the ridges above the river.

Part of the true watershed between the rivers that flow into the Mediterranean and the rivers that flow into the Atlantic came just west of the spectacular Pancorbo pass. Here the river Oroncillo, unseen from the train, has cut a deep, narrow defile into the mountains like a saw into wood. For hundreds of years it was the entry from Europe itself into the meseta of Castile.

'For myself, the passage through Pancorbo is the moment of conversion', wrote V. S. Pritchett. 'Now one meets Spain, the indifferent enemy. Out of this clear, rare air the sun seems to strike, the senses become sharper, the heart and mind are excited.' Pritchett felt the walls of rock of the pass close in here, for there was hardly room for the old road to find a way beside the river though the sheer gate of stone, and the railway had to duck in and out of short tunnels.

The church tower of Pancorbo is pressed towards the dinosaur ridge of the mountain. The 500 souls who inhabit the old village are squashed into tall houses, with arches of stone and great beams supporting walls of mud brick.

This is the route taken by Trevor Rowe in 1965 on a fortnight's holiday, described in his minor classic *Railway Holiday in Spain*. It contains much germane and accurate information about trains, but its real achievement is to turn Spain on its head and see it principally as a network of railways. Food, love, labour, architecture and art disappear into a dim background, and the light falls on 4-8-4s and engine sheds.

Rowe ticked off the viaduct at Pancorbo and noted that it had been depicted on the five-peseta postage stamp issued in 1948 to commemorate the centenary of Spanish railways. When the train reached Burgos he just found time for a 'quick visit to the small shed where locomotives of class 140 2505-26 are to be seen'. These were built by Babcock & Wilcox, Bilbao, between 1927 and 1929. 'Unfortunately, there is not time to visit the attractive city of Burgos', he adds, 'although the towers of the fine Gothic cathedral can be seen from the station.'

So they can, on the far side of the river Arlanzón. Further particulars can be found in *A Pilgrim in Spain* by Christopher Howse (2011). The train did not wait, but set off to follow the river westward among the pollarded willows that fringe the water and the mistletoe growing in airy balls on the boughs of the trees. Another 60 miles on, at Palencia, the track turned to the north-west to run endlessly across the miles of empty dry meseta to Sahagún.

The shepherd of Sahagún

THE BIGGEST CROWD in Sahagún was on the narrow, old stone bridge over the river Cea. The flock of sheep filled the road, as they trotted, their bony heads nodding horizontally as smoothly as the piston of some stationary steam engine. Two hundred sheep and lambs, the most ragged specimens limping at the end, swept past the pedestrian bays along the parapet above the cutwaters of the bridge.

The ruddy-faced shepherd in straw hat and overalls, carrying a simple cloth bag, said nothing but '*Hola*' as he went by, two dogs at his feet. The flock raised a cloud of dust as they hurried westward on the way that leads to Santiago beneath the poplar trees.

The very lamp posts here had the pilgrim emblems of the scallop shell. On the highest ridge of land in the town stood La Peregrina, the church of a former Franciscan convent, where the seventeenth-century polychromatic statue of the Virgin Mary is dressed as a pilgrim and holds a staff with a gourd-bottle attached, and topped, for devotional reasons, with a cross.

Some scientists from Bradford have blamed the lichen *Diploschistes scruposus* for eating into the thirteenth-century masonry here and spoiling its murals. At Santiago de Compostela, La Peregrina's assumed destination, the yellow-brown lichen *Xanthoria parietina* used to be credited with protecting the granite walls and pinnacles, but stone-eating acids have been extracted from this organism too. Five million euros had recently been spent on the restoration of La Peregrina, not all to repair lichen damage, and the local paper optimistically expected a surge of tourism to see the results.

Outside the church, brambles and teasels grew at the edges of the open fields and another kind of bright yellow lichen stained the trunks and boughs of the poplars, without obvious damage. A road sign pointing westward to Joarilla de las Matas had been edited by some wag with a spray can to 'Joarilla de Tomate'. A school of gnats danced in the evening air above the reeds.

The river Cea runs south on the west side of Sahagún. On the east side of the town the river Valderaduey runs in parallel, the two never meeting until their waters mix in the Duero, 70 miles on. The water of the rivers is welcome in this wheat-growing area, where the annual rain of between 16 and 28 inches is undependable. The biggest building in the town, higher than the famous Romanesque towers, bulkier than the bullring, is the grain silo near the station.

But agriculture is not enough to keep the people here. The population of less than 3,000, much fewer than in the Middle Ages, is ageing, as younger people leave for jobs, if they can find them, in León or in Palencia to the south, for Sahagún stands on the very southern edge of the province of Leon.

A thunder of falling bricks

AT SAHAGUN the warm and joky woman in the tobacconist's said: 'No, let me put the stamps for your postcards in a bag or you'll lose them'. The postcards showed the remarkable tower of San Tirso. This is the oldest Mudéjar church in Spain, the work of craftsmen whose ancestors had learnt their skills under Moorish rule.

The Christians who had stayed, on sufferance, under the Moors were called *mozárabes* (from the Arabic word meaning 'like an Arab'); the Moors who stayed, on sufferance, after the reconquest were called *mudéjares* (from the Arabic words meaning 'permitted to remain'). There was a pejorative element in both names.

Sahagún was the town where King Alfonso VI began his campaign to replace the Mozarabic liturgy with the Roman liturgy. Both, it should be realised, were conducted in Latin (though Richard Ford was under the illusion that the Mozarabic rite was in the vernacular). The Roman liturgy went together with the monasticism of Cluny that the king imported from France at the same time.

In 1080 Bernard de Sedirac from Cluny became abbot of Alfonso's refounded monastery at Sahagún, dedicated to Saints Facundus and Primitivus, reputed to have been martyred here in about 300. (From St Facundus – San Fagunt in the vulgar tongue – came the place name Sahagún.) Abbot Bernard was made Archbishop of Toledo, after its reconquest in 1085, and primate of Spain.

Stand outside the east end of the church of San Tirso, near the ruins of the monastery, and what you see is a triple apse in the Romanesque idiom. The lower courses are of squared masonry, laid about 1170. Everything above is in brick, the long, thin brick of a kind familiar from Tudela. The church was finished by 1200, so the construction was contemporaneous with the collegiate church at Tudela, but with no hint of Gothic here.

The tower is fat and tall, like a giant domestic chimney stack, pierced by round-headed arches in three storeys above the roof-line: four wide arches supported on columns for the first storey, with six narrower arches for the storey above and seven arches in the brickwork of the top storey, below the eaves of the tiled tower-roof. It looks tremendously heavy, and strong.

But at ten o'clock on the night of 29 February 1948, the tower fell, crushing the chancel within. The fall cut off the town's electricity supply, and Sahagún was enveloped in a fine dust in pitch darkness. Yet while it was still night, the townspeople dug out of the ruins the metal ciborium in which the Blessed Sacrament was reserved in the buried tabernacle, and a procession set off through the dark by the light of burning torches to provide reverent refuge for the ciborium in the church of San Lorenzo.

By 1960, the tower of San Tirso had been rebuilt in replica as exact as that of the brick campanile of St Mark's Venice after its own sudden fall in 1902.

San Lorenzo has an even more massive tower than San Tirso, square in plan where San Tirso's is rectangular, and tapering slightly as it rises. This church too is built of brick, with the same attractive blind arcading on the exterior of its triple apse. The tower of San Lorenzo still stands, but part of the south wall of the nave has collapsed and is held up by vertical props of wood inside and a row of timber buttresses outside.

San Lorenzo, Sahagún, drawn by Salvador de Azpiazu, 1927.

'It's been two years and they promised money, and nothing has been done', said a woman standing at the porch. A notice on the door of the chemist's in the high street advertised a public meeting to protest at the unforthcoming funds.

In the little Plaza Mayor, where children were playing, the seats outside the best bar, El Ruedo, were crowded. Inside a mother was dandling her toddler on her knee, singing to it, sometimes lifting it up and kissing it. On the large-screen television behind them, a matador was making rather a poor job of finishing off a bull.

Twice his sword fell out of its back. Then he plunged it in to the hilt, but perhaps not quite in the right place, for the bull, having fallen to its knees, made repeated efforts to get up again. The attendant *puntillero* gave the creature a coup de grace in the neck with his short knife.

Downstairs at 10 p.m. in the windowless *comedor*, cheered by ochre plasterwork, only a man and a woman were dining as a football match played on the television on a bracket high on the wall. They ate a plate of *jamón,* then a leg of lamb. There were kidneys on the menu too, a dozen or two from milk-lambs, served in an earthenware dish, cooked with diced garlic and eaten with fresh bread, elastic, with a crisp, dark, heavy crust. By 11 o'clock the town was empty under the bright stars.

Thirty-four minutes

THE TRAIN crossed the Montes de León, between the stations of Astorga and Ponferrada, seeming to seek out by sallies and roundabout diversions a narrow pass that was old when the Romans came. The four-hour journey had begun at Sahagún, in the Kingdom of Leon, and was to end at Monforte de Lemos, in the autonomous community of Galicia.

A long train journey has a regularity of movement combined with occasionally arresting sights that cannot be conveyed in writing, otherwise the reader, like the traveller, would periodically succumb to sleep. But here are 34 minutes of the ride, between Astorga and Bembibre, a distance of 30 miles, as the train chugged up over the watershed on the afternoon of 13 March 2012.

3.07 The train labours uphill from the open Maragatería, north of Astorga. This is where the strange, separate folk, the Maragatos, live, the women known by their black clothes when they come into town to the market.

Up from the little river Porquera (which flows south, towards the Duero) the slope is covered with broom and *Quercus robur*, the English oak, the first seen on this journey from Barcelona, in place of *encina,* the evergreen oak. The oaks still bear dead leaves from the autumn.

Pines are mixed in where the soil is sandy. Now oak woods stand on each side.

3.12 Porqueros station. No stop. Oaks and other bare deciduous trees, with birches and alders by the stream, amid heathy land.

3.18 Brañuelas station. No stop. Here, for the first time, the houses have slate roofs. The broomy heathland is greener than the treeless land we had been passing through up to now.

A tunnel, trees, a steep valley. Tunnel. Short tunnel. This is the ridge of the watershed.

We are now in a steep valley, hundreds of feet deep. Heather, white-thorn, deciduous trees. The steep valley down to the right is that of the river Tremor. This river flows down to the Sil, which makes its way between the mountains into Galicia.

Tunnel. Pines. Tunnel. Tunnel. *Encinas.* A long tunnel. *Encinas* mixed with deciduous oaks. Tunnel. *Encinas.*

The constant pace leaves no time to study the view. Tunnel. The deep valley runs north towards the peaks of the Sierra de Gistreo, its slopes covered with pines to the top, mixed with deciduous trees. Through them firebreaks are cut like a parting through hair.

3.38 La Granja station. No stop. The new motorway crosses the valley below us, on stilts. Tunnel.

The valley of the Tremor. The train begins to go downhill. Tunnel. Cumulus clouds fill the sky. *Encinas.*

A long tunnel. A cutting through slaggy soil. The motorway on stilts runs at our level. Tunnel. *Encinas* and deciduous oaks. We follow the valley, heading west, along its southern slope.

Encinas, with poplars by the river. The floor of the valley is the width of a small field.

A spoil heap. Tunnel.

3.34 Alders growing by spoil heaps. Tunnel. The village of Torre del Bierzo, with tall houses of uneven stone cramped in the narrow valley. Tunnel.

Village of Santa Marina de Torre. We cross a stream.

3.37 The valley side is rocky. Tunnel. High above us climbs a slope of *encinas*. Tunnel. *Encinas*, with sandstone crags beside the narrow road. Tunnel.

Alders grow by the water. Tunnel. Spoil heaps. Cut timber stands by the railway. Many spoil heaps. Power lines. Fir trees.

Poplars coming into leaf, the first spring leaves seen on the journey from Barcelona.

3.41 Bembibre. The train stops. Houses with pitched slate roofs and gabled ends. An abandoned coal yard. Grey clouds overhead. The eaves of the station gable end are rotten. Pitched slate roofs on a block of flats beside the river Boeza.

Mary Tudor's wedding guest

MONFORTE DE LEMOS, another two hours on, was dominated by a rounded hill like that in a child's drawing. That is the *mons fortis*, the mountain stronghold. The *lemos* element means 'mud', or more politely the silt that the river Cabe washes past its foot.

On one side of the hill stood the remains of the medieval town. The stone houses on the lower slopes had the upper two or three storeys clothed in glazed balconies, a characteristic of this rainy region. Here in Galicia the streets were *ruas* not *calles*. The older streets, higher up and now deserted by the commerce that gave them their names – the Shoemakers and Fishmongers, Zapaterías and Pescaderías – ran along a steep green slope, surrounded by walled kitchen gardens and small terraced vineyards with granite posts supporting the vines.

One house had a panelled door framed in a lovely ogee arch of stone.

The summit was marked by a square 100-foot tower, with the Renaissance palace of the Counts of Lemos and a great surprise hidden inside the walls of the old monastery of San Vicente do Pino.

The building had been taken over as a Parador, with all the usual distractions of soft furnishings and piped music. But the central two-storey cloister, although its arches had now been glassed in, remained a most peacefully balanced expression of Baroque classicism.

On the first floor, resting on the square pillars of the ground floor, double columns of pale stone supported round arches beneath the eaves. In an arrangement familiar in Venice, the paved courtyard sloped down a little to each side, collecting the rain, with at its centre a domed well-head, a simplified version of the courtyard fountains in the palace-monastery of El Escorial.

The town boasts a pocket Escorial of its own, down by the river, built by Cardinal Rodrigo de Castro (1523–1600), from the family of the Counts of Lemos. He was the eleventh of the 14 children of the formidable Doña Beatriz, who had married a bishop's son (legitimated, the records note carefully, by royal decree). A great beauty, she was celebrated in song: *De las aves, la perdiz; de las mujeres, la Beatriz* – 'The partridge among birds; Beatrice among women'. It was meant kindly.

As a courtier, her son Rodrigo accompanied his elder brother, by then Bishop of Salamanca, on the voyage of Philip II to England in 1554 to marry Queen Mary. By way of Santiago they journeyed to La Coruña and set sail with a fleet of 150 ships on Friday 13 July, landing at Southampton on 19 July in good time for the wedding at Winchester on 25 July, the feast of St James the patron of Spain.

Philip stayed in England for a little over a year, and Don Rodrigo went back with him when he sailed from Dover on 4 September 1555, en route to Brussels where the king's father Charles V was putting into effect his determination to abdicate as Emperor.

Don Rodrigo's life continued in parallel with that of King Philip, but from 1558 as a churchman, not a lay courtier. In 1574 he was made Bishop of Zamora, in 1578 Bishop of Cuenca and in 1581 Archbishop of Seville, being created cardinal in 1583. It was a glittering career in the manner of the Golden Age, for good or ill: from an official of the Inquisition to a patron of El Greco.

He wanted before he died to leave to the town of his family a splendid college of stone, dedicated to Nuestra Señora de la Antigua – Our Lady of Old – a patron of Seville. It was built in the 1590s. Its founder's aim was to promote by it the work of the Society of Jesus, the religious congregation founded in Spain that had grasped the initiative of the Counter-Reformation.

Today the people of Monforte call the school housed in this grand edifice Los Escolapios after the teaching order that has run it since 1873, for the Jesuits, here (as from Tudela and all Spain), were expelled in 1767. Certainly, the college is a reminder of the Escorial, its architectural model, when viewed from the wide granite *lonja* or esplanade in front of its strictly symmetrical 385-foot façade. But beside this silty river it lacks the truly monumental scale and the mountain-air, hard clarity of its inspiration.

Under the arms of its founder carved in stone, his intentions are recorded in an inscription that positively rejoices in contractions and diacritical marks. Expanded, it says:

> *Rodericus Cardinal de Castro Archiepiscopus Hispalensis templum Virginis Mariae Collegii Societatis Jesu in museum iuventute dotavit*
>
> Rodrigo, Cardinal de Castro, Archbishop of Seville, endowed this church of the College of the Virgin Mary of the Society of Jesus, as an academy for youth.

The incorrigible Duchess of Alba

THE BUILDING remains the property of the Counts of Lemos, whose title passed, in the strange way of Spanish titles, to the Dukes of Berwick and Alba. The 1st Duke of Berwick was

James II's son by Arabella Churchill, and his title was created in the peerage of England in 1687, in the nick of time before James fled the country.

It was James Francis Edward Fitz-James Stuart, 3rd Duke of Berwick (1718–85), who inherited the Lemos title. By then England was distinctly cool about his dukedom.

The 7th Duke of Berwick inherited the dukedom of Alba in 1802, at the age of eight, on the death of the 13th Duchess – the one painted by Goya in white with a red sash, red bow in her wildly curling hair, red bow on her bosom and red bow on her white unruly-haired little dog. She looks like a madwoman in her own waking dream. After that the titles began to snowball.

Born in 1926, the 22nd Countess of Lemos in her own right was the 18th Duchess of Alba, María del Rosario Cayetana Paloma Alfonsa Victoria Eugenia Fernanda Teresa Francisca de Paula Lourdes Antonia Josefa Fausta Rita Castor Dorotea Santa Esperanza Fitz-James Stuart y de Silva Falcó y Gurtubay. She inherited 7 dukedoms, 19 marquessates, and 23 titles as countess. She attracted attention by her wealth, gusto and mischievous disposition.

In youth, the Duchess of Alba had dash and beauty; in age, lovely clothes and the expression of an inscrutably defiant monkey. Her palaces and works of art were breathtaking: the sixteenth-century Palacio de Monterrey in Salamanca, the Palacio de las Dueñas in Seville and the Palacio de Liria in Madrid, rebuilt after its complete destruction in the Civil War.

She shocked the shockable sections of Spanish society with her second marriage in 1978 to a former Jesuit priest who happened to be illegitimate. Illegitimacy was not unknown, as we have seen, in earlier centuries in the descent of the Counts of Lemos, and was the very foundation of the house of Berwick. In the case of the Duchess's ex-Jesuit it had been the subject of an ecclesiastical dispensation allowing the poor man to be ordained in the first place.

Even after his death in 2001, the Duchess continued to receive wide coverage in *Hola!* and less reputable celebrity magazines, with a crescendo of interest when in 2011 she married as her third husband a man 24 years her junior, after squaring the worried children about their inheritance. At the wedding, she kicked off her shoes to dance more energetically.

The street of disillusionment

IN BETANZOS, the town council had put up a helpful sign in English outside the historic church of Santa María del Azogue: 'Temple with a popular sling from old, counts on a basilical plant formed by three ships, and in their interior innumerable coffins dedicated to a large extent to the third estate'.

Betanzos, journey's end, 680 miles from Barcelona, looked its best when the sun came out between showers, and lit up the pale, lichen-dappled granite of the tall houses with their glazed balconies in the streets running round the little hill on which the town was built, closely embraced by the confluence of the rivers Mandeo and Mendo, which flow into the long ria, the drowned estuary leading to the wild Atlantic between La Coruña and El Ferrol.

Stone paving encased the hillside between the houses like a carapace. The town had something of the air of Totnes in Devon, with fine buildings left from its times of greatest prosperity from the fifteenth to the seventeenth centuries. Both towns had suffered from fires, 600 houses in Betanzos being burnt in a single conflagration in 1596.

Betanzos did not lose its walls until 1872, and retains some of its medieval gateways, such as the Puerta de Cristo, 15 steps up from the riverbank. Over its arch a Romanesque crucifix surrounded by the instruments of the Passion was sheltered from the rain in an alcove.

Some heavy double corbels had been cannibalised from the crenellated gate-towers to support balconies of nearby houses, such as those in the pretty street that runs steeply uphill to the church of Santa María. This is the Rua do Desengano, a curious name.

The Castilian equivalent is Calle del Desengaño, as a street in Madrid is called. It lies at the crook of the Gran Via, which it predates, and was for long a pocket of poverty, still being seedy today. Tourists are sometimes alarmed to see prostitutes on the streets there.

Goya lived in Madrid's Calle del Desengaño in the 1780s, as well he might, since he has his place in the great Spanish artistic endeavour of distinguishing appearances and reality, deception and enlightenment. The notion of *desengaño* is an awakening from a deceitful dream, the counterpart of the proverb *La vida es sueño* – life's a dream – as Calderón de la Barca called his play a century or so before Goya was born.

The opposite of *desengaño*, *engaño*, trickery, is the very life and business of the picaresque anti-heroes of Spanish literature, of Rinconete and Cortadillo (Corner Boy and Cutter) the two young ne'er-do-wells in Cervantes' short story, or of Guzmán de Alfarache in Alemán's long novel from the same period. Not only do street boys deceive us, the writers of the Golden Age assure us, so do our eyes and our own hearts.

Miras? – do you see? – Francisco de Quevedo begins one of his sonnets later given the title '*Desengaño de la exterior apariencia*' (Seeing through outward appearances). 'Do you see that great giant walking along with such gravity and pride? Well, inside there's just a framework of split sticks and scraps of cloth held up by some drudge.' The poet is referring, as Tyler Fisher rightly points out in a paper on the sonnet, to the giants on wicker frames that parade and dance at Spanish festivals, especially Corpus Christi.

At Sangüesa, for example, an old town in Navarre, they bring out the giants, and the *cabezudos*, the big-headed figures of lesser stature, several times a year. There are a king and a queen among those giants, and they dance with surprisingly lifelike grace, the operator within, with the figure on his shoulders, looking out through a mesh panel let into its front.

So Quevedo (who himself published a volume of satires called *Los Sueños*) makes a commonplace point, in well-turned verse, that such is the apparent grandeur of vain plans of tyrants, those '*fantásticas escorias eminentes*' – fantastically piled slagheaps. As Dr Fisher reasonably enough notes, few of Quevedo's audience would have heard the word *escorias* without being reminded of the Escorial where the king and his courtiers dwelt.

In Spanish, *ilusiones* are generally good things – the word is a false friend for English-speakers, and usually means 'ideals'.

But for Quevedo's courtiers these ideals have become corrupted from the inside and all their plans are turned to ash heaps.

As for the Calle del Desengaño, a nineteenth-century guide to the place names of Madrid gives a tall tale of two men about to fight a duel when they are interrupted by a beautiful woman who fixes her eyes upon them from beneath her veil as she passes by. They sheath their swords and follow her, only to find the mysterious figure seated, and beneath her veil the hideous face of a mummified corpse. A likely story.

But its name still inspires lyricists, among them Manu Chao, the streetwise, world-music singer, who in his song '*Malegria*' asks María in the Calle del Desengaño for a glass of wine, and he'll pay her tomorrow.

Earlier in the twentieth century Amália Rodrigues, the Portuguese fado singer, had some success with the song '*Tres Ruas*', in which the imaginary heroine progresses from first love in the Rua da Esperança, 'Hope Street', then lives for a short time on the corner of Rua do Desengaño, before misfortune consigns her to the Rua da Amargura, 'Bitterness Street'.

Turnip seed and birdseed

THE CHURCHES within the circuit of the old walls lent solidity to the charm of the hilly streets of Betanzos. Every visitor is struck by the tomb, in the church of San Francisco, of the fourteenth-century magnate Fernán Pérez de Andrade (known to Galicians as O Boo – the Good), with its effigy of the knight recumbent on a sarcophagus carved with chunky hunting scenes, which rests at either end on the backs of a free-standing boar and bear.

These are his heraldic beasts, but it is impossible not to be reminded of *verracos*, those prehistoric monoliths scattered over the bare surface of Castile, which could be meant for either bulls or boars but certainly assume an animal nature by twilight.

Just next to San Francisco is the fine church of Santa María del Azogue, begun at the time of the death of O Boo, and now supplied with that helpful sign for English-speaking visitors. Azogue does not here have its ordinary meaning 'mercury', but means 'market', coming from the Arabic word that gives us *souk*.

A little to the west of the hilltop stands the church of Santiago, with a pentagonal, sixteenth-century, town clock-tower at its east end, built of great granite blocks and looking like a lighthouse topped by bells in place of a light.

The interior of Santiago exceeded the promise of its reconstructed west façade. Lovely east windows lightened its dimness, their slender lancets rising into deeply hooded vaulting. The priest, although anxious to lock up after an afternoon wedding, first wanted at least to show off a Romanesque carving of which he was particularly fond: an expressive depiction of the Resurrection carved over a doorway deep within the walls leading to the sacristy.

Outside the church of Santiago, the Rua dos Ferreros, 'Blacksmith Street', lined with stone houses with white-framed, glazed balconies, ran through the middle of the town, downhill towards the river Mendo. A big horseshoe hanging from the wall half way down announced the seedsman's shop: Sementes O Horreo.

An *horreo* is a very Galician thing, a little house on granite legs with a cross at one gable end, and side walls made of slats to let the air through, since it is intended for grain storage. It looks like a medieval reliquary or a pagan shrine. So the shop-sign incorporated a model *horreo* inside the loop of the hanging horseshoe.

The shop window itself displayed packets of seeds desirable for a Galician garden: chickpeas of two varieties, 'Castilian' and 'Milk White'; two kinds of maize, one for popcorn and a sweet maize called 'Golden Bantam'; three kinds of peas, the low growing 'Lincoln', the tall 'Alderman' and the middling 'Rondo'; most importantly it sold seeds to produce *grelos*.

Grelos are the proudly Galician greens feebly translated as 'turnip-tops'. As the seed packet boasted, the best plants for the purpose produce hardly any root, and no big leaves. The greenery eaten is of that of the small leaves and the flowers just before their buds are fully formed. *Grelos* are eaten with *lacón*, which is ham shank, or in *caldo gallego*, a broth of ham fat to which cabbage or spring greens and potatoes are added.

Above the vegetable seeds was fixed a shelf with packets of birdseed such as Kiki Cantor, its cardboard container bearing pictures of a goldfinch and a canary. 'Strengthens and restores song', said the label hopefully. At the window of many a city flat, the sadly cheerful song of a cage-bird pierces the sound of the morning traffic.

But, for horticulturalists who are more troubled by wild birds than comforted by tame ones, Sementes O Horreo also offered Spant, 'liquid repellent against birds and rodents'.

At the bottom of the hill, the muddy wet sides of the river were shrinking as water filled the channel, flooding back up with the tide, bringing a fresh salt tang of the vast Atlantic.

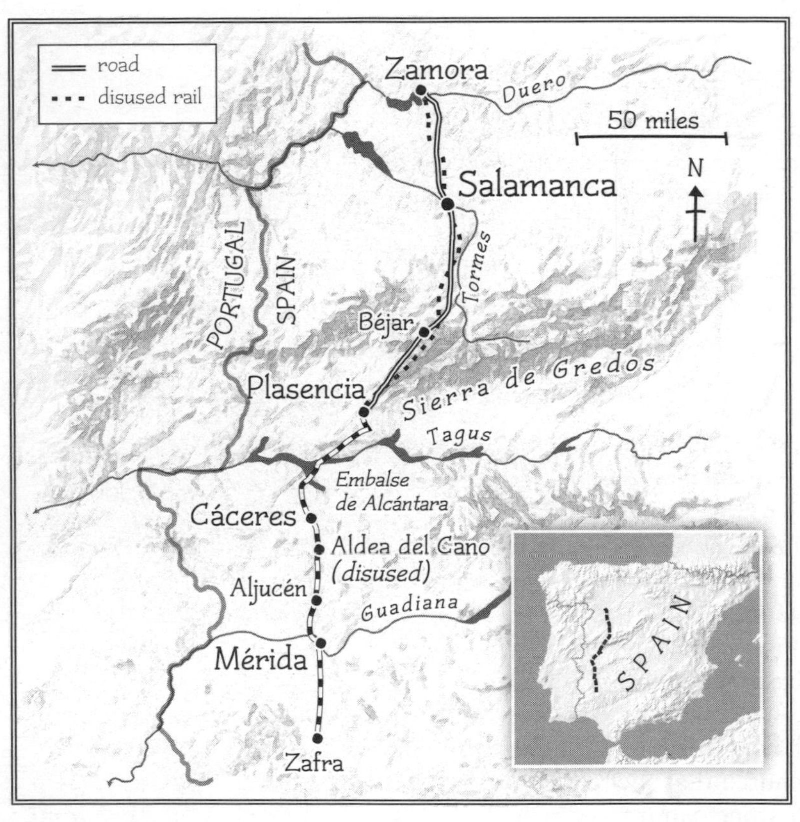

road
disused rail
Zamora
Duero
50 miles
N
Salamanca
Tormes
PORTUGAL
SPAIN
Béjar
Plasencia
Sierra de Gredos
Tagus
Embalse
de Alcántara
Cáceres
Aldea del Cano
(disused)
Aljucén
Guadiana
Mérida
Zafra
SPAIN

3

Bellotas – Acorns

ZAMORA TO ZAFRA

One thing in Zamora – The weekly train – The policemen's saints' day – The ever-present pig – A recipe for acorn pie – A country without houses – Mérida's stupendous Roman remains – The little oven of St Eulalia – Suspected body-snatching at Zafra – Night in a hot castle – A touch of the Escorial – The beautiful handmade shoes

One thing in Zamora

IT IS WORTH GOING to the pleasant little city of Zamora, on a ridge above the river Duero, even to see one thing alone: a tomb. It was called 'the most notable tomb in Castile and Leon' by the brains behind the multi-volume *Encyclopaedia of the Romanesque in Castile and Leon*, José Manuel Rodríguez Montañés. If it has a rival, he says, it is the cenotaph of San Vicente in Avila, a structure which is indeed astonishing. In any case, the visitor can go to Zamora and take time and look.

No one knows whose tomb it is, but it shows every sign of having been built at the same time, the twelfth century, as the church that shelters it, St Mary Magdalen. The tomb lies under a stone canopy supported by three thin pillars along the front edge. The capitals of the pillars are remarkable, but first the visitor can lean in and examine the memorial of the woman buried here.

There she lies portrayed in stone, dead in bed. The coverlet is sharply pleated. Her arms, outside the covers, are stretched out along her body, with the palms of the hands resting on the bedclothes. Her feet peep out at the end of the bed. So far, all is quiet and rest. On the wall behind her something is happening.

Two angels reach down from heaven, holding either end of a cloth, and lift up within its folds the soul of the dead woman in the form of a naked child, her hands uplifted in prayer, in the conventional sign of the time, with the palms facing outward, as if in surprise. The angels beckon upward with their free hands to heaven. Another two angels stand on either side censing the action with thuribles, from which the smoke rising to heaven can almost be smelt.

This would be enough: a calm, composed survival from 800 years ago or more. But then in addition, a sculpted canopy gives a dimension of restless activity. Each half of the stone canopy (in the form of a Romanesque church, with fish-scale roofs, like the cathedral at the end of the street outside) rests on a wide ogee arch. The arches overhang panels depicting fighting beasts – fabulous monsters that the world has never seen.

The two under the left arch are dragons, with fire rising from their toothy jaws. Their necks are knotted together as they fight. These dragons are far more vigorous than the Chinese-looking dragons in the cathedral that hang from the north transept arch – although those are striking enough. On the front of the tomb, the other ogee arch harbours a panel of two fighting harpies, with faces that are genteel, perhaps, though they bear goats' hooves beneath their feathery bodies. Their necks too are intertwined in combat.

This intertwining of necks is a repeated feature of the menagerie of monsters that inhabit the capitals at the tops of the tomb's twisted columns. Who can tell their species? There is a pair of dog-headed birds with goats' feet, and a pair of cat-headed feathered creatures whose talons grip the astragal, the moulded ring of the capital.

At the west end are a male and a female harpy, if that is what they can be called, and near them two eagles, not fighting but reaching up with their hard beaks to grasp foliage. Apart from the reckless invention, it is the energy of the ensemble that impresses. It writhes wildly, in contrast with that tranquil upward journey of the rejuvenated soul in its heaven-sent blanket.

So there it is. Some historians think it might be the tomb of Queen Urraca, the wife of King Ferdinand II of Leon. Urraca means 'magpie', or rather the magpie was given the woman's name Urraca, just as in English the pie was given the prefix *mag-*, short for Margery. No one knows the origin of the name Urraca, but it definitely does not come, as some had tried to derive it, from the Latin *furax*, 'thief'. It is a pre-Roman word, from some language of old Iberia, just possibly Basque.

Anyway, Ferdinand had a penchant for marrying Urracas. It was also the name of his third wife, in the last year of his life. His first Urraca, the daughter of the King of Portugal, was put away on the grounds that she was his cousin, but not before she had conceived a son, whose own son was Ferdinand III – the celebrated San Fernando.

That first Urraca lived thenceforward as a nun attached to the monastery of St John of Jerusalem, which was the original owner of this church of St Mary Magdalen, while the father of her child went to war against her father, the King of Portugal. Urraca died, like Ferdinand II, in 1188, but all the archives of

Tomb in Santa María Magdalena, Zamora, drawn by G. E. Street, 1865.

the church have been destroyed, and with them proof of the ownership of the tomb.

Having seen it, the visitor can leave now for another town, where nothing quite like this can await. But if there is a day or two to spare, Zamora – with its lop-sided Plaza Mayor, two dozen Romanesque churches and fish-scale domed cathedral – is an agreeable place to spend them.

The weekly train

ZAMORA BOASTS some rare trains. Until June 2012, there was one that arrived on Sunday afternoons from Avila and returned the following Saturday. It is difficult to think that it could have suited many passengers' travel plans, although that would probably not have been the reason for discontinuing it. The replacement train runs daily but arrives at 1.47 a.m.

Traditionally the Spanish were said to favour night trains, as Gerald Brenan noted, since they saved a day's hotel bills, but the small hours, *madrugada* as the time of day is known, is an inhumane moment to arrive laden with luggage in a strange town. Yet in Spain, with its wide distances, the timetables do not fear the deadest hour of night.

At Chinchilla, where the station is a long and lonely walk from the town, two trains a day used to stop, minutes apart, but both in the small hours. Anomalies still abound. There is a direct train from Cuenca to León, but none from León to Cuenca. From the southern highland village of Fregenal de la Sierra ('Mountain Ash Grove') a rare train runs towards Seville, but none returns.

Travellers must beware the footnotes on timetables too, which all too often conceal the vital information that the train runs only on 5 January, or on Fridays, but only in Holy Week. For those who have learnt to love timetables, the internet has brought them into their own. Gone are the days when the Spanish tourist office in London refused to keep a timetable on the curious grounds that Renfe did not have an office in London to sell tickets.

The 200 yards of the street running to the station at Zamora, the Avenida de las Tres Cruces, were punctuated with closed-down shops. A clothes shop had closed next to a shop that was offering to buy gold (a thermometer of increasing hardship). A youngish man sat on the pavement with a cardboard sign: *Asturiano sin recurso* – 'From Asturias and with no one to turn to'.

A travel agency had closed down, its offers of Canary beaches and South American adventure fading in the sun. Next to it another gold-buying shop had opened. A man sat begging outside the Dia supermarket ('Quality and value are very near'). Then came a closed-down jeweller's and a closed-down croissanterie. Another clothes shop had closed, after devoting its last days to the offer: 'Everything must go due to retirement'. In Spanish, retirement is *jubilación*, another example of a linguistic false friend.

Things do change. The Avenida de las Tres Cruces was still a place for everyday shopping. The most charming street in Zamora, the Calle de Balborraz (marking a Moorish gateway), with overhanging enclosed balconies and its long series of steps running down towards the river, was a prosperous stretch of shops in the Middle Ages. Near its upper end, close to the Baroque arcaded town hall, a shop that sells shawls, La Rosa de Ora, the Golden Rose, founded in 1882, was offering the best Manila shawls from €78. The label still stated the price in the peseta equivalent: 12,978. In this part of town there are, surprisingly, several impressive Art Nouveau buildings. An elderly woman was mopping the terrazzo floor of the old-fashioned shop Lucio Astudillo. It had two windows, strictly separated by the doorway: one displayed brassières, the other men's hats.

The railway station at Zamora is not far from the bus station. The railway line from Astorga to Plasencia via Zamora was opened in 1896. It was closed to passengers in 1984. Today, if you want to go by rail from Zamora to Plasencia, you have to go all the way to Madrid and out again. There are times when buses, for all their inherent deficiencies, serve a purpose.

A coach sails happily southward-bound from Zamora – following the line taken by the Romans from Asturica Augusta (Astorga) to Augusta Emerita (Mérida) – now parallel with the disused railway, reaching Salamanca, that golden city, within the hour.

Another coach continues further south, up the valley of the river Tormes, over the ridge of the sierra near Béjar (where the railway went through tunnels) and into Extremadura. Then it's downhill, along the outer side of the ridge that hems in the valley of Plasencia.

The small city itself, as pleasant as its name suggests, sits inside its ancient walls above the river Jerte. The walk from the bus station to the railway station is a long one, but seems shorter by the roundabout route through the Plaza Mayor, where there is always something going on and something to eat and drink and a cracked bell chiming the hours. The railway station over the river is the gateway to a new world: the plains of Extremadura, deep within which lies the city of Cáceres.

One train from Plasencia leaves for Cáceres before dawn, and one after dark, but the other two leave in the bright morning and arrive an hour later, in time for lunch.

The policemen's saints' day

AT CACERES, in the deserted and monumental old town, surrounded by walls on its hard stone mound, a road-sweeper in a peaked cap kept a sprig of some sweet herb between his teeth as he scritch-scratched the granite surface of the street.

The previous night there had been a cheese-coloured moon low over the churches and truncated signorial towers, where storks stood and clattered their bills. Now at noon the pavements near the church of St John were crowded with men in strange uniforms, with riding boots and frogged tunics, some with round patent leather hats peaked at the back.

'It's the policemen's saints' day,' an onlooker explained, and so it was in a way, the feast of the Guardian Angels. If they looked like painted wooden figures from a child's toy-box, well, policemen do generally make awkward worshippers, especially in stiff dress uniform.

Cáceres is a city that from a single visit could easily be taken as better or worse than it is, simply by choosing the wrong turning. The Plaza Mayor has the same steady charm that makes its counterpart in Plasencia so attractive. The walled nucleus of ancient churches and stone houses can seem an enchanted survival from past centuries. But the new suburbs that triple the 30,000 population of the old central parts are dull and featureless blocks of high flats, which stretch the mile or two to the station and beyond.

Cold and foggy in winter and violently hot and sun-blasted in summer, Cáceres shares in the extremes of Extremadura, a region the size of Switzerland inhabited by few more than a million people. To half the region, Cáceres acts as a proud provincial capital. It is provincial for good and ill, rusticated but not rivalled in its identity by any near neighbour. Its church of Santa María shares cathedral status with Coria, 45 miles away and a seventh of its size, compared with which it possesses an air of sophistication.

The ever-present pig

THE HAMS OF Cáceres hung patiently in bars, waiting to be eaten. Their fat, dripping at geological speed, was caught in a variety of little vessels designed for the purpose. The grandest was a little round tray like a paper holder for a cupcake, only made in tin, with a spike going up from its centre, like an upturned umbrella, its sharp end stuck in a promontory of ham. Other arrangements were surprisingly ad hoc: a plastic cup attached with a butcher's S-hook, or more pathetically a folded paper serviette nailed on with a wooden toothpick.

The parts of the pig not hung up as hams are preserved as *chorizo* with red *pimentón,* or eaten bit by bit: its ears with a tomato and onion sauce; its cheeks, *jeta,* baked or fried; its subcutaneous fat, *tocino*, added in cubes to a stew; its liver mixed with fat as pâté; its blood, darkened into *morcilla*, encased in its intestines; its fat rendered into lard serves in the South, instead of butter or olive oil, to spread on breakfast toast, flavoured with *pimentón* or garlic.

The pig can hide in the most innocent guise: as lard in *polvorones,* the almondy sweetmeats with a hint of cinnamon and sometimes aniseed that are unwrapped from thin paper at Christmas time and burst into dust at one bite. Nothing could seem more Arabian in their spicy sweetness, yet no Moorish princess would bake with pig's fat. Even a rich pudding dish of egg yolks and sugar with no trace of pig products is called *tocino de cielo*, heavenly bacon. And the best pigs are reared on acorns.

A recipe for acorn pie

IN THE LITTLE restaurant off the Plaza San Juan in Cáceres, at the end of a lunch of salad and then meatballs with flaccid chips cooked in olive oil, the acorn pie, when it arrived, came with a dollop of honey and ginger ice cream. The worry, no doubt, was that it would be too dry on its own. But acorn pie is meant to be dry.

It is not made with pastry and not boiled like a pudding, but contains flour and eggs and is baked, like Madeira cake, and is eaten cold. It most closely resembles *tarta de Santiago*, which contains ground almonds instead of acorns and is regarded as sufficiently Spanish for the European Union to have granted it a Protected Geographical Indication label.

In reality *tarta de Santiago* is chiefly recognisable by the pretty outline on its icing-sugar-dusted surface of a Cross of Santiago, the dagger-shaped cross with arms ending in fleurs-de-lis, as seen on Velázquez's breast in his painting *Las Meninas*. (Philip IV had had to overcome a certain amount of resistance from the Order of Santiago to enrol the painter as one of its knights.) A *tarta de Santiago* without the stencilled outline of a Cross of Santiago tastes far less exalted. No such difficulty is presented by acorn pie.

To make one, first collect your acorns. You could use the acorns of *Quercus robur*, the English oak, called *roble* in Spanish, but they are quite bitter, though the bitter tannins can be reduced by soaking broken acorns overnight.

Do not, say people who know, use the acorn of the *quejigo*. *Quejigo* is not a name that often troubles a tourist, or indeed most Spanish people, but it greatly excited the great lexicographer Joan Corominas, who devoted to it three pages of his *Critico-Etymological Dictionary of Castilian and Hispanic*. He leant to the opinion that, like the French *chêne* it derived from the Celtic word that in Greek appeared as *kastanos*, 'chestnut'. Today, it definitely applies to the Portuguese oak,

Quercus faginea, the acorns of which pigs much enjoy, but not pie-eaters.

No, you want acorns from the *encina*, the evergreen oak, *Quercus ilex*, with which the meseta of Spain is sprinkled. More particularly it is the subspecies surnamed *rotundifolia* in Latin, and called in Spanish *encina dulce*, sweet oak, that is to be sought. It loves heat and drought so much that it won't grow on the rainy Atlantic coast of Galicia. It is an amiable tree that tolerates salinity, cares nothing for nitrogen and positively laps up alkalinity.

So, then, armed with its pattering fruit, make:

Acorn pie

Ingredients

12oz acorn kernels	4oz plain flour
4oz butter or lard	zest of 1 lemon
12oz sugar	juice of 1 lemon
6 eggs	icing sugar

Loosen the acorn shells by boiling for a couple of minutes or baking at a low heat for 15 minutes. Shell dextrously with the help of a hammer. If the acorns need to be made less bitter, chop roughly and soak overnight, or boil, transferring the pieces, uncooled, from one boiling pan of water to another until the water clears.

Dry in a low oven until crumbly, then grind finely. Now, cream the butter or lard and sugar together. (Tradition specifies lard.) Beat in the eggs gently, one by one. Stir in the flour and the ground acorns. Add the lemon zest.

Cook the mixture a finger thick in a greased sandwich tin in a moderate oven (180°C) for perhaps 45 minutes, or until a knife thrust in the middle comes out clean. While still warm, sprinkle with the lemon juice. When cool, dust with icing sugar. A couple of flat English oak leaves make a very pretty stencil.

Try it out once or twice before inviting guests, for the variable effects of the acorns, eggs and oven are so great that some adjustment may well be necessary.

A country without houses

NO FRESHER, RICHER brown exists than that of the trunk of a cork oak newly stripped of bark. It is a smooth, even chestnut colour. The unstripped bark higher on the tree is rough and grey. The tree does not die from the removal of its corky jacket.

Just such harvested cork oaks stood at one spot near the line as the train passed slowly on its hour's journey, south from Cáceres to Mérida. In that time it went past not a single inhabited house.

From Cáceres the train had quietly laboured uphill to the ridge of a low sierra of 2,000 feet which divides the rivers that flow north to the Tagus and those that flow south to the Guadiana, on which Mérida lies. The land on the slow ascent was empty, the railway crossing no road for 20 miles.

If there had been a tree on this stretch of bare moor, storks would have built nests in it, just as they balance nests on both sides of one electricity pylon after another near Carrascalejo on the south-facing slope towards the Guadiana. (Carrascalejo takes it name from the *carrasca*, one of the words for that sweet *encina* ideal for acorn pie.)

In 1996, Red Eléctrica, the operating company for Spanish power transmission, counted 239 white storks' nests on 172 pylons in this part of south-west Spain. Storks have been thriving in the past two decades, even more here than in Tudela, the edge of their territory. Abundant food in winter has increasingly persuaded many Spanish storks not to bother flying south for winter to Africa.

A census in 1948 found 14,513 pairs in Spain. A low point came in 1984 with 6,753, but the numbers had risen to 32,215 pairs by 2004, 11,900 of them in Extremadura. In 2006, the autonomous region of Extremadura adopted as its trademark a green stork in flight with a black shadow – picking up the green, white and black of the regional flag.

But here between Cáceres and Mérida, the occasional flock of sheep had the treeless plain to themselves. Then some black cattle looked up as the train went by. After a few miles, at Aldea del Cano there was a station. The train did not stop. Trains never do stop here any more. Even when they had stopped, the station was five miles away from the little town, with its castle and church and shrine and 699 inhabitants. In the census of 1842, it had returned a population of 1,250.

None of its surviving houses was visible from the train, which shuddered into silent motionlessness under the afternoon sun, taking the opportunity of a length of double track to wait for a train coming in the opposite direction to pass. A bird of prey hovered.

There are kestrels round here, and Montagu's harriers and black kites and red kites. Small birds generally prefer to make themselves unseen, though Spanish sparrows flock on bushes, and invisible larks are heard overhead in the open air. A strange magpie with azure wings is common in these parts and the ginger bouffant-headed woodchat shrike attracts attention when it is found. Bustards run on the bare moorland that naturalists call steppe.

Later, just before Mérida, among some olive groves, came an even more extreme example of a settlement separated from its station. Aljucén has a population of 260. In the last year for which figures have been filed, a baby was born and three old people died. The station is 15 miles from the village, and the route by road goes through Mérida. In any case the train did not stop at the Estación de Aljucén, which properly belongs to the west-east line from Badajoz. There is a train, though, that does stop at Aljucén, one a day via Cabeza del Buey to Madrid, arriving in the capital in 6 hours 48 minutes.

Even for the trains that don't stop, the station has a stationmaster on hand, as visible as a woodchat shrike, with a peaked cap and a red flag, which he holds up to let the train go by on its way to Mérida.

Mérida's stupendous Roman remains

IN CACERES THE WALLS of granite turned golden in the evening sun. In Mérida the walls of houses shone white. In Cáceres men from the country brought in wild spears of asparagus to sell. In Mérida there was lard for your toast at breakfast. A divide had been crossed. This was the South.

Most people know Mérida for the 'stupendous and well preserved monuments of antiquity' in Richard Ford's words. They are indeed memorable. The 6,000-seat Roman theatre, turned into a bullring in the seventeenth century, was restored in the twentieth, with a reconstruction of the Corinthian marble pillared *scaena*, the building behind the stage against which the action took place.

Next to the theatre are the remains of the great arena. Beyond the railway is the hippodrome, 4 furlongs long, now shorn of the crops that grew there in its centuries of abandonment. Visible from the railway stands the tall, spindly aqueduct – Los Milagros – a dozen arches of it still rising miraculously to 80 feet or more. Its alternating layers of brick and granite give it something of a Victorian air, as if it were more closely connected to the railway than by propinquity.

Overlooked by many visitors, because it stills fulfils triumphantly the task for which it was built, is the Roman bridge stretching half a mile across the Guadiana, on 60 arches (Ford somehow counted 81). Its pillowy great blocks of granite, resembling those in the aqueduct at Segovia, resist the floodwater as stoutly now as in the reign of the Emperor Augustus. Then, for the modern cultural tourist, the national museum of Roman art in the middle of the city shows off hundreds of items of beauty and historic interest.

The little oven of St Eulalia

A SUNBURNT, BAREFOOT woman with a silver bracelet on one ankle stood praying quietly before the monument of Mérida more famous to her than any other: the *hornito* of Santa Eulalia. An *hornito* is a little oven, and this by tradition is the furnace in which Eulalia was burnt in martyrdom in the days of Rome, as the classical carvings and inscriptions on the building must surely bear witness.

The people of Mérida think St Eulalia is familiar the world over, but her legend was not much known in England in 1885, when John William Waterhouse submitted to the Royal Academy summer exhibition in London a painting 6 feet high of her martyrdom. With it he sent a note: 'Prudentius says that the body of St. Eulalia was shrouded "by the miraculous fall of snow when lying in the forum after her martyrdom"'. When it was chosen to be hung at the exhibition, the painting caused a sensation, though some found it 'horrifying' or 'bizarre'. The painter was elected an Associate of the Royal Academy.

A keen student of Lawrence Alma-Tadema, he had already made a name for seemingly correct representations of the classical world, as in his *Sick Child Brought into the Temple of Aesculapius* or *The Favourites of the Emperor Honorius*, in which the Roman Emperor is shown feeding doves that perch upon his hand and throne. Doves feature in *St Eulalia* too, 16 of them, half of them white and half the variegated grey of London pigeons. They flutter about the dead and semi-naked body of the 12-year-old martyr of Diocletian's reign.

The backdrop is a façade of Corinthian pillars, more like the tall granite columns of the Temple of Diana at Mérida than the smooth marble columns of its theatre. In the painting a Roman soldier stands guard, and so the friends and family of the dead girl are kept in the background.

Between the soldier and the foreshortened body that lies with its head towards the viewer stands a sort of cross, lashed unsteadily to a stone post with thick cords. The ropes that had bound the saint are cut away. Her hair lies spread out on the marble paving and already the snow that falls is beginning to cover her tresses and the reddish cloth that covers her lower parts. The white of the snow, the white of the doves and the white of the stone are masterfully differentiated.

As for the dead body of St Eulalia with its girlish breasts, it is notable that the painter possessed an unflagging ingenuity in finding scenes in ancient myth and literature, from Ovid's *Metamorphoses* to Keats's *Lamia*, that allowed him occasion to depict nymphs, mermaids, naiads and other unclothed female figures.

A year after *St Eulalia*, Waterhouse painted his celebrated *Lady of Shalott*, Tennyson's heroine who dies longing for a corporeal kind of love, since in her mirror 'when the moon was overhead, / Came two young lovers lately wed; / "I am half sick of shadows," said / The Lady of Shalott.' In 2009, the Royal Academy mounted a retrospective of paintings by Waterhouse, and the critic Richard Dorment wrote: 'His work is slick, professional and completely empty of real feeling or thought. A pleasant void.'

It is not that the Latin poet Prudentius, to whom Waterhouse referred his Victorian audience, was unaware of the earthly interest that might be taken in the girl martyr. Prudentius was born in Spain (in Tarragona, some think, or perhaps Zaragoza or Calahorra, all important Roman cities) in 348, 44 years after St Eulalia's martyrdom. So he was familiar, in a way that Waterhouse could not be, with the civic setting of her death and the realities of Roman capital punishment.

He chose Eulalia as the subject of one of the five hymns that, with seven other poems on martyrdom, made up his book *Peristephanon* – 'On Crowns' (crowns of martydom). A mosaic of St Eulalia holding a glittering crown of martydrom is to be seen on one side of the sixth-century church of Sant'Apollinare Nuovo in Ravenna. At least in those times she had international fame, for she is the only Spanish saint among the 22 female martyrs shown there.

Prudentius makes his young heroine very sure of her strength in relying on the God whom she yearned to proclaim aloud. Her parents prudently kept her at their house in the country a safe distance from the rich and powerful city of Emerita. But she stole out by night and, thinking nothing of the thorns that cut her feet, walked all the way to the city, so that early in the day she stood in its courthouse right next to the magistratc's token of authority, the fasces, the sticks bundled up with an axe, and raised her voice to question the madness of worshipping polished stones and denying God the father of all.

Quaeritis, o miseranda manus, / christicolum genus? En ego sum – 'Are you searching for the people that follow Christ? Well, here I am.' Maximian, the co-Emperor, she declared, was just as bad as Isis, Apollo and Venus, for they are wrought by human hands and he makes himself their client.

The Praetor responded in a gratifyingly intolerant way, hardly pausing to mention the sorrow she was causing her noble family before turning her over to the torturers, from whose terrors she might still save herself just by touching with her little finger one grain of incense for the state-approved offerings.

Prudentius gives his account of her martyrdom vivid violence, in his tight Latin verses, but does not, like Waterhouse, gaze on her body as an object of desire. When the executioners lacerated her flesh with metal claws down to the rib-bones, she spoke to Christ and said that the bleeding marks were letters spelling out a message that told of him. When she was covered in burning lamp-oil, the long hair that had cloaked her modesty caught fire, engulfing her head. She eagerly drank down the flame.

And, before the snow began to fall in the forum to cover her dead limbs, a snow-white dove issued forth from her mouth. *Spiritus hic erat Eulaliae / lacteolus, celer, innocuus* – 'This was the spirit of Eulalia, milk-white, innocent and swift.'

The *hornito* at Mérida is not really the furnace where Eulalia drank flame. It was built 400 years ago from the ruins of a temple to Mars. 'Sacred to Mars', MARTI SACRUM, says the lettering on its façade, with another Latin inscription added in 1612: 'Consecrated anew, not now to Mars but to Jesus Christ.'

Ford in the 1830s found it in use as a pig-sty. Now it is a shrine where flowers and prayers can be left for St Eulalia when the church next door is closed. Archaeological investigations beneath the church found remains of a Visigothic church from before the Moorish invasion and, under that, walls with murals from the church that Prudentius would have known from the fourth century.

Suspected body-snatching at Zafra

THE BODY OF the Duchess of Zafra arrived at the church she had founded there at half past five on the afternoon of 2 February 1612, the day of Candelemas. It had taken nine days for the heavy coffin of wood enclosing an envelope of lead to be brought by coach from her house in Madrid.

'If I should die now,' she had said in the cold stormy days of December, 'what trouble I should give my servants to carry my body.' As it turned out, the journey, even over the high mountains separating Castile from Extremadura, where the funeral party expected tempest and bitter storms, proved 'as pleasant a voyage as could be wished', according to a trusted member of her household, Henry Clifford.

For the Duchess had an English name too, Jane Dormer. She had left London 52 years earlier, the bride of the favourite courtier who had accompanied Philip II to Winchester (like Rodrigo de Castro of Monforte de Lemos) when he had married Queen Mary in 1554, on the feast of St James, the patron of Spain.

Jane Dormer had become Juana Suárez de Figueroa, Duquesa de Feria, almost reigning as a sovereign's consort in the endless lands around Zafra, and then as a powerful widow for 40 years after the Duke's death. It was an exile in an almost utterly alien place. She was isolated all the more by the unceasing network of conspiracy and espionage among supporters of the Emperor, supporters of the Pope, exiled Catholics and agents of Queen Elizabeth's spy-masters. Yet she never complained – except of the heat.

That night in chill February, her body lay at the church of Santa Marina, which she had built close against her fortified palace in Zafra. But it was intended to bury her in the family tomb in the church of the Poor Clares, the Franciscan nuns who lived all their lives enclosed by the walls of their convent in the middle of the town.

The Poor Clares' abbess, a duke's niece herself, delayed the funeral by insisting on one measure before she accepted the coffin for burial. Who knew whether, during the night that the coffin had rested in Santa Marina, the pious nuns might have stolen the body of their foundress and stuffed the coffin with other matter? That indeed was what Henry Clifford learnt had been their plot, hatched in all the unreasonable innocency of family entitlement. Only the lock on the coffin lid, it transpired, had prevented them going through with the scheme.

Perhaps the Abbess of Santa Clara had wind of the plot, for, not satisfied with the unbroken lock and the undisturbed covering of black velvet fastened with gilt nails, she insisted the coffin lid be opened and the lead envelope pulled apart.

> So the coffin was opened and the face seen, which was twelve days after her death, still remaining fair, so seemly and sweet and with so lively colours as if she had been living; her hands tender, flexible and white, as they were while she lived. And out of her nostrils dropped a little blood, so fair, fresh and red, as if it had been from a lamb; which a priest standing there took in his handkerchief.

Night in a hot castle

FOUR HUNDRED YEARS later, in June 2012, at five in the morning (or, because of Spanish double summer time, three o'clock by the sun that would rise in a few hours), it was cool in the night breeze on the flat roof jutting from the castle walls of the old palace of the Ferias.

To the left, the ghostly white shapes of a pair of storks stood unmoving on their nest on the apex of the belfry of the church of Santa Marina, now a concert hall. Far away to the right, above the rooftops, shone the four illuminated faces of the clock above the Collegiate Church of Our Lady of Candlemas (built by a sixteenth-century Count of Feria). From it rang the quarters, to the tune of the Westminster chimes of Big Ben. The great size of the church is said to have been calculated by its architects to accommodate the citizens worshipping there, the space they needed being taken to equal the size of their graves: 7 by 3 Castilian feet.

Ahead, on the horizon above the deserted little streets and palm-tree fronds of Zafra, a cockscomb ridge of rock left an outline of deeper darkness against the night sky. Immediately behind the roof terrace, the pointed merlons of the battlements gave the high, fat towers of the castle an Arabian air. By day, the June sun had struck hard on the thick fifteenth-century walls. By night, the heat radiated into the rooms inside.

The Ferias' castle, once the *alcázar* of Zafra, is now a Parador de Turismo. Today it bears once more the name of the

Dukes of Feria, but upon its conversion into a hotel in 1965 it had been given the name of Hernán Cortés, for here, they say, the conqueror of Mexico took counsel with the Count of Feria before setting sail.

How stifled they must have felt in their high-collared doublets in the tapestry-hung oven of the state room. Tourists can now sleep in the very room in which they met, the *salón dorado*, with its lofty, coffered ceiling painted with heraldic devices. And since the main window of the room is heavily shuttered and barred, the guest may make his way out on to the roof terrace only by way of some steps from the bathroom. Perhaps, long before there was a bathroom, Jane Dormer, the Duchess of Zafra, took the night air here in a respite from the furnace of summer.

A touch of the Escorial

ON 11 JUNE 1571, the Duchess's husband Gómez, 1st Duke of Feria, joined Philip II and a band of 15 friars at the half-built palace-monastery of the Escorial. It was eight years since the foundation stone had been laid and four years since Juan de Toledo, the first architect had died. Juan de Herrera was now the chief architect, and to him has been attributed the remodelling of the interior of the palace at Zafra.

The attribution seems to be without foundation, but the spirit of the rebuilding is Herreran in the sense that it takes in elements of Italian Renaissance architecture adapted to Spanish taste.

The work at Zafra was done in the Duchess's lifetime. From the outside, the nine strong round towers and brown-faced staring walls remained. Inside, a wide staircase of 40 steps led to the new state rooms ranged round an arcaded courtyard with a fountain. Unlike the granite of the Escorial (or of the lovely courtyard at the monastery of San Vicente do Pino at Monforte de Lemos), the two-storey cloister of the Ferias' palace at Zafra makes use of white marble, lightly veined in black. Even the rainwater spouts on the façade are of marble.

The courtyard at Zafra is tighter than that at San Vicente do Pino, being of three arches each side, supported by classical

The design by Sebastiano Serlio that inspired the palace at Zafra.

pilasters with correct detailing of triglyphs and guttae. The inspiration was clearly *The Fourth Book of Architecture* by Sebastiano Serlio, published in Florence in 1537 and in Toledo in 1552. (It was not to be translated into English until 1611, when the author's name is given on the title page as Sebastian Serly.)

The illustration of the use of the Corinthian order in Serlio's book (folio 52 in the 1611 edition) bears a recognisable likeness to the courtyard at Zafra, but Corinthian is replaced by plainer Doric and Ionic, and the arches on the first floor are the same width as those on the ground floor instead of being half the span. Even the marble balusters of the first floor are square in section, (not round), a pleasing tapered shape, set diagonally.

While the Duke attended the King at the Escorial, talking of architecture and the future of England, the Empire and the things of God, it was decided that he should be the next Governor-General of the Netherlands. It would be no sinecure, since the Iron Duke of Alba had met nothing but rebellion and reverses in the past four years. But suddenly Gómez was taken ill, and died on 7 September. His body was taken on the long journey to Zafra where he lies with his widow in the church of the convent of Santa Clara, beneath a stone shield carved with fig leaves, the rebus of the Figueroas.

Of his wife, the English Duchess, perhaps the most touching relic is not the church of Santa Marina nor the grand architecture of her palace, but a little rock crystal cross kept in the (hardly visited) museum of the Poor Clares. It was once honoured in the Duchess's private chapel, while she despatched the business of her vast estates and played off the intrigues of foreign agents. It stands 9 inches high on a curved triangular stand outlined with small pearls. Lodged in the crystal lie tiny relics of the saints who helped her most, and, in the centre, a fragment of the True Cross.

The beautiful hand-made shoes

THERE USED TO BE a train from Atocha station in Madrid that left for Zafra in the middle of the morning and arrived for *merienda*, teatime. It had two carriages full of acrid fumes from the noisy, throbbing diesel engine. Perhaps because of its battered rolling stock and sluggardly ways, it had been banished beyond the stable of swish Ave high-speed trains to the platform at the furthest extreme of the station. No direct train runs today.

On 1 January 1889 the Compañía del Ferrocarril de Zafra a Huelva opened the last stretch of its 115-mile line, with 18 tunnels and an insubstantial-looking trestle bridge 140 yards long crossing a valley, at a height of 216 feet above ground.

The first president of the company was Práxedes Mateo Sagasta, at that time between his third and fourth term as Spanish Prime Minister, out of the eight terms that he eventually clocked up. His successor in the company was Antonio Cánovas del Castillo, who often alternated with Sagasta as prime minister, at that time serving his sixth term, a few months before his assassination.

The old station building at Zafra, with brick latticework over whitewashed walls, surmounted by a central roundel between conical finials, declaring 'ZH 1917', still stands behind locked gates, opposite the simpler, newer station building, white-washed, with oxblood-painted facings. One train now goes to Huelva from Zafra, at six in the morning, but only on Mondays and Saturdays.

The Avenida de la Estación feels very long for a pedestrian with any luggage in the heat: a mile from the deserted tranquillity of the station to the populated tranquillity of the town. Some elm trees survive of those that once lined the dusty road with their shade. Some fields on the way now have had *chalets* built on them. A takeaway pizza shop with moped delivery has opened. This is typical of Spain, but not what tourists think they have come to see.

Zafra delights the foreign visitor because it is small, historic and very Spanish. This is the town that the Hispanophile Simon Courtauld recommends to connoisseurs of small Spanish towns. Since 1920 its population had grown from 6,000 to 16,000, but before that it had been saved by decline from industrial development. The narrow, white-painted streets fill the tight area once surrounded by walls. There are paintings by

Zurbarán hardly noticed in the dimness of the Colegiata (as the people still call the church of Nuestra Señora de la Candelaria, though its college of clergy was dissolved in 1835).

No high-rise buildings rival the tower of the church. The charming, arcaded Plaza Mayor gives out on to the charming, arcaded Plaza Chica. The shoppers in the narrow, pedestrianised Calle Sevilla are by and large Spaniards, not tourists, and they take a morning glass of wine or perhaps decaffeinated coffee (a sachet poured into a glass with hot water) in the friendly Bar Sevilla, or buy ice-creams or a waxed-paper cup of *horchata* from the kiosk at the end of the street opposite the children's playground in the municipal park.

An old-fashioned shoemaker's had put in his window a special offer of supple-looking brown shoes, handmade at a remarkably low price. Inside, the shop had a bare boarded floor and shelves heaped with rolls of leather and shoes and bags to mend and tools and paper bags and boxes and unidentifiable shapes.

The shopkeeper was conversing, of course, with someone who had just popped in, but he soon turned his attention to trade and fetched down a cardboard box with the beautiful handmade shoes. There was a stool for the customer to sit on and the shopkeeper held out a plastic bag. That was for covering the foot while trying on a shoe for size.

'Shoemakers won't pull off shoes,' wrote Samuel Pepys in a little list of oddities headed 'Spain Praeposterous' (by which he meant 'topsy-turvy'), observed during his visit in 1683. Today, customers who don't wear riding boots can usually manage to pull off their own.

The shoemaker was happy to make a bargain and threw in a little pot of dubbin, called in Spanish *grasa de caballo*, 'horse grease'. He unscrewed the lid and proffered it to be smelt, remarking on its sweet savour.

Later, the antecedent thought behind this performance become apparent. For the fact was that the beautiful shoes smelt. It wasn't just a smell of new shoes. It was not just a strong smell of leather. They stank, and their smell stuck to anything with which they shared space: socks, a bag, clothes, a cupboard, a car. Something must have gone wrong in the tanning. The moment of truth arrived and the beautiful handmade shoes were abandoned.

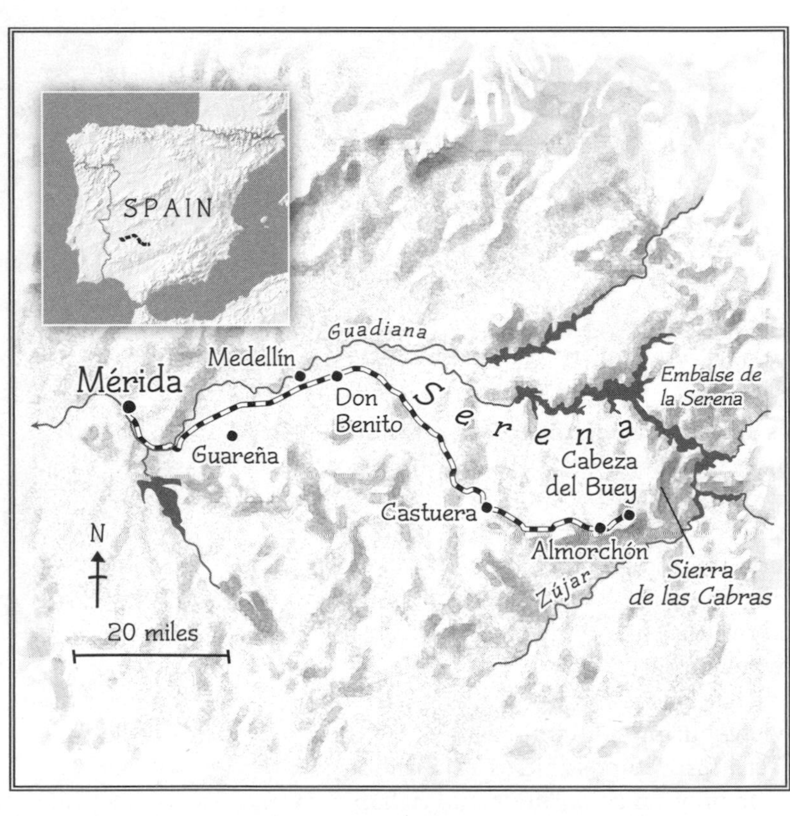
SPAIN
Guadiana
Medellín
Mérida
Don
Benito
Serena
Embalse de
la Serena
Guareña
Cabeza
del Buey
Castuera
Almorchón
N
Sierra
de las Cabras
Zújar
20 miles

4

Buitres – Vultures

MÉRIDA TO CABEZA DEL BUEY

The imaginary Oxhead – The far towers of Medellín – Statue of a conquistador – Through the Serena with song – Crags full of vultures

The imaginary Oxhead

'IF YOU WENT via Cáceres, you could be in Madrid by six o'clock,' said the guard as he made a squiggle of ballpoint on the ticket. Instead, the line from Mérida via Cabeza del Buey is slow, but penetrates eastward into the heart of Spain, up the river Guadiana into less and less populated countryside until, near the border of Extremadura with La Mancha, it passes vast tracts of empty grazing land and follows open valleys where, first the roads turn into ribbons of sand, then no roads run at all. From the window of the train you may see an eagle high above the mountains and antlered deer coming to drink at the water's edge.

'The line is not good,' the guard added, referring not to the view, but the jolting provoked by the unevenness of the track. Yet it proved possible to sit without having to hold on.

It only takes an hour and a half to reach Cabeza del Buey from Mérida, and then another hour and a half to escape from it further east to Puertollano, which, as a former mining town, is not somewhere to be taken as a destination. It does have a railway junction, though, from which fast trains hammer towards Madrid or, just as fast, south to Seville.

The railway authorities are a little undecided about the exact name of Cabeza del Buey. In recent years they have taken to calling it Cabeza de Buey – 'Oxhead', or 'The Oxhead', what difference does it make? In origin, it is not Oxhead at all. Buey does not mean 'ox', as it seems to, but 'gateway', from the Arabic *buwayb*, a diminutive of *bab*, 'gate'. Cabeza is 'head' all right, so it is the head of the little pass or gateway through the serrated mountains here. Its 5,000 or so inhabitants number no more than in the mid-nineteenth century, and 2,000 fewer than 30 years ago.

The far towers of Medellín

THE WALLS and towers of Medellín castle had appeared on the horizon to the left of the train after half an hour or so of chugging from Mérida, on its high rounded hill, above the river Guadiana, like an earthwork raised by giants. On one side of the town, 28 round arches of the seventeenth-century stone bridge spanned the wide river. On the other side a new motorway bridge crossed, like a racetrack on stilts.

The landscape of the river valley had so far been of olives and vines and ploughed fields, with groves of fruit trees and flooded fields of rice, from which a heron flew off. The train never stops now at Medellín station, which has the battered look of an abandoned mission-post in Baja California, whitewashed, with arches painted in ochre and half the roof fallen in. So if you want to see the birthplace of Hernán Cortés and the castle which gave its name to the Colombian city, you must get off at Don Benito and walk back for five or six miles, a dull walk if you keep to the road.

A rhyme goes:

Don Benito por bonito,
Guareña por las bodegas,
Medellín por el castillo,
Por las tinajas Castuera.

Don Benito for tuna fish,
Guareña for its cellars,
Medellín for the castle,
And Castuera for its jars.

Tuna fish hardly seems right for a place so far from the sea, though that is what *bonito* usually means. There is, to be sure, tuna in the bars of Don Benito, as there is in the cellars or bars of Guareña, or anywhere else. It comes in cans the shape of cake tins and sits in oil on trays under glass canopies on the bar, sometimes as little square chunks with sticks in, or with slivers of raw onion.

'Don Benito' sounds funny in Spanish as a place name. It is the name of a person, a local magnate who settled the land in the late fifteenth century. In the 1950s another attempt at settlement was made under the Franco regime. The 'Plan Badajoz' dammed rivers such as the Zújar, a tributary of the Guadiana upstream from Don Benito, for hydroelectricity and irrigation.

People were brought in to start new towns such as Guadiana del Caudillo, downstream from Don Benito. It was established in 1951 with 276 settlers. By 2008, despite all sorts of difficulties, the settlement had grown to a population of 2,499, and its citizens wanted to establish independence from the provincial capital of Badajoz. The regional government of Extremadura gave permission as long as it ditched the suffix 'del Caudillo'.

After all, it was argued, that was what the Law of Historical Memory, passed in 2007, stipulated: that public bodies should take steps to remove shields, insignia, plaques and other objects, or commemorative personal or collective references, which exalted the military uprising, Civil War and the repression of the dictatorship.

The people of Guadiana del Caudillo, not because they had any warm feelings about the dead Caudillo, but perhaps because they did not like being bossed about, decided in March 2012 to have a local referendum, in which 495 voted to keep the full name, and 310 voted to drop the 'del Caudillo'. No doubt in 500 years' time, El Caudillo will be as forgotten as Don Benito.

Statue of a conquistador

WHEN HERNAN CORTES was born at Medellín in 1485, it was not in the castle, for his father was a less exalted hidalgo. He was sent away for his education in law to the premier university of Salamanca, but threw up his studies after two years in favour of adventure.

What is to be made of his conquest of Mexico? Who could applaud the bloody shock that won a new empire? But who could find the enterprise any less than stupendous? Yet the notable element in the life of Cortés after he became the first Governor of New Spain was his inability to convince the Emperor in Old Spain of his importance.

'Who are you?' Charles V is said to have asked when the conqueror returned to Spain and forced himself into the royal presence. 'I am a man,' Cortés replied, 'who has given you more provinces than your ancestors left you cities.' (This exchange was not invented, like much else, by the American historian W. H. Prescott, but emerged from somewhere as a commonplace earlier in the nineteenth century.) Far from becoming a gilded viceroy, Cortés spent his last years back in Spain frustrated and embittered.

In today's Medellín, the raised area of paving in the Plaza Cortés, around the tall bronze statue of the first Governor of New Spain, looked grand enough. But it was surrounded by modest two-storey houses, whitewashed, with shutters closed against the sun. On the hard ground, the wind moved the dust about with a few dead leaves from the municipal shrubs. Nothing was open.

Not that there was much that could be open, apart from the little shop near the town hall at one end, with a sign promising, 'Books, stationery, gifts, sweets', and its steel shutters down. Above everything, stood the castle on its hill. On one side of the square rose the blank stone apse of the parish church of St Cecilia (closed) and beyond it the tower of the church of St Martin (closed), which boasts the font in which Cortés was baptised, as if it were the future conquistador who lent dignity to the waters of life.

When the heroic statue of Cortés in the square was set up in 1890, the last traces of his house were by an irony swept away with the accompanying improvements. The town had been left ruinous by the French, who in 1809 slaughtered 10,000 for the loss of 240 men, as Richard Ford noted two decades later, and massacred the wounded, giving rise to the phrase 'à la Medellín' for such atrocities. The bodies were 'left to the vulture, the Iberian undertaker'.

The statue of Cortés was the work of Eduardo Barrón, a shoemaker's son from the province of Zamora, whose father (like the father of Santiago Ramón y Cajal, his contemporary) tried to beat his artistic ambitions out of him.

Luckily for Barrón, his father died when he was 14, and he was sent off to Italy by a patron to learn classical sculpting according to the ideas of his time. Today, the city of Zamora boasts a statue by Barrón representing Viriato (the Lusitanian equivalent of Asterix) in the pleasant square named after this 'Terror Romanorum', as it says on the base.

Barrón's work shares the twin characteristics of much public statuary of the period: absurdity and patriotism, a delicate mixture for a visitor to comment on. Viriato holds one arm out in an unwitting proto-fascist salute. Barrón's Christopher Columbus in Salamanca (1893) holds one arm out too, but ending in a finger pointing to the unseen New World.

Here at Medellín, one hand of the statue of Cortés, in full armour, holds a baton, the other a banner surmounted by a cross. The difficulty comes with his left foot, which rests on the head of a fallen Aztec. In 2010 red paint was thrown over the statue and pamphlets that were left nearby denounced 'the cruel glorification and arrogance of the genocide' perpetrated by the Spaniards against the indigenous people of America. The statue, they said, was 'an insult to the people of Mexico'. The government of Mexico, however, called the paint incident 'an act of intolerable and unjustifiable vandalism'.

Through the Serena with song

AT DON BENITO a crowd of gypsies filled a carriage of the train. They were seeing off a mother and her ten-year-old son. She had large, ornately figured, gold earrings hanging against her dark, sunburnt skin. The large farewell party having got off again, the two began their lunch at half past two, once the train was well under way – bread of course, with chorizo, done up in a crackled aluminium foil wrapping inside a white plastic bag.

There was no one else in the carriage. The sun shone and the train swayed. It seemed more like the gondola of a balloon in its disembodied motion as the endless expanse of the Serena stretched out like a tawny sea. Serena, like *serene* in English, meant originally 'clear and cloudless', the air that Keats breathed in his sonnet 'On First Looking into Chapman's Homer'.

As in English, too, there is a subsidiary meaning of 'night dewfall', and the better known sense of 'calm'. The *sereno* in Spain used to be the nightwatchman who noisily cried the quiet hours of the night and patrolled the streets of tenements with his bunches of huge keys. He is no more remembered in the city than the *arriero*, the muleteer, in the country.

But serene the Serena remains: perhaps 400 square miles of rolling grazing and *dehesa* north of Castuera and its famous jars, towards the unseen river Zújar. Here in January can be seen wide white patches like the remnants of snow. They are spiders' webs on the short sheep-bitten grass still holding the dew of the night.

The bare land was called, by geographers and ornithologists who took an interest in it, 'steppe', after the Russian example, and it is here that dinner for the kites and eagles lives: sand-grouse, larks, wheatears. These prefer to make themselves inconspicuous.

From the train, vertical fangs of stone were visible, 1 foot high or 5 feet high, penetrating the moor in different places: dogs' teeth, the people of the region call them. Among them, sheep as tawny as the dry surface looked like rocks too, scattered on the land.

Outside the huge area of bare steppe, the land took the form of *dehesa*. The word comes from the late Latin *defensa*, for the land thus set aside was prohibited from general use as pasture or for the gathering of firewood. There, very widely spaced *encinas*, evergreen oaks, would stand amid wheat in one year, then for several years of fallow they would cast their shadow on pasture and scrub. It was this slow, unreliable system of rotation that such technocratic schemes as the 'Plan Badajoz' hoped to replace with irrigated annual crops. Today, where the wheat ends, cistus blossoms white, and oleander pink, beside dry watercourses.

Having finished his lunch, the boy in the carriage, to pass the time, started singing songs. They were of the traditional southern kind: *la luna* and *amor* featured in their lyrics, and *ilusión*, that unfamiliar concept to English visitors, an ideal, something to live for, or die for, but perhaps the prelude to *desengaño*.

The singer was unembarrassed, not seeming to care whether anyone heard or not. When he faltered his mother prompted him. The train, having gradually eaten up its ration of miles, slowed and stopped at Almorchón, population 32, up against its own sierra. No one got off. No one got on.

The stationmaster in his red-crowned peaked cap, his sleeves cuffed with oak-leaves, his furled flag held aloft, stepped forward to allow the train to go on its way. Behind him, the station clock had stopped, its cracked glass face crossed with thick black tape. In five minutes, the train was at Cabeza del Buey.

Crags full of vultures

IT WAS IMPOSSIBLE, the next afternoon, to climb the ridge by way of the *barranco*, the dry watercourse marked on the map, for it was choked with thorns. But on the high cliffs, roosting in the afternoon sun were 40 or 50 vultures. They looked like barnacles, or perhaps, with their hunched shape, like those unpleasant red pouch galls that you find on sycamore leaves.

Suddenly there was a sound of bells, and scores of white goats appeared on the horizon of the crags, followed by the black silhouette of a man. The goatherd shouted sharply: 'Hai! Hai!' Above, a half-crescent moon rose as the sky turned orange and grey.

This colony of *buitres leonados* was well established on the rocks to the east of Cabeza del Buey. Their crags were visible from the train, once it had passed the ruined station of Las Cabras, disappeared into a tunnel beneath the sierra and reappeared again into the sun. These griffon vultures, *Gyps fulvus*, may look scabrous when roosting, but in the air they are effortless and elegant, and big. The wingspan is 8 or 9 feet – wider than the red kite or the golden eagle, or the Iberian imperial eagle.

In most of Europe they are rare, but in 2008 there were estimated to be 25,000 pairs in Spain, three times the number a generation earlier. In Castile, near Sepúlveda, in the strong thermals above the limestone canyons of the river Duratón, a dozen may be seen at once, gliding, turning, traversing the broad landscape at great speed.

'The cliff where I obtained my first Griffon Vulture's egg,' wrote Colonel Willoughby Verner in *My Life among the Wild Birds of Spain*, 'is a very imposing mass of sandstone which rises over six hundred feet from the stream at its base.' He was writing in 1909, when it was still counted a virtue among naturalists to collect birds' eggs.

Colonel Verner, the inventor of the Luminous Magnetic and Prismatic Compass and the discoverer of the Palaeolithic painted caves at Tortosilla, was a brave man. In 1882, aged 30, he risked his life to save a man from drowning in Totland Bay, winning a bronze medal from the Royal Humane Society, a month before Bram Stoker won another for saving a man from the Thames at Chelsea. It was the thing to do.

Verner saw action in the Sudan at the desperate battle of Abu Klea in 1885, where 1,100 of the Mahdi's men were slaughtered in a quarter of an hour, and 74 British officers and men lost their lives, including Fred Burnaby, the strongest man in the Army, speared in the throat.

Burnaby's image is preserved in the languid painting by Tissot in the National Portrait Gallery: waxed moustaches, red-striped uniform and chintz sofa. Verner's portrait, by an unknown artist, shows him standing in a scarlet tunic, looking quizzically out from above luxuriant moustaches, with a gauntleted hand on the hilt of his sword. It is kept more obscurely than Burnaby's at the Royal Green Jackets (Rifles) Museum at Winchester. Verner survived the Nile Expedition, to be severely wounded in the South African campaign of 1900.

All this time, from the 1870s, whenever he had leave, he followed his interest in the birds of Spain. Within a few miles of his house ('El Aguila', near Algeciras) was an old Bonelli's eagle's nest taken over by a pair of griffon vultures. It was there that he shot, skinned and later preserved the big female with outspread wings that took pride of place in the case of stuffed vultures at the Natural History Museum in London.

He was fond of griffon vultures, which he insisted were the cleanest of birds in their habits. The chief delight of one that he kept for two or three years 'was to be played upon with a garden hose, when it would expand its wings and gyrate slowly so as to let the water strike every part of its body'.

The same cleanliness applied to their nesting. 'The appearance of these great birds steadily winging their way to some crag with a leafy branch of cork or ilex or wild olive, a foot or more in length, held in the beak is absurdly suggestive of the curious medieval pictures of the dove returning to the ark with the olive branch,' he wrote.

> One day, after seeing a Vulture enter a cavern, branch in beak, I climbed up to it and found a newly-lined nest, the infant Vulture in it having been provided with an entirely new change of bedding in the form of freshly cut branches of green ilex and heath placed on top of the dirty and much used nest.

Verner frankly admits that his lack of preparation for bold acts of cliff-climbing nearly cost him his life on several occasions.

> Once I let myself drop on to a ledge whence it was impossible to return, for it is one thing to drop neatly with one's feet on a few square inches and another to use the same restricted area to spring from, so as to recover one's hand-hold even a foot above one's reach overhead; more especially if there is a matter of 300ft or so between the place where one is standing and the next step below.

Worse, he recalled, was another mistake:

> the result of even more unskilful conduct, for I swung myself round a projecting crag into a cavern which did not admit of egress by the same route. Here I nearly remained for all time, but fortune once again favoured me, and by means of emulating the action of the chimney sweep of old I managed

Entering the nest of a griffon vulture, a drawing by Willoughby Verner, 1909.

> to scramble up a fissure for some 50ft and thus make good my escape. To this day I can recall the sensation of the start from that nest at a point where the fissure was widest and up which I had to spread-eagle, back to the cliff, and with nothing in front except the fresh air and a magnificent view.

A similar 'craze for nests' was confessed by the future scientist, Santiago Ramón y Cajal, who was born in the same year, 1852, as Verner. While still a boy he was keen to examine an eagle's nest on a tremendous cliff in the Sierra de Linás in mountainous Aragon.

He climbed with difficulty down a series of ledges till he was able to observe close at hand the nest of some eaglets 'which stared at me in terror'. Then,

> fearing attack by the eagles, whose screeches I thought I could hear, I tried to escape from the projecting ledge on which I was perched, but on attempting the ascent I met insuperable difficulties. The shelf to which I had got down by a foolhardy jump projected from a high and almost smooth wall. There I remained for hours, as if caught in a trap, consumed by terrible anxiety, under a burning sun.

Luckily he always carried a knife with him, and he used this to enlarge some narrow cracks until they provided holds for his hands and feet. For Verner, survival meant the opportunity to beat the armies of the Mahdi; for Cajal it was the opportunity to undertake work that won him a Nobel Prize.

20 miles
N
SPAIN
Guadalquivir
Seville
Marchena
Osuna
Genil
Granada
Fuente de Piedra
San Juan
de Aznalfarache
Antequera
San Francisco
de Loja
Sierra
Nevada
Mediterranean Sea

5

Sol – Sun

SEVILLE TO GRANADA

San Juan de Aznalfarache – The Rogue's home town – The field of the gypsies – Thirty-four ramps to the sky – Florence bore him; Seville starved him – Osuna's street of palaces – Olives all the way – The man who sold the Alhambra – The deserted gallery – Shabby old Granada – The game of birlimbao – Sugar and spice

A SECURITY GUARD in a brown and yellow uniform stood on duty at the entrance to the new funicular railway at San Juan Bajo, on the banks of the river Guadalquivir. Two youths with a bicycle and a young mother got into the brand new glass cabin and it glided up the inclined plane with a surprisingly wobbly gait.

The Most Excellent Municipal Council of San Juan de Aznalfarache had spent €4.79 million on the latest technology from the ThyssenKrupp elevator company to transport its citizens, free of charge, from the metro station at the water's edge, 100 feet or so up the escarpment overlooking Seville two or three miles away.

It was a relatively modest undertaking, just over half the height, for example, that the celebrated Tünel in Istanbul (built 1875) raises passengers, or, if comes to that, half the height which the Hay inclined plane (built 1792) hauled boats up the side of the Ironbridge Gorge in Shropshire. Show mankind a slope and the desire is be pulled up it.

The funicular at Aznalfarache was an improvement upon the zig-zagging steps climbing the steep slope below a brick tower (which from a distance looks like warm stone) surmounted by a gigantic statue of the Sacred Heart of Jesus (erected in

1942). At the top of the funicular ascent lay the hideous Plaza Otto Engelhardt, an uninhabited space marked off by blank white concrete, surrounding a splattering fountain. As a nod to nature, two small mounds had been clothed in artificial grass, to which a bulldog strained, on a lead held by a man in a tracksuit.

This is the site of the Moorish palace that gave Aznalfarache its name, Hisn al-Faraj, 'Lookout Castle'. It was restored and beautified by Abu Yusuf Yaqub al-Mansur, 'The Victorious', directly after his victory over the army of Alfonso VIII in 1195, at the battle of Alarcos, in which the thousands slaughtered included the Bishops of Avila, Segovia and Sigüenza. Al-Mansur was building his palace where the Visigoths had built their city of Osset, on the ruins of the Roman settlement of Julia Constantia. Its height above the river always made it a strategic site. The remains, partly unearthed during the building of the funicular, have been neatly enclosed in high walls for the benefit of archaeologists and the discouragement of vandals.

From here, wrote Richard Ford, 'the panorama of Seville is charming. On the opposite side of the river is the fine Naranjal or orange grove.' He was moved to quote Byron: 'Seville is a pleasant city, famous for oranges and women,' adding: 'There are two sorts of the former, the sweet and the bitter.' The panorama had changed. No orange groves were visible. In January, at the edge of the escarpment, the bright yellow flowers of toxic goat's foot oxalis bloomed thickly, and some of the 20,000 citizens of the dormitory town of San Juan de Aznalfarache exercised their dogs.

From here, two motorway bridges could be seen spanning the river, and, on this bank, the warehouse shopping outlets of El Corte Inglés, Hipercor S Juan de Aznalfarache and Conforama, kitchens and *electrodomésticos*. Birds twittered against the moan of fast traffic. Beyond the Guadalquivir stretched, not orange groves, but featureless rough grazing. In distant Seville, above the flats clustering around the centre of the city, rose the cathedral's tangle of flying-buttresses, like mangrove roots, and, breaking the horizon, the Giralda.

The Giralda is the cathedral tower, given its name by the Renaissance weathervane of Faith personified as a female figure, 14 feet tall, cast in bronze, holding in her left hand a palm branch and in her right what is meant to be a shield, but looks more like a bullfighter's cape, designed to catch the wind and rotate the heavy sculpture. It is a strangely mobile emblem for Faith.

The weathervane was only erected in 1568 to top the latest additions to the 250-foot tower that had been erected by the same al-Mansur who lived here at Hisn al-Faraj. Built as a minaret, it followed the style of the square-built tower of the Kutubiyya mosque at Marrakesh, with the same trelliswork brick decoration, like the patterns on a Fair Isle jersey, and called *ajaracada* in Spanish, a word of Arabic origin meaning 'ribboned'. A third great minaret, at Rabat, was left truncated at al-Mansur's death in 1199. In the *Handbook for Spain*, when Richard Ford comes to Seville, where he lived for three winters from 1830, he says decidedly: 'First visit the cathedral tower.'

The Rogue's home town

TO VISIT the cathedral tower meant a walk of an hour or so back from San Juan de Aznalfarache into Seville. The route must pass the spot where Guzmán de Alfarache was conceived. Guzmán is the hero of the smash-hit picaresque novel of the same name published in 1599. Alfarache is the place name with the *Azn-* (representing Arabic *Hisn*) lopped off.

The popularity of the book outran that of *Don Quixote*, in its time, with 30 editions being printed within six years. The author was Mateo Alemán, born in the same year as Cervantes, 1547. His novel, once translated and handsomely printed in folio in 1622, a year before Shakespeare's First Folio, and brought out by the same publisher, sold faster in England than the plays of England's foremost dramatist.

Just as the translator, James Mabbe, was to contribute a prefatory poem to the Shakespeare First Folio, so Ben Jonson wrote a commendatory verse to his translated novel, noting that it:

Hath the noblest marke of a good Booke,
That an ill man dares not securely looke

> *Upon it, but will loath, or let it passe,*
> *As a deformed face doth a true glasse.*

If that is so, we must belong to a generation of ill men, for *Guzmán de Alfarache* is in practice unreadable. It might be studied by the dogged, but few voluntarily read the four volumes of the English version. One obstacle is an element praised in its day, a leisurely sort of sermonising upon virtue. For the modern reader, there stand out from this smooth surface, like bright stones shining on wet sands, the incidents of vice and trickery that define the picaresque. Recognising this essential, James Mabbe gave the novel a new title *The Rogue*.

As in *Don Quixote*, some of the violent mishaps that befall the hero repel us today instead of making us smile. So the young Guzmán, having run away from home, was sold by a dishonest landlady an omelette, or 'froize', of stale, half-incubated eggs. He was so hungry that 'all went up together without any great chewing, howbeit, to speake the truth, I felt the tender bones of those untimely chickens to crackle between my teeth, that they made my gummes to tickle againe'.

As he went on his way,

> eructations and belchings did come and goe from my stomake to my mouth, till at last I fell a vomiting, till there was not any thing left within me. And even yet to this day, me thinkes I heare those little chickens, those poore pretty fooles, cry still peepe, peepe, within my bowels.

On the road, Guzmán met a carrier, who told him how this dishonest hostess met her comeuppance. A young fellow who was served just such a rotten omelette of embryonic chicks at her inn 'with all the force that he had, threw it full in the face of her, seeling up both her eyes therewith, which looked like an old wall all to bedawbed with rough-cast', while his companion threw a handful of hot ashes in her face.

> She was toothlesse, chap-falne, hollow-eyed, and wappering withall, her haire sluttishly hanging about her eares, unkempt, and as greazie as it was knotty; a fouler Swine no man ever

> saw: mealed she was all over, like a Mullet dressed with Flowre, or a Flounder that is ready for the frying-pan; with a gesture so graciously scurvie, a looke so pleasantly fierce, that as oft as you shall but thinke either of it or her, you cannot (if your life should lye upon it) but you must needes burst foorth into laughter.

Did James Mabbe chuckle as he set about his vigorous translation? He was, to be sure, a fellow of infinite jest. He had adopted a play on words as his Spanish pen-name, Don Diego Puede-Ser, 'may-be' or Mabbe. We know something of his life, but he remains hard to place.

A Fellow of Magdalen College, Oxford, a clergyman of the Church of England and an official of the university, he also translated a work by the Augustinian mystic Cristóbal de Fonseca under the title *Devout Contemplations*. In 1631, under a title of his own devising, *The Spanish Bawde*, he published a translation of the classic Spanish drama *La Celestina*, in 21 acts, a work that in a modern edition fills 250 pages of close set text. It did not enjoy as much success as *The Rogue*, but is admired for its language.

Certainly Mabbe knew Spain and its ways well, as his notes in *The Rogue* demonstrate, for he had spent some years in Madrid from 1611 as secretary to a college friend from Magdalen, the ambassador Sir John Digby, who had been sent to negotiate a marriage between Henry, Prince of Wales, the heir of James I, with Ana, the daughter of Philip III of Spain. The negotiations definitively failed in 1612 when the prince suddenly died, but Mabbe stayed on. He had travelled to Spain in the company of a younger graduate of Magdalen, Leonard Digges, whose place in English literature may be larger than generally recognised.

Leonard Digges, born in the year of the Armada, was the son and grandson of mathematicians. His father was mixed up in the world of the astronomer and alchemist John Dee, whose speciality was conducting conversations with angels believed to have charge of the cosmos. Leonard made poetry his sphere. On the flyleaf of a copy of Lope de Vega's *Rimas* (sent from Spain by Mabbe to a friend in Oxford and now kept at Balliol College) he compared the Spanish poet's sonnets to those of

Shakespeare. Digges' own commendatory verses are printed both in Mabbe's *Rogue* and in Shakespeare's First Folio.

The chief publisher of the First Folio, Edward Blount, was also the publisher of *The Rogue* and, in 1622, of Digges' translation of a Spanish play under the title *Gerardo the Unfortunate Spaniard*. It was Blount who had brought out the first English translation of Cervantes' *Don Quixote* in 1612, the work of Thomas Shelton. In Spain the second part of *Don Quixote* came out in 1615. Blount was to publish an English translation of that too, in 1620.

It is the contention of Anthony G. Lo Ré, a professor at the University of North Carolina, that the translation of Part II of *Don Quixote* is the work not of Shelton but of Digges. The argument depends not just on style, but also on the translator's habit of leaving out bits he felt not worth translating and on his obviously Protestant attitude to Catholic practice, which differed from the Catholic Shelton's.

The field of the gypsies

THE GUADALQUIVIR, which Guzmán would have crossed with the help of the ferryman, was spanned now by motorway bridges not open to pedestrians. Nor was the bridge for the new Seville metro, Linea 1. ('Please take care not to put the foot between the platform and the train,' said a solicitous notice on this expensive new transport system, in other words, 'Mind the gap.') The iron-girdered swing-bridge of San Juan could, however, be walked over. A cast-iron plaque on the Aznalfarache side declared:

LA MAQUINISTA

TERRESTRE Y MARITIMA

BARCELONA 1934

It was closed to motor traffic, except for buses bound for Seville. Occasional bicycles joined in. The pedestrian lane proved unnerving. It was tacked on to the side of the bridge, poised 50 feet above the greeny surface of the river. The footway was of thin, warped iron plates. A handrail of metal tubing ran along it on the river side. When gripped energetically it wobbled rhythmically back and forth, the whole walkway acquiring a reverberation. The nervous hand, irrationally gripping the iron harder, as if that made anything safer, soon gained a shiny glaze of sooty dirt.

A man showing signs of poverty cycled past on a bicycle that made a clanking noise each time the pedal turned. Seville, to the east, had disappeared over the scrubby horizon. In the distance to the south a flock of hundreds of sheep grazed the land sometimes flooded by the great river. Somewhere near here Guzmán had been conceived, for his father had cunningly made an assignment with a woman who had caught his eye in one of the garden-houses hereabouts, cuckolding the old knight who was then her protector.

'Watery gullets purling along the bankes inrich and adorne all those gardens and fields that confine thereupon,' Alemán explained, 'so that with reason (if there may be a knowne paradise upon earth) sure the name therof properly appertaines to this particular seate.'

Four hundred years or so later, notices hung below a motorway on stilts crossing the bare land, declaring it an offence to set up camp under its shelter. In the sky, yellowish birds of prey patrolled for unseen finches peep-peeping from tangles of thorn.

Which was the way to cross the Chinese Wall of the north-south motorway between here and Seville? A woman and her husband appeared, from nowhere near, walking towards Aznalfarache. Yes, they knew the way: go past the gypsies, towards the trees, then right across the old fairground site – no don't try to cross the motorway there, it's too dangerous, he said, keep to the left and in a kilometre or so, after the round-about, there's a crossing.

First, then, on the far side of the wide field, stood five shacks, 50 yards apart, presenting a bizarre patchwork of improvised construction: tarpaulin, black plastic, blue sacking, an old advertising hoarding, packing-cases, fork-lift pallets, flattened metal drums. A mother sat on a plastic chair in the open air, her toddler running about among the scrap.

It was normal January weather, chilly in the shade, cold at night, but here there was no shade, and by day the sun warmed all. *El sol es hogar de los pobres*, goes the proverb: 'The sun is the hearth and home of the poor.' A dark man walked away across the field, towards a pale column of smoke. They had their own lives on this side of the motorway, away from Seville.

The sandy expanse of the old fairground stretched out beyond the eucalyptus trees. On an asphalt path a goldfinch lay dead, apparently uninjured, its yellow marking very yellow in the afternoon sun and its feathery splash of red very much like blood. The crossing appeared at last, a set of traffic lights that held up the traffic speeding to Córdoba or Cadiz.

On the other side, suddenly, was the Triana, the district separated from the centre of Seville by the eastern branch of the Guadalquivir. The gypsies here have long lived in houses. It is an area of local shops, not chain stores: bike shops, discos, ironmongers, builders' merchants, tile shops, fish shops, travel agents, *locutorios* for cheap telephone calls abroad, pet shops and, along the street called Castilla, the coral and white Baroque belfry of the church of Nuestra Señora de la O.

This is the seat of the Pontifical, Royal and Illustrious Archconfraternity of the Most Blessed Sacrament, Our Father Jesus of Nazareth and the Most Blessed Virgin Mary of O, founded in 1566. The statue of the Virgin venerated here, and carried through the streets in Holy Week, is dressed in a red dress and blue mantel. She clutches the crown of thorns in her hands and looks sorrowfully into space. The image dates from 1937, the eyes of the old statue having been gouged out in an incident during the Civil War.

The odd-sounding dedication of the image, Our Lady of O, is attributed to the Advent antiphons for the Magnificat at vespers on the last seven days before Christmas – *O Sapientia*, *O Adonai*, *O Radix Jesse*, and so on. To English-speaking Christians, they are familiar too from the hymn *O come, O come, Emmanuel*, translated from Latin by the indefatigable Victorian liturgist John Mason Neale.

All this makes Our Lady of O the object of devotion as the expectant mother of Jesus at Christmas. Her feast day is 18 December. But it is worth noting that the confraternity in the Triana first met at a chapel dedicated to Saints Justa and Rufina (patronesses of Seville) and to St Bridget. One of the most popular devotions of the late Middle Ages and Renaissance period was the Fifteen Oes of St Bridget.

These prayers to Jesus during his suffering and crucifixion, each beginning *O Jesu* or *O Domine*, though associated with the fourteenth-century St Bridget of Sweden, were probably not written by her but by Bridgettines in England. They were printed by William Caxton in a prayer book or primer in about 1490 and they spread widely, in Latin and translation. So Nuestra Señora de la O has more than one possible etymology.

The Calle de Castilla led on to the bridge of Isabel II over this branch of the Guadalquivir. In 1852 this replaced the bridge of boats first constructed by al-Mansur's father in 1171 and renewed through the centuries. On the parapet youngsters had fixed padlocks inscribed with the names of the one they loved: Juanjo y Lupe; Paz ♥ Kiko. This is not an age-old custom special to Seville. It spread from Rome with the success in 2006 of a romantic novel *Ho voglia di te* by Federico Moccia, turned into a film the following year. And from here on the bridge in plain view, quite close, was the Giralda.

Thirty-four ramps to the sky

THE TOP OF the tall, thin bell-tower of the cathedral at Seville is reached not by a spiral staircase but by a ramp, which runs by right-angled turns up the inside of the square structure. The sound of hoofs could be heard from outside at the beginning of the ascent, for open carriages are for hire for tourists, like gondolas in Venice seldom for the use of citizens. The ramps too are said to have been ascended by a horseman for a dare. They were paved with herring-bone bricks, long and thin – a work that a little plaque records was begun on 27 January 1813 and completed on 25 August.

The rise of the slope from one corner to the next was to about chest height. The light was subdued here, but at the occasional windows it dazzled white to the eye, bleaching the world outside. High on the wall at each corner, the ramps had been numbered on glazed tiles, with mannered blue digits on a white ground.

Thirty-four ramps, slightly less steep as they went up, brought the visitors to a final flight of 17 steps up to the platform under the bells. The names of the bells were inscribed on the girders supporting their stocks: San Miguel, Santa Cruz. On 14 February 1981, one of the ring suddenly broke: San Cristóbal. Its fragments remain on display in an alcove halfway up the tower. It had been cast in 1663 by Juan Gerardo, whose name can be seen on one shard. Its weight had been 19 quintales and 55 libras. Notionally, a quintal is a hundredweight, though pre-decimal Spanish measures are notoriously variable from place to place.

From the top of the 300-foot bell-tower, the strongest impression given by the view was the tangled complexity of old Seville's narrow streets. Just as in Venice the canals are invisible from the top of the campanile, so here the surface of the streets themselves was hidden by the tight jumble of roofs. But it proved a good place to examine the exoskeleton of the cathedral that John Harvey, the great English historian of Gothic architecture, called 'the highest overall achievement of Gothic Europe, and possibly of European culture of all times'.

On 8 July 1401, the dean and chapter had resolved to build a new cathedral which, one of them declared, would be 'so great and of such a kind that those who see it finished will think we were mad'. The cathedral is 454 feet long, and an ample 295 feet wide, for on each side of the central nave were built not one but two aisles, as at Toledo. This produces an extraordinary interior sense of space.

From the tower above, the outer surface of the roof below looked like a sea with a high swell as it followed the shape of the internal vaults that supported it. Above the double aisles, double flying buttresses leapt up to the top of the higher nave walls, and at right angles to these, others supported the tall transepts. These intersecting buttresses were weighted down and adorned with tall spindly pinnacles, giving the inter-branching stonework an organic sense of movement. Far, far below, the Court of the Orange Trees still lay in fresh morning shade, its golden fruit shining between the dark green leaves.

Florence bore him; Seville starved him

SEVILLE LONG THOUGHT itself the first city of Spain. Much of that perspective remains, to a stronger degree than for the citizens of most towns and even villages in Spain, for whom the world seems naturally made to be viewed from the place of their birth.

A reflection of Seville's elevated status is the street number displayed outside the cathedral. As in France, every house in Spain must display a number, often set into the wall on blue glazed tiles. Here at the cathedral, although there is no letter box for the postman, the number is cut in stone on a slab the size of a tabletop: 'The Holy Patriarchal Church, Number 1'.

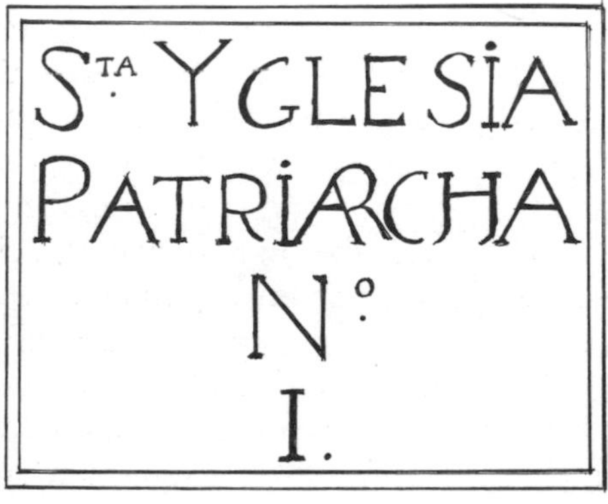

In the 1520s, Seville in its splendour attracted a man who had constructed for Henry VIII of England an *orbis miraculum*, 'wonder of the world', as the antiquary John Leland called the tomb of the king's father, Henry VII, at Westminster Abbey.

The artist was Pietro Torrigiano, a Florentine by birth. He was 40 when, in 1512, the King of England had commissioned him to make 'well, surely, cleanly, workemanly, curiously and substantially, for the sum of £1,500 sterling, a tombe or sepulture'. The price was enormous, but the result so satisfactory that the sculptor was persuaded to make the high altar for the chapel too. What remained of that after its destruction in 1644 hints at his success.

He was persuaded by royal patronage to leave for Spain in the early 1520s, portraying Isabella of Portugal in a terracotta bust for her husband, the Emperor Charles V. Other patrons were the Jeronimite monks much favoured by the Spanish crown. Torrigiano modelled for them two terracotta statues of their patron St Jerome, one for the shrine church of Our Lady of Guadalupe in Extremadura, and one for their monastery of Buena Vista in Seville.

The latter became one of the most powerful influences on Spanish art, leaving its mark on the work of Velázquez, Zurbarán and Goya. After the monastery of Buena Vista was broken up by the *desamortización* of 1835, the statue found its way to Seville's Museo de Bellas Artes.

It shows Jerome life-size as an old man with shaggy grey locks and beard. He kneels with his left leg on a block of stone, staring steadily at a cross made of two knobbly twigs. His sinewy right hand hangs at his side with a stone clasped in the hand. His chest bears flecks of blood where the stone has beaten it. His robe, paler than his flesh, is gathered round his thighs and loins. The big toe of his bare left foot is bent back with the two toes next to it braced against the ground, as the little toe and its neighbour hang loose. His body, revealed to view, is thin but muscular, the chest sagging a little with age. The whole is an essay in naturalism, in tones of brown. Classicism has been absorbed and remoulded as a vehicle of Christian feeling.

Shortly after completing this work that defined an age, Torrigiano fell into a dispute with the Duque de Arcos over payment (presented by the duke, as though in some variant of the old tale of the coffer of the Cid, in heavy sacks full of what turned out to be worthless maravedis) and was thrown into jail, where, according to Vasari's *Lives of the Artists*, overcome with melancholy, he starved to death.

Osuna's street of palaces

AT HALF PAST EIGHT the sun had not yet risen above the roof opposite the palace of the Marqués de la Gomera in Osuna, 35 miles from Seville. On a January morning, it was chill behind the curtains, chiller behind the shutters, sharply cold when the window was opened, for frost had descended during the night. But surely it was warmer in 2012, now that the place is a hotel with heating, than it would have been in the eighteenth century, when the Marquess crouched over a copper dish of charcoal to warm his hands.

On 25 September 1764 an agreement had been signed for the services of the master mason Juan Antonio Blanco to build a doorway to the designs of Don Andrés Tamayo, who was soon to be raised to the marquessate of Casa Tamayo (with the extra title Marqués de la Gomera arriving in 1817). When it was finished the following year, the Marquess would have had the pleasure, under the violent sun, of seeing his front door encased in a Baroque fantasy that would make all Andalusia stare.

The door-case rose the full height of the two-storey, white-washed palace façade. The door was set in a stone frame below an architrave with wandering mouldings of marine shape. Above the door, a wide balcony was supported by pairs of fluted pillars, its balustrade pierced in a way that suggested chinoiserie. The window that opened on to the balcony was flanked by pairs of barley-sugar-twist columns. Here the columns were of a deep-cut screw, supporting a sinuous, broken pediment topped by pairs of urns. The space left on the wall above, below a cornice like a breaking wave, was encrusted by a high-relief coat or arms between bold volutes and topped with an urn. One more urn for luck perched on the parapet above, outlined by the bright blue sky.

That was not the only brave doorway in Osuna. James Lees-Milne in his book on Spanish Baroque notes that all buildings of this style in Spain are ecclesiastical, 'apart from a very few town palaces'. For these, Osuna was the place to look. The Calle San Pedro, in which the palace of the Marqués de la Gomera stood, had, according to Unesco, more palaces per foot than any street in Europe. These, apart from the hotel, were all private dwellings, not open to visitors. You might think of them as ornamented town houses rather than palaces, but they were intended to impress.

The Spanish nobility did not build houses in the middle of open country like the aristocracy of England. They might have a big house in the capital, but their country houses stood in the streets of towns like Osuna. At No 2 Calle San Pedro the door, beneath a lintel of monumental stone blocks, was flanked by rusticated pilasters, the window above it set between fluted pilasters, with the family coat of arms carved in stone above.

The whitewashed walls of No 24 were varied with Doric pilasters on the ground floor and Ionic pilasters on the first. At No 21 the pilasters of the door-case were decorated with a trellis pattern; a large wrought-iron balcony resting on its cornice. At No 27, built in 1773, all in stone with no whitewashed wall, half pillars on each side of the door supported a heavy jutting cornice, with a zigzag edge, and a first-floor window, between attached urns, looked out on to a bow-fronted iron balcony. The dark, wooden double door of No 25 opened into a sixteenth-century courtyard.

A favourite feature of Spanish Baroque was the Solomonic column, the *salomónica* in Spanish, or barley-sugar column in English. Ancient columns of this kind, supposed to have been brought from Solomon's Temple, were incorporated by the Emperor Constantine into old St Peter's, Rome, and Bernini used four vast Solomonic columns to support his baldacchino over the altar there. *Salomónicas* were first employed in Spain in 1597 at the church of the Sagrario, attached to the cathedral in Seville.

Round the corner from Calle San Pedro in Osuna, in the Calle Sevilla, a splendid pair of *salomónicas* in high Baroque style were deployed at the entrance to the Palacio de Govantes y Herdara, built in 1738. They were tall, and flanking the balcony they supported a pair of large obelisks. The helical form of the columns was deeply incised, giving them a lively serpentine profile. The protruding surfaces were carved with vine leaves and thick bunches of grapes of a strangely conventional variety, like giant blackberries (as was often the case in medieval carved grape-bunches in England, as on the misericords at Newark, Nottinghamshire, or on a roof-boss of birds eating grapes at Sherborne, Dorset.)

If the effect of this porch was luxuriant, the façade of a house near the end of the Calle San Pedro was overwhelming. This was the Cilla del Cabildo, the granary of the chapter of canons, rebuilt in 1773 to house tithes from landholders. That was not a use its appearance suggested. Made of a biscuit-coloured stone, its façade was divided by double-height pilasters divided horizontally into panels, with geometric shapes looking as though they were made with pastry-cutters. Windows and doors were framed with the most eccentric moulding. The projecting bays of iron bars over the windows were supported by sinuous carved stone brackets. Above the double doorway, framed by a lavish cartouche, stood a model of the Giralda at Seville, flanked by its two patrons, Saints Justa and Rufina.

Among its Baroque finery, Osuna bore few scars of intrusive modern development. The Calle San Cristóbal ran uphill towards the old university, a four-square, sixteenth-century building resembling a toy castle with corner turrets like sharpened pencils. All up the streets, the two-storey, white-washed houses stretched, shoulder by shoulder. Each house had a double door. Some were left ajar or kept on a loose chain. Inside each was a *zaguán*, a lobby neither outdoors nor indoors, more or less square, large enough to house a moped and lined to waist height with coloured tiles. The houses bore an air of established prosperity.

From the top of the hill, wide green fields of springing wheat and regular groves of olives stretched out below. The collegiate church of Our Lady of the Assumption stood near the brow of the hill, a little knocked about externally, by French artillery practice in the Peninsular War and by a thunderbolt that brought down its tower in 1918. The big bare church was, it transpired, now used as a museum of art.

The bossy guide was worth putting up with in order to be allowed to see the crypt where the dukes of Osuna had been buried since the sixteenth century. A little set of 11 choir stalls were ranged about the underground altar beneath a gilt and blue coffered ceiling. A programme of restoration was under way, though it was hard to think that the new gold paint came up to the standard of the old gold leaf.

The plateau above the collegiate church had a strong smell of pig manure. A large patch of rough grass by the road to the Roman necropolis was strewn with bits of rubbish. On the far side, an old man sat on a canvas chair in the late sun, with a boy beside him playing with a grey cat. A dozen chickens and six big turkeys pecked amid the rubbish. On the edge of the Cañada Real, the sheep drove from Estepa to Marchena, a row of houses ended in waste land. A family was enjoying a party in a building like a store for agricultural machinery. Drink stood on trestles. All the time, near and far, dogs barked.

Olives all the way

FROM THE TRAIN, the landscape was of ploughed fields and groves of olives. The distance as the crow flies from Seville to Granada is a 160 miles – much further as the train wanders – and it's olives all the way.

The computer that governs the allocation of seats on the train loves to cluster passengers together, but it was possible, on the two-hour leg of the journey from Osuna to Granada, to find a section of carriage with all 16 seats empty. The speed was moderate, the air heated but not oppressive, the countryside like a constant projection of colour film. The low winter sun emphasised the variations in shade of the unwalled, hedgeless, ploughed fields, where the surface had dried in the wind. When the olive leaves were viewed looking into the sun they were silvery; looking back, greener. It was like the pile of a brushed carpet.

As the engine laboured to conquer an incline (old Spanish lines being far steeper and more sharply curved than is usual in England), it was possible to see the train's tail of carriages following round the bend, and the trajectory of the line ahead bending along one side of the valley. At Fuente de Piedra, the stationmaster held his furled flag ritually aloft against a background of lemons hanging on the trees by the platform. In the open country far from human habitation, little birds flew up from the olive trees and birds of prey hovered and circled above.

Twelve wind turbines stood on a ridge, a rarity on this journey, though as common throughout the land as windmills were in Don Quixote's La Mancha. Then came a field where nothing was cultivated but solar panels, before the train went for a while through land with red earth, a striking contrast with silver where it lay bare beneath rows of olive trees. Near the old town of Antequera rose a steep and isolated rock like a broken molar.

This being a single track railway, like most lines on the old network (separate from the high-speed routes), the train waited at Archidona station, not a scheduled stop, and apparently never a scheduled stop, till the service in the opposite direction passed. Single-track working (and the poor durability of the track-bed) always limited the number of trains that could run each day in Spain, even when there was enough rolling stock.

Entering the province of Granada, the train passed under a ridge of sharp, broken boulders dotted with broom bushes and *encinas*, the first seen on the journey from Seville. Above a white village, olives climbed the steep slopes until they gave way to *encinas* on the upper crags of the ridge. The train crossed a narrow ravine on a box-girder bridge.

Just before San Francisco de Loja, kitchen gardens were neatly laid out in a little valley with a rushy stream between rocks. A cemetery stood on an isolated hillock, hugged by high walls, whether to keep the dogs out or the spirits in, who could say? At half past two, a few minutes before reaching Granada, the dot-matrix display in the train said that the temperature outside was 9°C. The train made its usual noise of compressed air brakes as it slowed to its last stop at Granada.

The passengers in the next carriage pressed the green button to be released from their comfortable moving prison and breathed the air of the Sierra Nevada. From the platform, looking east, a ridge of mountains rose above the hilly city with its churches and walls. The mountains were bright with snow, and from the high, knife-blade summit the wind blew its icy particles into the air like veils.

The man who sold the Alhambra

EVERYONE READING THIS will have seen the Alhambra, or no doubt intends to see it. In 2011 it was the most visited tourist site in Spain, with 2.3 million paying visitors. The man who ensured that it is the destination of first importance was Owen Jones.

Jones spent six months in 1834 examining the Moorish palace minutely, with the French architect Jules Goury. Goury died of cholera; Jones came back to London and spent the rest of his career pursuing what he had seen in Granada, culminating in the Great Exhibition of 1851, of which he was a superintendent. Jones decided upon the bold colour scheme inside Paxton's vast glasshouse on the basis of his ideas about colour as an element in architecture, developed through his studies of the Alhambra.

Of course, Jones was working with a conception of Spain that had already caught the imagination of literary Britain. It was the work of his own century. When Joseph Townsend had arrived in Granada in 1787, the Alhambra delighted him, having taken him by surprise. 'As long as I continued in Granada,' he wrote, 'I seldom passed a day without returning to contemplate an edifice so perfectly different in its stile of architecture from every thing I had seen before.' He even spent time drawing the Court of the Lions, unaware of the drawings made a few years earlier by the English traveller Henry Swinburne.

The greatest populariser of Spanish travel, Richard Ford, had actually lived in the Alhambra during the summers of 1831 to 1833, while researching his *Handbook for Spain*, which finally came out in 1845.

That book was published by John Murray. In 1812, the publisher (under John Samuel Murray, 1778–1832) had brought out the first two cantos of *Childe Harold's Pilgrimage*, Byron's account of his travels through Spain towards the Orient. It was the book of which the author remarked: 'I awoke one morning and found myself famous.' The publisher sold 500 copies, at the high price of 50 shillings each, in three days.

Murray was also the chosen publisher in England of Washington Irving, who had taken up residence in the Alhambra two years before Richard Ford, and written his very popular *Tales of the Alhambra*. Murray then reinforced the romantic image of Spain in 1841 with a richly ornamented edition of J. G. Lockhart's *Ancient Spanish Ballads*. These had first appeared in 1823 but were now printed with coloured borders to the pages and full-page decorative devices by Owen Jones.

It was the most sumptuous use of colour in a mass-market book of its day. At the back, Murray advertised their popular range of illustrated books: Edward Lane's new translation of *The Thousand and One Nights*, Lady Calcott's *Little Arthur's History of England*. It was to this readership that Jones was appealing in his first essay in the theories of colour and design that his studies of the Alhambra had stimulated.

These were to be fully developed in his *Grammar of Ornament* (1856), one of the most influential works of the nineteenth century in its field. But from 1835 Jones was busy producing the chromolithographic plates that would illustrate his *Plans, Elevations, Sections and Details of the Alhambra*. The last volume was not finished until 1845, for Jones had to set up presses for the colour work at his own home in John Street, Adelphi, in London. Jones was helped in London at this time by the Spanish Arabist Pascual de Gayangos, probably introduced by Richard Ford. It was Gayangos who translated for him an inscription in the Alhambra: 'Observe how I am adorned, and thou wilt reap the benefit of a commentary on decoration.'

This inscription was given a central place by Jones at his Alhambra Court for the Crystal Palace after its move to Sydenham in 1854. The construction of the court (alone, among such features as the Byzantine Court, the Assyrian Court and the Medieval Court, in being devoted to one building, the Alhambra) was beautifully recorded in black and white photographs by Philip Delamotte, but the finished exhibit, centred on a facsimile of the fountain in the Alhambra's Court of the Lions – with water splashing into the wide basin supported on the backs of 12 archaic lions – was characterised by its

Boabdil presenting the keys of Granada to Ferdinand and Isabella, from Lockhart's Ancient Spanish Ballads, 1841.

dazzling colours. Although the pillars of the Court of the Lions in Granada are plain marble, Owen had his gilded, convinced that this was their original state.

With limited headroom and unavoidable iron pillars encroaching on his plan, Jones admitted he was 'driven to *bungles* or imperfect finishings which no Moorish eye could have endured'. The first façade that visitors encountered was of Jones' own invention, a fantasy of geometric polychromatic tiling, made up of ornaments that were 'repeated in the various halls in different positions'. The Court of the Lions took up half his space, with the Hall of Justice beyond, leading to the Hall of the Abencerrages.

Here he constructed a kind of dome with stalactite-like geometric pendants called *muqarnas,* originally made by Moorish architects as an intricate repeating pattern of prisms of plaster. Instead of building up the pattern prism by prism, Jones found it saved time to produce sections from moulds formed with the help of firm gelatine. 'It is difficult to conceive to what extent the Moors would have been led by their vivid imaginations,' Jones wrote, 'had they been acquainted with gelatine moulds.' By 1882, the Alhambra Court was being used to display a great electric chandelier, another advance with which the Moors had been unacquainted.

For Jones, the Alhambra was the perfection of Moorish architecture, as the Parthenon was to Grecian. In his book *The Alhambra Court in the Crystal Palace*, published in 1854, to go with the exhibition's re-opening, he reproduced J. G. Lockhart's 'Flight from Granada', taken from his *Ancient Spanish Ballads* and recounting the departure of Boabdil, the last Moorish King of Granada. Lockhart had chosen the language of old Scottish border ballads to tell his Spanish tale: 'There was crying in Granada when the sun was going down; / Some calling on the Trinity, some calling on Mahoun.'

By invoking Lockhart, Owen Jones ensured that the Romantic connections between Spanish history, literature and architecture were complete. The Alhambra was fit to be a pattern for architectural design, and the prime destination for cultural tourism. 'It is impossible to conceive anything more exquisite than the Alhambra,' wrote Lady Herbert of Lea during her

Iberian tour of 1866, 'of which no drawings, no Crystal Palace models, not even Washington Irving's poetical descriptions, give one the faintest idea.' But she had known to put it high on her list of expectations.

The deserted gallery

THERE WERE NO tourists in the Museo de Bellas Artes inside the walls of the Alhambra. From the first-floor window of the gallery, the sunny hills of Granada could be seen though the linen blinds, as if painted in faint watercolour on a canvas.

This is, it may be said, a despised part of the Alhambra, for it is housed in the palace built by Charles V that invades the Moorish space of the fourteenth-century Nasrid architects. There was no entrance fee, no queue and no one inside, to speak of. Yet as a palace it was very fine – a simple square enclosing a circular courtyard bounded by a two-storey arcade or cloister of 32 monolithic pillars on each floor, all in opulent Renaissance style. The picture gallery was at the top of 34 broad steps. The paintings and sculpture were not at all despicable.

In one room hung a canvas from the beginning of the seventeenth century by Juan Sánchez Cotán, of a bristly bare cardoon and carrots in a stone window opening against a black background. It seemed to take still life to the stillness of contemplation. In another room stood four life-size statues by Alonso Cano, made in the 1650s for the Poor Clares' convent, from which they were taken on its closure in 1933. Among them, the statue of St Diego de Alcala perhaps shows how far towards naturalism great polychromatic sculpture can go.

A canvas by Alonso Cano (1601–67) depicted two heads against the bold design of a forked, pale-cocoa pennant flying in front of a black background. The pennant was grasped firmly by St John Capistrano, for this was a picture painted for the Franciscan friary of Granada, and the other saint is another Franciscan, St Bernardino of Siena. He held a book with the device IHS on the cover. That was his life's theme, the name of Jesus, represented by its first three Greek letters, iota, eta, sigma. Cano's double devotional portrait demonstrates that the Spanish Baroque could muster the boldest simplicity to alternate with its love of complication.

In the same room a head of St John of God also made by Alonso Cano followed the convention of naturalism established by the funeral effigy of Henry VII by Torrigiano that is kept in the museum of Westminster Abbey. These portrait heads resemble neither a waxen death-mask nor a cold marble sculpture. With both, the coloured surface gives an impression of a head cut from a living body, like contemporary devotional heads of St John the Baptist (St John of God's patron). Alonso Cano gave his subject a frown, a beaky nose, hair combed forward and a stubbly chin.

This same St John of God is the subject of a gold-framed, nineteenth-century canvas 10 feet high, towards the end of the museum's itinerary. It was painted in 1880 in a grand, historic, Venetian manner by Manuel Gómez Moreno, an historian of Granada. He painted it in Rome and abided by the best conventions of history painting of his day. The result is amiable and not a little absurd.

It shows a fire at the Hospital Real of Granada on 3 July 1549. With a burning beam in the act of falling towards them, a group of figures makes its way down the grand staircase towards us. In the middle, the barefooted saint in his dark habit carries a thin-limbed old man wrapped in a sheet, not at all helped by another man with a bandaged foot grasping his right arm. A sweet little boy in velvet breeches and blue hose, with a bandaged head, looks up with well-founded anxiety. The picture remains as popular among Granadans as the saint it depicts.

Shabby old Granada

THE CALLE DE ELVIRA in Granada is old, narrow, shady, shabby, smelly and seedy, in other words, far preferable to the parallel Gran Via that was cut through the neighbourhood in 1895 to link the station to the cathedral and the Alhambra. Perhaps with horse traffic and new shops, the Gran Via once seemed modern and fashionable. With motor traffic and graffiti on empty shops, it now seems bare, noisy and commonplace.

The very year after the Gran Via was opened, the eleventh-century, fortified, Moorish gateway, the Puerta de Elvira, was declared an historic monument. Through the horseshoe-arched gateway under its crenellated tower, the road made a kink to the right. There, next to Rashid Ahmed ('Comida Pakistani') and opposite the Carnicería Elvira halal butcher, stood a single-storey stone chapel with a Gothic parapet and a single arched doorway, barred and glazed.

This marks the site of a shop opened in 1538 to sell pamphlets and books of chivalric romance, like those mentioned by Cervantes as having turned the brains of Don Quixote. The proprietor was the man one day to be known as John of God, but at this time known simply as Juan. If he had a surname at all, it was Ciudad, or his native Portuguese equivalent, Cidade.

In the next 12 years, this extraordinary man gained a reputation for insisting on the humane treatment of the sick and mad, but not before he had led a rocky, wandering life himself. Born in Portugal in 1495, he first gained employment as a shepherd in the province of Toledo, before going off to serve as an infantryman with Charles V's army, against Francis I of France. He narrowly escaped death twice: once after being knocked unconscious from a horse near enemy lines, then under sentence of death because some of the goods he was meant to be guarding went missing. The noose was round his neck when an officer interceded for him.

He followed a picaresque life, on a road all the rougher for his reluctance to pick up money by trickery. After some freelance shepherding near Seville, he went into service with an exiled Portuguese knight, perhaps with the thought of going to the New World. They only got as far as Ceuta in North Africa before running out of money. Juan supported the knight's family for a time by working as a day-labourer on the reinforcement of the city's fortifications.

Juan next turned to life as a pedlar, selling books and pamphlets in the country near Gibraltar. Settling in Granada he established a stall in the busy market, here inside the Puerta Elvira, when it was a main entrance to the city. On 20 January 1539 his life changed. It was the feast of St Sebastian, he remembered, and in a sermon by Juan de Avila he heard something that struck his heart. This preacher, declared a Doctor of the Church in 2012, had, like Juan Ciudad, lost his parents while he was young, and had been moved to give all his possessions to the poor. On that day, outdoors on the slope leading up the Alhambra, Juan heard Juan de Avila declare that the rich were not to be envied, but that it was the poor, the hungry, the sorrowful, the despised and reviled who were blessed.

Juan's immediate response made him appear mad. He ran down the hill, shouting for God's mercy and rolled on the ground. Back at his bookshop he tore up his romances and gave away his pious books. He ripped off his clothes, leaving himself in shirtsleeves in the freezing winter weather. Over the next two days he rolled in the mud in the Plaza Bibarrambla (on the other side of the cathedral from his lodgings), and shouted his sins aloud. He was mocked as a madman (in the convention of the times). Perhaps he was mad. But Juan de Avila soon had a long conversation with him and became a lifelong friend and supporter.

Juan was taken by a well-wisher to the Royal Hospital, founded by Ferdinand and Isabella. It offered care to those with venereal disease, but its limited endowment did not run to sufficient supplies of mercury, the only medication available. In spare wards, the mad were confined. Once Juan's Good Samaritan had disappeared, he was beaten by the warders. In the enthusiasm of his new found penitence, he accepted this treatment for himself, but was indignant at the brutality inflicted on his fellow patients. 'Grant me the favour,' he prayed to God, 'of finding a hospital where I can receive the poor and homeless mad folk and be of service to them.'

Juan's comportment gradually grew less outlandish. He was released from his fetters, and allowed to act as an unpaid orderly. In May, Juan de Avila, in Granada to preach at the Empress's funeral, secured his discharge. He made his way on foot the 80 miles to Baeza, where Juan de Avila had established a college, and spent five or six months learning what he could there, before walking another 200 miles to Guadalupe, the pilgrimage town where the Jeronimite monks had established a number of excellent hospitals. Brian O'Donnell, an expert on John of God, quotes the stipulations for the hospital contained in the fifteenth-century Book of Offices at Guadalupe: 'Good food, comfortable, clean beds; a good physician who knows the patients; a good administrator and charitable carers.'

The game of birlimbao

ON HIS RETURN to Granada, bearing a bundle of firewood he'd gathered to sell, Juan felt ashamed to appear in the streets gaunt and ragged, when everyone would remember him as the ludicrous madman. It was his honour, that powerful Spanish motive for gallantry and revenge, he realised, that was under threat. But he braved it out and declared to the mocking people of Granada that they knew no more of it all than in a game of blind man's buff. (The children's game he named was *birlimbao*, in which the one blindfolded apparently guesses the number of passing ships impersonated by the other players.)

For spiritual advice Juan contacted a reliable priest recommended by Juan de Avila, but for the time being he had nowhere to sleep but the street. He was rescued by Miguel Abiz Venegas, remarkably enough a grandson of Boabdil, the last Moorish king of Granada, celebrated in Lockhart's ballad. Don Miguel allowed Juan to sleep in the *zaguán* of his palace – the entrance lobby closed to the world at night and also closed to the inner house, neither public space nor private. Forty years later, just such a knight was to give John of the Cross shelter in his *zaguán* after he escaped from prison in Toledo.

After Don Miguel came home one day and found he could not get through to his own front door for all the poor people that Juan had given shelter there, he persuaded him to join other followers of Juan de Avila who had set up a refuge for the sick and poor in or near Calle de Lucena, round the corner from Plaza Bibarrambla. Since he turned no one away, Juan had to beg food and money to support them, walking the streets with a large basket crying out an unconventional request for alms based on the dictum that it is better to give than to receive: 'Who wants to do themselves a bit of good?'

One of John's regular activities was to help prostitutes who wanted a life outside the brothel to find husbands. Often all they lacked was the money to pay off the brothel-keeper and to use as a dowry to set up in married life. It was still the same, all over Spain, within living memory. In his remarkable memoir *The Perfect Stranger*, the poet P. J. Kavanagh remembered prostitutes, many of them unmarried mothers, that he'd met in lodgings in Barcelona in 1958. 'They'd all sit and say the Rosary together before the day's work, praying always for a rich husband. These they sometimes found when the American Navy put into port.'

Another incident characteristic of Juan's times was the story of Antón Martín, who had come to Granada to take revenge on the man who had killed his brother. Juan begged him on his knees in the open street to forgive the killer, which he was moved to do, and moreover to join Juan's work with the poor. He outlived Juan and was to give his name to a hospital in Madrid, after which a station on the Madrid metro was named, which is what Antón Martín means to most people today.

As for Juan, who had gone mostly by his Christian name, the Rector of the Royal Hospital where he had once been confined, Miguel Muñoz, now a bishop, came up with a new name for him: Juan de Dios, John of God. The name caught on. Royal Granada, full of energy and of poverty, was proud of its brother to the poor, who also called the proudest nobleman 'Brother' and addressed him by the familiar *tú*.

Half an hour after midnight on Saturday 8 March 1550, Juan, who had been sick for some weeks, crept out of bed and knelt on the bare floor. 'Into your hands I commend my spirit,' he said, and those with him heard no more. He did not fall down, but he was dead.

Sugar and spice

ABOVE THE DOOR of No 48 in the Avenida de la Constitución, a sign said: 'Piononos'. The Avenida de la Constitución was not pretty, being a main road running past Granada railway station, lined by modern flats above shops. No 48 was a pastry-cook's and coffee shop.

It sold *suizos*, cleft buns with a crystal sugar glaze; *napolitanas de chocolate*, made of puff pastry and sown with chopped nuts on their sticky tops; *barquillos*, which are cream horns;

glorias, sandwiches of confectioner's custard between pastry and *cabello de angel*, 'angel's hair', a sweet fruity pulp. The speciality of the house was the *piono*no.

This little item of confectionery is associated with the town of Santa Fe, to the west of Granada. That is where Isla, the company that ran this shop, had its factory, which had been turning them out since Ceferino Isla invented the sweetmeats in 1897, naming them after Pope Pius IX on account of his devotion to the Blessed Virgin Mary, the dogma of whose Immaculate Conception the Pope had solemnly defined in 1854.

Even if Don Ceferino did invent them from scratch, they convey an ancient oriental Moorish savour. They are constructed of a little cylinder of rolled up sponge-cake, like a tiny swiss-roll on its end. (Swiss roll in Spanish is generally called *brazo gitano*, 'gipsy's arm'.) The cylinder, moistened with a sweet liquor (as with *borracho* or tipsy-cake), supports a thick mushroom-cap of egg yolk, mixed with sugar and toasted. The whole is flavoured with cinnamon.

It is impossibly sweet, and popular for *merienda*, the meal that fills the gap between a late lunch and a later dinner. A *pionono* is a mouthful or two, and its consumption is helped by a little cup of strong, bitter coffee. The woman behind the counter was proud of the product, but even prouder of the glass of water she proffered to accompany it. 'Whoever,' she said, 'tastes the water of Granada will return.'

Yellow cable cars being hauled up 1,800 feet to the ancient monastery of Montserrat near Barcelona

St Eulalia, martyred in the snow at Mérida, by J W Waterhouse (1885), which some in his day found 'bizarre'

Pineapple and hothouse grapes for the *Last Supper* by Francisco Salzillo, 1763, carried through Murcia in Holy Week

The spindly ironwork bridge, fixed on Renaissance footings, over to houses clinging to the Huécar gorge at Cuenca

Deeply incised Solomonic column, with stylised bunches of grapes, 1738, at the door of the Palacio de Govantes y Herdara in Osuna

Modernity in the form of a train rushes over a Good Friday procession, in Darío de Regoyos's *Viernes Santo en Castilla*, 1896, on show in Bilbao

A mastiff laps from a shepherd's bowl as he hears the angel's Christmas greeting – 12th-century murals in the church of San Isidoro, León

The price of fish: a mortally wounded seafarer in Joaquín Sorolla's large canvas, bought for the Prado in 1895

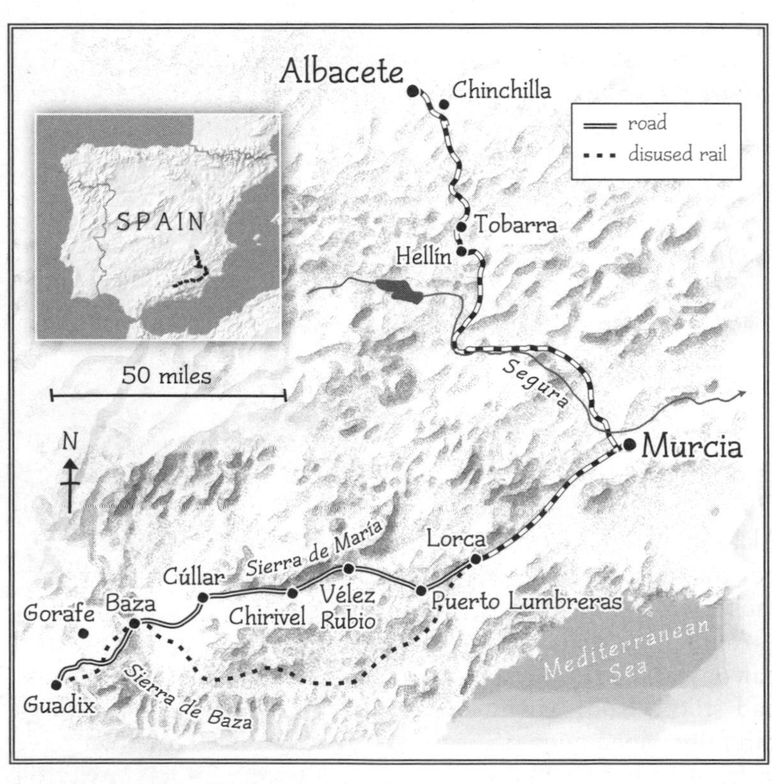

Albacete
Chinchilla
road
disused rail
SPAIN
Tobarra
Hellín
50 miles
Segura
N
Murcia
Sierra de María
Lorca
Cúllar
Vélez
Rubio
Chirivel
Puerto Lumbreras
Gorafe
Baza
Mediterranean
Sea
Guadix
Sierra de Baza

6

Cuevas – Caves

GUADIX TO CHINCHILLA

Ten thousand troglodytes – The old town of Guadix – A journey by ghost train – By bus across the badlands – Lorca, after the earthquake – Where the poor of Lorca live – Open-air card-players – The Roman milestone – Murcia: a taste for richness – 'I regret you were that man's wife' – The makings of a tobacconist – No tomatoes to be had for lunch – The Last Supper, with pineapples – Chinchilla: an appointment with death

Ten thousand troglodytes

IN GUADIX, 10,000 people live in caves. Climbing the narrow old streets of the little city from the cathedral to the Moorish Alcazaba was hot work. These streets had the marks of a neighbourhood prosperous 300 years earlier but now abandoned by those who prefer modern conveniences.

An old man glared from the open window of his second-floor balcony at the car parked on rough ground where once a house had stood, from which loud techno music blared. A woman carefully wiped fine dust with a damp cloth from the iron grille in front of her ground-floor window, though 20 feet away on the other side of the street the house opposite was nothing but a pile of rubble.

Even the reddish bulk of the Alcazaba, built from compacted clay and reused Roman tiles, was giving way. The grand gateway beneath the square, battlemented tower had sagged and cracked, and was now held up only by steel jacks.

Next to the Alcazaba clustered tiny whitewashed houses, and at the top of a street that ended in steps, the view to the west opened up. The eye was baffled. Nearby, traditional tall white chimneys, with smoke holes near the top like the eyelets of a knight's helmet, rose up from red-tiled roofs. Beyond, there were chimneys but no roofs. The chimneys were the only straight verticals. Everything was a jumble of bare, jagged, rock hummocks, like broken sandcastles, running to the horizon.

This was where the cave-dwellers lived. It was as though an Arctic landscape of fissured icebergs had turned into dry sand. Looking out over this prospect in 1787, the Rev Joseph Townsend speculated that 'horizontal strata, for ages covered by the waters of the ocean, were lifted up' and, the land being subjected 'to violent and heavy rain, it was soon torn in every possible direction by gullies, which, in process of time, became deep ravins'.

Richard Ford was astonished by the sight when he saw it in the 1830s:

> The whole country about the town resembles a sea whose waves have suddenly been transformed into solid substances. The hillocks rise up fantastically into conical and pyramidal shapes: their marly sides are excavated into caves, the homes of the poor.

At first sight it looked unsettling and alienating.

Many a comfortable cave home had a whitewashed front wall behind which the rooms burrowed into the soft rock. With wood-smoke rising from the chimney piercing the domed ground above, they resembled the holes of Hobbits. Some tourists like to come and inspect these caves where people are living; others even stay in cave hotels.

Perhaps the idea of living in a cave is more romantic than the reality, which, with tiled floors and a television, differs not much from the common Spanish habit of sitting in bare rooms behind shutters blocking the sun, and cooking tripe and peppers in an earthenware dish in a windowless kitchen from which the fumes disappear via some old chimney flue or Vent-Axia through the wall into an unknown cavity.

Caves lie deep in the Spanish soul. A shrine nestles in a mountain cave at Covadonga, far in the north in Asturias, where the Christians were supposed to have won their first victory against the Moors, in 722, 11 years after the conquest. The name Covadonga is popularly derived from *cova dominica*, 'cave of the lady', after the Virgin Mary, although the more likely derivation is from *cova d'onga*, where *onga* is a Celtic word for a spring.

In a cave in Catalonia the image of the Virgin of Montserrat was found. At the cave of Nájera in La Rioja the kings of Navarre were buried a thousand years ago and more. In a cave beneath the church of San Vicente in Avila the Virgen de la Soterraña, Our Lady Underground, is honoured. Deep below the cathedral of Palencia lies the ancient crypt of St Antonin. These are the ancestral foundations of a culture.

But here in Guadix, the caves are for the living. Safe from the terrible sun, the air keeps an equable temperature. Rain does fall – hardly at all in the fiery months of June, July and August when the thermometer is in the nineties Fahrenheit – but an average of about 14 inches a year.

The caves remain dry because the rock is not merely loose sand. It is often called tufa, but it is not volcanic rock, rather a consolidated bed of alluvial deposits. It is into this that the rivers, *barrancos*, *arroyos* and *ramblas* have eaten, over thousands of years, to carve gullies that are themselves cut into by gullies, leaving spurs, mounds and pinnacles of rock.

From the surrounding high land, Guadix can be seen hugging these wildly eroded walls of its river-basin, above which a sunlit shelf stretches out, like the fields of heaven, at the foot of a distant, higher wall of mountains. In the haze of a hot day, it possesses a look of unreality. Below the cathedral, the river Guadix is contained in a deep, walled channel a hundred feet wide, but the single puddle that could be seen on a June day only emphasised the long months when it remains dry.

Even so, to its conquerors this was a wadi, the Wad-Acci, Guadix. Acci was a place name old when the Moors arrived, when the Visigoths before them came, and the Romans before them. It is thought to be a Carthaginian name, possibly related to Himilce, the Iberian wife of Hannibal. In his day a fat strip of land all along the south coast of the Iberian peninsula was Carthaginian territory, east to Cartagena (New Carthage), and beyond. The narrow seas of the western Mediterranean did not divide Europe and Africa but united them.

The old town of Guadix

IN CALLE ANCHA, 'Broad Street', curving downhill from the Alcazaba towards the cathedral, a very black African man was trying to sell Spanish football shirts for Euro 2012 from the heavy bag slung over his shoulder. No one bought any, but a middle-aged woman enjoying an evening glass of wine at a table outside a bar engaged him in conversation for a while.

A gypsy, not nearly so black, asking for money, with his little daughter at his side, was met with blank stares and curt refusals, and disappeared into a nearby shop. The barman brought out drinks and added unbidden a *tapa*, a little saucer of sautéed kidneys with a few chips.

The *jamón* shop on one side of the bar was closed for the evening, the shop on the other was closed permanently, its roof fallen in. Hardly any cars passed by, for few live up in the old town, and the highest streets climb up steps. On the other side of the road, the door of the little Costurero de María Gracia was open for customers, offering to make curtains and *fundas nórdicas* – duvet covers.

Opposite the chemist's, stood a palace from the sixteenth century, six bays wide, divided crudely into two shops at ground level, with the upper three storeys retaining their dignity and balconied windows beneath splendidly heavy eaves of seven courses of centuries-old brick, each projecting further than the one below.

At 9.15 p.m., with the heat of the June day growing less hostile, the swifts flew low over the houses to catch the evening insects then, quick as the wind, up against the blue sky, shrieking past the black, green and red glazed tile spire of the church of Santiago.

The parish of Santiago was one of the four into which Guadix was divided when it was reconquered in 1489, after the best part of eight centuries of Moorish rule. The church, built on the ruins of the Arab baths, had a cool whitewashed interior with a dark wooden roof of intricately geometric

Mudéjar work. The arches cut through the thick nave walls had a Moorish contour.

That evening in 2012 the parish had combined their regular 8.30 Mass with a novena to the Sacred Heart. The Poor Clare nuns from the neighbouring convent sang from behind the stout squared grille at the back of the church.

Diego de Siloe, the architect of Granada cathedral, had a hand in building the church of Santiago in the early sixteenth century, at the behest of Bishop Gaspar de Avalos, the son of the commander of the forces that took Guadix, and nephew of the first Archbishop of Granada. Don Gaspar called in Siloe too for the amplification of the cathedral, which in its first decades had occupied the shell of the principal mosque of the city.

The cathedral today remains easily the dominant building of Guadix, elevated above an ugly traffic intersection, with its high, fat tower seeming to glow like the native sandstone when seen from the long, straight road leading down from the railway station, but from nearby revealing its upper storeys to be made of brick.

The tower was among the later parts of the cathedral to be completed in its three centuries of construction, along with the extravagantly Baroque façade. When he came this way, the Rev Joseph Townsend remarked laconically: 'The front is whimsical, yet pretty.' Work had come to a stop after the rebellion in 1568 of the Moriscos, the Moors who had ostensibly become Christians, and the expulsion in the early seventeenth century among these of many a skilled workman.

Inside, the cathedral gave an impression of heaviness and weird eclecticism. The heaviness came from the relatively low vaulting over a nave the same height as the aisles (and largely blocked by the usual walled choir). Thick Gothic ribs sprang from the Corinthian capitals of the Neoclassical piers.

The cathedral did not see itself as a latecomer to Spanish Christendom, for here lie relics of St Torquatus, reputed to have brought Christianity to Spain in the first century and to have become the first bishop of Guadix. Legend has him as one of the 'Seven Apostolic Men', ordained by Saints Peter and Paul themselves. The other six bear names of which any Spanish parent with a taste for the outlandish at the font (as many have) would be proud: Ctesiphon, Hesychius, Euphrasius, Indaletius, Caecilius and Secundus.

St Torquatus' relics (apart from a bit of his jaw, preserved in a rock-crystal ostensory in the cathedral museum) are honoured in one of the six chapels radiating from the central point of the high altar at the (ritual) east end of the cathedral. The chapel looked dim in the afternoon light, with only a glinting suggestion of the Baroque splendours within.

A little notice for tourists proudly drew attention to the *cuerno de toro* arch across its entrance – starting thick and ending thin, like a bull's horn, as it curved up and skewed over to the right, following the line of the ambulatory behind the high altar. It would be a rare tourist, though, who came to obscure Guadix for the sake of this curious architectural detail.

If, to the outside world, St Torquatus is just as obscure as the see he founded, then a saint honoured in one of the other chapels behind the high altar is obscurer. This is St Fandila, a native of Guadix martyred in the ninth century in Cordoba by order of the Emir. Obscurity, of course, depends on your starting point. St Fandila is not obscure to the 3,623 inhabitants of San Fandila, named after him, in the state of Querétaro Arteaga in Mexico.

In any case, there is a pattern in the people of Guadix honouring Torquatus as a saint martyred under the rule of pagan Rome, and honouring Fandila as a saint martyred under the rule of the Muslim Emirate of Cordoba, for, on each side of the retrochoir are inscribed the names of 24 local clergy *imolados por Marxismo*, as the wording puts it – 'killed as victims of Marxism'. The reference is to the Civil War.

Chief among those killed was Bishop Manuel Medina Olmos, now honoured in the same chapel as St Torquatus, since he was beatified in 1993 by Pope John Paul II. An oil painting of him and those who were martyred at the same time hangs in a nearby chapel. He was not killed in the heat of battle, but five weeks after his arrest, along with 16 others, shot by a firing squad at Almería on the coast on 30 August 1936. His last words were taken down: 'We have done nothing to deserve death, but I forgive you so that the Lord will also forgive us. May our blood be the last shed in Almería.' It wasn't, on either side.

A journey by ghost train

GUADIX IS EASY enough to reach by train from Granada, but not so easy to leave. A line runs south to Almería, through the badlands, most spectacular between the stations for Gérgal and Gádor. Beside these bare mountains of the moon, Spaghetti Westerns were made in the 1960s, but the railway eastward from this fantasy Wild West was closed in 1985, a hundred years after work on its construction began.

On this line, in the 1960s, when Trevor Rowe took his holiday here, used to run locomotives built by Kitson, Sharp Stewart and North British between 1889 and 1905, bearing circular works plates inscribed 'Great Southern Railway of Spain' – in English.

The traveller by train who wants to reach Lorca, on the eastern side of this barren region, would now have to make a detour of hundreds of miles, via Linares and the junction deep inland at Alcázar de San Juan. So the great train journey from Guadix to Chinchilla is a ghost-train ride. The starting point is a dead end; the finish at Chinchilla is a ruined station, as so many small stations now are, left abandoned beside a high-speed track.

Chinchilla was once at the heart of railway development in Spain, for it lay on the first stretch of line to be completed by the Madrid-Zaragoza-Alicante line, the MZA. The company, nationalised by Franco, along with the other railway enterprises in 1941, had been set up in 1856 (with the backing of Rothschilds) by the astonishing figure of José María de Salamanca.

José María de Salamanca was in his forties then, having been born in 1811, the son of a provincial doctor, in Malaga. By 1856, he had already been exiled twice, made millions by obtaining the state monopoly in salt, made more millions by rigging the Madrid stock exchange, and had presided over the failure of the Banco de Isabel II (which was saved from utter destruction by a merger with the Banco de San Fernando, soon after to become the Bank of Spain). Perhaps the richest man in Spain at one point, he was called by his political enemies the *bestia negra*.

He left two marks on Madrid, the smart district known as Salamanca, which he developed, and the palace at 10 Paseo de Recoletos, near the Prado, which he was forced by financial pressures to sell. It was later acquired by the bank BBVA. He was created the 1st Marquess of Salamanca in 1863 and died with vast debts in 1883. But the MZA, powered by locomotives from Stothert Slaughter of Bristol, steamed on.

Chinchilla had become the junction that connected the line between Madrid and the coast at Alicante with the line that branched south to Murcia and Cartagena. The station was never easy to use, being two miles from the hilltop town of Chinchilla de Monte-Aragón. Today, passengers from the coast to the provincial capital of Albacete see the romantic silhouette of the ruined castle of Chinchilla on its hilltop and the less romantic ruins of the station of Chinchilla close by.

Castles, which gave Castile its name, the instruments of Spanish rule through centuries of warfare, remain pleasing eye-catchers in the landscape. Railway stations, which enabled Spain to act as something like an industrialised European state, fall into ruins that seem nothing but an eyesore.

By bus across the badlands

THE SMILING PLAIN of almond trees and ripe barley a few minutes outside Guadix gave little hint of the desolation to come during the three-hour bus journey to Lorca. The bus followed a highway striking eastwards along a valley parallel with the line of the old railway. Before the routes diverged, the bus paused at the disused station for Gorafe – a village (population 474) 6 or 7 miles away, surrounded by deeply eroded cliffs and 240 Neolithic dolmens. No one, alive or dead, got on or off here.

For the next half an hour, the bus passed a plain planted with almonds to the left (north) and mountains clothed with pines and *encinas* under dark clouds to the right. The mountains belonged to the Sierra de Baza, part of a designated Natural Park. At Baza, a dull town of 20,000, 13 people got off and 4 got on, leaving 6 on board. One of the newcomers was a young woman whose grandfather in a pork-pie hat and sandals, who had come to the little bus station to see her off, kissed his hand as the bus pulled away, holding up his palm flat, as though it were pressed against a glass window.

Just outside Baza, at the junction with the A92N, stood the Club Los Rosales, with parking spaces and shuttered windows – a brothel, typically situated. Like a hotel, it has a website dedicated to customers' opinions. 'The situation is good and the rooms are in order,' wrote antonio41 in Spanish, 'I went with a dark, podgy Romanian girl. I wouldn't recommend it.'

Ten minutes later, the bus was passing acres of land so intersected with eroded channels that spurs were cut through by lateral gullies. Some hillocks isolated by the process bristled with chimneys from cave dwellings. The nature of the badlands varies: sometimes the surface is a crust with a mass of cracks, sometimes the crust is covered with lichen and widely separated perennial shrubs. The ancient silt that makes up the eroded ridges contains different kinds of mica: hard, sharp minerals with silicon, potassium and aluminium. It doesn't rain much here, but when it does rain, the water just runs off.

On the bits of land where cultivation is impossible, the biggest shrub looks like a kind of broom, with spherical yellow flowers. Of all crops here – figs, barley, vines, acorns, olives – almonds seem most resistant to drought and absence of soil. Another 20 minutes on, below the town of Cúllar, a smoothly domed field of newly planted little almond trees showed its flank to the highway: the field was moon-grey and the sprigs of green almond trees nestled inside blue plastic protecting sleeves. It was an abstract composition in colour.

The landscape remained bare, except where short-stemmed barley grew, between plantations of almonds. Townsend's local guide told him that the last league to the next town, Chirivel, was 'as long as Lent'. The town (of 2,000 people), once reached, proved unattractive. Its name derives from the Latin *silvella*, 'little wood', but that must long ago have been cut down.

An air of stupefaction fell upon the six passengers on the bus, as its engine laboured on uphill stretches, making the seats vibrate. Sometimes the air-conditioning sent gusts of cool air through the nozzles above the seats; sometimes it saved up the stale, hot air until sweat broke upon every brow. Yet if the journey had been attempted on foot, it would have been a series of terrible scrambles up dry, rough, boot-shredding ridges and down the other side, again and again, in still, hot, dusty air, with no water to be found and no path to be discerned, but one short gully looking like the next till the head throbbed and the knees gave way.

The halfway point came at Vélez – Vélez Rubio, at the foot of the road up into the Sierra de María. (That road led to Vélez Blanco, with its spiky-headed castle and hidden Neolithic cave painting.) At Vélez Rubio, the bus passengers had half an hour to take a beer under umbrellas outside the bar, which must rely greatly on these refreshment breaks.

On the ridge around which the town had been built, rose a fine big Baroque church – 'a beautiful church,' thought Townsend, 'built by the Dutchess [*sic*] of Alba'. It was of light-coloured brick with stone facings, and dominated a quiet square, looking like a grand colonial church in Mexico. Inside it, the huge, dark wood retable of the high altar had little mirrors set into it that must have caught the candlelight in the years when it was new.

There was time to buy some stamps at Correos, the post office. No, they didn't have stamps of 70 *céntimos* to send to England, but they did have 35 *céntimo* stamps. See, you put two on each letter. Two. Now then, ten you want? That means ten lots of two. Let me see. Five. Five. Five. And two more. No, that's not enough. Conchi, Conchi, have you any 35 cent stamps? No? Oh, you've got some of 70 cents in the cupboard? So, five and five and five and one more and two at 70. How much will that be? Where's my calculator. Let's see. No, that's not right. Five times 35 plus five times 35 plus five times 35 plus 35 plus 70 plus 70. Total – €7.

She took the ten-euro note proffered, passed it through a counterfeit detector, keyed into the till the seven euros due and the ten euros proffered, hit the transaction key and counted out the change: one, two, three euros. At the foot of the hill the bus was still there. Inside, as it waited with the ventilation off, the smell was not just of sweat but like the greasy clothes that a tramp had not taken off for many days.

By way of ash-grey hillsides banded with ruddy strata of harder rock, of little fields of dwarfed barley bordered by tough, pink-flowered oleanders, of isolated white houses protected by hedges of prickly pear – the bus swung cheerfully downhill on to the plain by Puerto Lumbreras, that dry, dull town, for some years inexplicably the site of a Parador state hotel, and towards its terminus, through the meagre light-industrial zone of Lorca. The square silhouette of the old defensive tower on the ridge very high above the town looked the same as ever. But barely a year earlier Lorca had been devastated by an earthquake.

Lorca, after the earthquake

The first shock had struck at five past five in the afternoon of 11 May 2011. At 6.47 p.m. another, stronger shock sent loosened masonry crashing down. Spanish television viewers saw a church bell and belfry smash into the ground feet away from a news crew reporting on the first shock.

Eight were killed. Aftershocks followed. To the world it was merely a 'moderate earthquake'. To the people of Lorca, the world had changed. Although the magnitude of the biggest shock was only 5.2, the earthquake was shallow, the epicentre just outside the town and many buildings were susceptible to damage. A boy walking his dog was killed by falling rubble. His mother called to passers-by for help, but there was nothing anyone could do.

The scenes of damage for the television cameras were banal: parked cars with their roofs crushed, concrete floors concertina'd, families wrapped in blankets spending the night in open squares. 'Lorca looks like Beirut,' the mayor said the next day. 'There's rubble on the ground and huge cracks in the walls.'

A year later the damage was less apparent at first sight. It was not like a carpet-bombed town. Here and there in the old streets a site was empty where a house once stood, the exposed walls on either side daubed with the yellow waterproofing with which Spanish engineers like to cover such surfaces, just as childhood grazes were always anointed with a yellow iodine solution.

But many a Spanish town bears such scars where old buildings have been demolished or have fallen through neglect.

The cruel difference in Lorca was that its proudest cultural masterpieces were the worst hit. The earthquake shook the roofs and domes of the Baroque churches till they fell in. 'Lorca has been abandoned by the gods of the Baroque,' said the local writer and historian José Luis Molina Martínez, six months after the disaster. With the churches closed, there remained little to draw tourists, and, as the Spanish economic crisis deepened, prospects dwindled for the restoration of Lorca's fortunes.

The golden stone façade of the church of Santiago, on its railed masonry platform on the steep hill of the town, appeared whole at first glance. Behind it the church lay open to the sky, its dome turned into a mound of rubble before the high altar. Sunday Mass was held in the sacristy, under old, white-painted vaulting that in some past decade had been so strongly pulled together with iron rods between its piers that it resisted ruin.

The benches and stacking chairs were all taken by worshippers. An old man laid his walking stick gently on the top of the old polished vestment-chest next to his seat. A mother knelt on the floor with two little girls swinging slightly on the bench-back next to her, one holding a cloth bag embroidered with studious rabbits.

The decoration of the makeshift church was an odd mixture of mannered, eighteenth-century statuary and cheap, twentieth-century prints and plastic. The people still came day by day, week by week, but it was a cramped space, cheek by jowl. There was no opportunity to light a candle at a side altar, say a prayer before an image of Christ crucified, take holy water with two fingers from a stoup to make a sign of the cross or kneel at the side of a Baroque confessional to receive the words of absolution for their sins.

Where the poor of Lorca live

IT WAS NOT the first time that the church of Santiago had been reduced from a building for people to the bare gathering of people who had once made it their own. The building had been burnt by the anarchists in the Civil War, depriving some parishioners of the only place of light, space and beauty to which they had free entry. The poor and ragged could not pass through the doors of the nearby Casino of Lorca, the club for solid citizens (itself occupying the old building of the Hospital of St John of God sequestrated at Mendizábal's dissolution of the monasteries in 1835).

Another church destroyed in the Civil War was Santa María, high above the town, up the zig-zag streets, at the entrance to the complex of buildings fortified by the Moors before its capture in 1244. Santa María was then built on the site of the main mosque. Today, the esplanade outside the roofless ruins commands a wide view of the plain beyond Lorca to the south, dotted with houses and shut off from the Mediterranean by another ridge of mountains.

Immediately below the esplanade, tiny houses held on like barnacles to the rock, higgledy-piggledy. Some had corrugated roofs. Some had been fitted up with flat roofs of red tiles, so that their inhabitants could sit and take the breeze of the evening. These must once have been shacks, put up on land that was unvalued. Over the years their owners had made them their own, with wrought-iron trellises for security, minuscule cement terraces, little metal-framed windows, postboxes, flowerpots. Some had air-conditioning units.

The paths between had been cemented into narrow roads, some ending in steps, some joining the road up from the plain to the castle. There was electricity, water and sewerage underneath the main road. A girl lugged two carrier-bags full of rubbish to the big, plastic municipal bin on wheels at the roadside and placed them beside it. 'Put the rubbish inside,' cried a middle-aged man, of Latin American appearance, from the other side of the road. 'I can't,' she replied. Then she did. 'Fat cow,' shouted the man without hostility – not that she was fat. A smell of rubbish hung over the town, but it was not limited to this little *barrio*.

On an oppressive, hot Sunday afternoon few people passed by. A very tanned fat man walked across the empty esplanade and said: '*Buenas tardes*.' An old lady in a loose print dress for the heat, leading a woolly dog, walked in the opposite direction and said: '*Buenas tardes*.' Two no-good-looking men in their thirties, one gap-toothed, with his hair in a ponytail, went by conspiratorially. The uglier one said: '*Buenas tardes*.'

A house directly below Santa María was perhaps 20 feet long and 15 wide, narrowing to 10 feet at one end. An open window behind bars betrayed signs of activity in the kitchen. The steepness of the hill allowed space for another room underneath this, its outer wall covered in crazy paving, with chickens pecking in a yard one pace wide, closed by a wrought-iron gate opening on to steps down the hill.

Under a corrugated roof, behind a chicken-wire grille decorated at strict intervals by three cement-cast horses' heads, a plastic clothes line aired a load of washing: two dozen pairs of knickers and underpants segregated by sex. The earthquake had made cracks open in houses like these, but the dangers of multi-storey tenements were absent here. The postman still called here, while many inhabitants of other, hazardous areas had to collect their mail from the main post office.

A couple of hundred feet down the hill, swifts wheeled about the tall, red crane outside the splendid Baroque church of San Patricio, closed since the earthquake. The crane was weighted by piles of concrete blocks each marked '3,000 kg'. Six great beams of wood lay neatly outside the west door, a tape-measure left lying on one. Work was in progress.

It was in slow progress too at San Mateo, and at San Francisco, its bell-tower bisected by a deep crack, and at Nuestra Señora del Carmen, where the vigorous Baroque façade was bound up with giant steel girders like a surgical cage round a broken skull.

From this church of Nuestra Señora del Carmen, Our Lady of Mount Carmel, goes forth annually the confraternity of the Most Holy Christ of Forgiveness, every Maundy Thursday and Good Friday, bearing on their shoulders a heavy float with an image of Christ carrying his cross. Lorca, like so many Spanish towns, is transformed in Holy Week, the streets full, day and night, with crowds watching the rival confraternities go about their penitential acts.

This confraternity is known as the Paso Morado, from the purple colour of its robes. Other confraternities include the Paso Negro and the Paso Blanco. But *morado* also means 'bruised' and *pasar morado* means 'to have a hard time of it', as the object of their devotion had, as he walked his Way of the Cross.

The statue is eighteenth-century, with real hair and beard. It is in an artistic idiom that the Anglo-Saxon world has often found in poor taste. The people of the parish of Nuestra Señora del Carmen hid the statue during the Civil War to prevent it being burnt. The confraternity now declares its intention of seeing its church restored. But where's the money to be found?

Some prosperity remained in Lorca. On the other side of the railway from the old town, just where a poor district is be expected to be found in many Spanish towns, Lorca still boasted a suburb of large detached houses, many designed by architects in Modernist, Art Nouveau, even in Renaissance style. They were separated by sandy paths with stone benches overhung by elms and palm trees.

These houses occupy the *alamedas*, formal walks first laid out in the seventeenth century. 'I was delighted with the public walks,' Townsend declared a hundred years later, 'resembling the parks at Oxford, but upon a more extensive scale and more beautiful.' The modern houses there were clearly desirable residences and were protected by high railings, shutters and alarms.

Lorca had not been entirely spick and span before the earthquake. A visit in November 1992 found mothers nursing their babies on the steps of the upper town, sitting in the sunshine for warmth, while their older children played football on waste ground. Everything higher up the hillside than San Patricio seemed then marked by poverty. There were roofless old houses.

Open-air card-players

LORCA HAD BEEN STRUCK by earthquakes before. One in 1674 led to the construction of the elegant town hall, with its arcaded balconies, on the hill opposite San Patricio.

Just where the earthquake damage from 2011 looked worst, in the Calle de la Corredera, the historic high street of Lorca, a saddler continued to trade. Casa Durante ('Everything for the horse and rider'), founded in 1895 by the present owner's great-great-grandfather, showed off in its window – among the harnesses and bridles, the riding-boots and breeches, the stirrups and girths – in pride of place the Zaldi saddle, fashioned by craftsmen from box-calf and beechwood, strengthened with steel and cushioned with rubber, all for €1,300.

In the window of a nearby bar a chirpy handwritten notice announced: 'We have *torrijas* on Fridays.' *Torrijas* are a sort of eggy bread fritter, once a recourse on religious days of abstinence from meat, and now regarded as something of a treat.

Outside another bar along the street, in the Plaza San Vicente, six old men were playing cards – or four were playing and two sitting with them. A *toldo* or canvas canopy gave their table shade, and on top of the rectangular base holding up the *toldo,* three walking sticks were carefully laid down, as the stick had been laid down on the vestment-press by the old man at Mass the evening before. Each of the card-players' sticks had a rubber ferule and was made in the pattern of a real cane of bamboo, though one was clearly metal. One had a curved handle and the other two crutch handles.

Each man had bought a drink but none took a sip. Their drinks were put out of harm's way in a row next to the sticks, not on the black tablecloth where the cards were dealt. Each of the men wore a short-sleeved shirt in the noon heat. One card-player wore a grey baseball cap. One of the men watching wore a straw hat. He was holding a transparent polythene bag of spice that he must have bought earlier. Five wore sandals – either ones with straps and no socks, or the kind with openwork uppers over socks. One man wore slip-on, brown leather shoes like moccasins, clean, as older men's shoes always are clean in Spain.

This was plainly a regular card school: sociable and economical, a variation on the old *tertulias*, the circles of male friends that characterised the life of the casino and café in the days of Unamuno before the Civil War. Today, other varieties include the endless games of dominoes, slapped down in bars that used to be smoky before the law forbade smoking on 1 January 2011, or the equally endless games of *petanca* on gritty pathways among shady trees in parks.

The Roman milestone

BEHIND THE CARD-PLAYERS of Lorca was a red-washed building held up by a steel framework, its window spaces empty and staring. On the corner with the Calle Corredera stood a Roman milestone from about the time of Christ's birth, a plinth and column 10 feet high, inscribed:

IMP CAESAR DIV
AVGVSTVS CO
FIEYNICPOTE
IMPXIIIIPONTII
MAX
XXVIII

Before the earthquake, under a serrated metal canopy or halo, an expressive stone statue from the seventeenth century was elevated on the column, depicting St Vincent Ferrer, reputed to have preached at the spot. He was the son of William Ferrer, an Anglo-Scottish soldier, the story goes. Vincent became a Dominican friar and during the papal schism of the fourteenth century spent his days wandering Europe in penance, preaching reconciliation and devotion to Christ. At the death of Christ on the cross, he said in one sermon on Good Friday, 'There was darkness over the whole face of the earth, the sun took off his robes of brightness and was clothed with black. The earth quaked and the rocks were rent.'

A stone plaque 400 years old remains, let into the wall, next to the place where he preached in Lorca, inscribed with six lines.

Hic, ubi consuevit praeco Vincentius illud
Clangere terribili voce Timete Deum.
Terribilis locus iste! Dei domus ista Tonantis!
Sit sacer iste locus sacra columna Deo.
Sitquoque et hoc nostri monumentum et pignus amoris
Semper in (outinam) posteritate ratum.

The preacher Vincent one time made his pulpit here
And cried with awe-filled voice: *All you the one God fear.*
How awful is this place, the God of Hosts' own home.
To God hold this place sacred and this standing stone.
May this our monument and this our loving token
Never by men in times to come (please God) be broken.

On the first-floor balcony above, a much newer sign was written in black paint on a bedsheet billowing a little in the breeze: UN ANO SIN CASA Y SIN SOLUCION – A year homeless and nothing done.

Murcia – a taste for richness

MURCIA SEEMED smart, metropolitan and busy after the bleakness of Guadix and Lorca. That is not at all how Murcia looks from Barcelona or Madrid, whose citizens tend to regard it as dull, provincial, obscure and dusty. It's a question of perspective.

Richard Ford, in the 1830s, thought it 'the dullest city in Spain, which is no trifle', and wrote that it had fallen under the rule of 'Murtia, the pagan goddess of apathy and ignorance', though in truth its name derives from the Arabic Medina Mursiya, 'strong city'.

Murcia is a provincial capital. There are 48 provinces in Spain, rather like the old counties of England. But Murcia is also an autonomous region, of which there are 19, if one counts the little enclaves in North Africa of Ceuta and Melilla. Murcia comes halfway up, with a population of about 1.5 million, about the same as Northern Ireland, though Murcia is 1,000 square miles smaller.

The biggest of Spain's autonomous regions by population is not Madrid (7.5 million), but Murcia's neighbour to the west, Andalusia, with a population of 8.5 million, about the size of Austria's. In the first quarter of 2012, one in three people in Andalusia were out of work; Murcia was closer to the national average of one in four. For the previous four years, Murcia's economy had been shrinking, doing worse than any region, apart from Extremadura perhaps. People at café tables referred to the economic position as ‘the crisis’. A common social enquiry in 2012 was not ‘How are you’? but ‘Have you got a job?’

Yet Murcia, at the end of an arid hour’s railway journey from Lorca, over sandy *ramblas*, as some of the dry watercourses here are called, and past ugly patches of light industry, still retained a taste for richness. It was quite normal in a bar to take chocolate for breakfast, so thick, strong and sweet that only those habituated to it could finish a cup. The counterpart in art here is the Baroque, taken to Rococo extremes. It can be hard to digest. To see how this flamboyant art grew from medieval roots, the best place to start is the cathedral.

Murcia revealed itself as a largely low-rise city of narrow streets, little troubled by hills, following a bent grid pattern on either side of the river Segura, a proper river with water in it. The cathedral, as is often the case, was the most impressive building in the city. The Baroque domelet and cupola at the top of the 300-foot tower was visible above the plane trees by the river. Closer to, the only aspect to be seen across an expanse of stone paving was the western façade, likened by the architectural historian John Harvey to stage scenery.

It was built in the middle of the eighteenth century by Jaime Bort y Meliá. Sumptuous, ample and imposing are among the adjectives that Harvey applies to his work here. The central part of the roofline high above the main door looked as though a segmental pediment had been broken into three by the sudden hydraulic lifting of the middle section. There were deeply encrusted areas of carving, plenty of heavy Corinthian capitals on pillars, forming sentry-boxes for gesticulating statues, and angels lounging between classical urns on the skyline. The stone was of reddish gold.

On one side of the façade rose the tower, ‘in compartments, like a drawn-out telescope’ thought Richard Ford. It took a long time to draw out, having been begun in 1521 and finished in 1792. Perhaps it demonstrates that Spain never really took to pure Renaissance architecture. At ground-floor level a carved plaque declares that *Anno Dni M.CCCCCXXI die XVIII Octobris inceptum est hoc opus* – This work was begun on 18 October 1521 – in the eighth year of the pontificate of Pope

Leo X, the Emperor Charles and his mother Joan reigning in Spain (that being Joan the Mad, already 12 years into her 46-year confinement at Tordesillas).

By 1525 the first stage, designed by two brothers from Florence, was completed, with pilasters carved like the borders of the frontispiece in a book of the time, rising to a cornice encrusted with stone vegetation. The second stage, which took another 20 years to build, was of slightly lighter stone. In the middle of the wall a satyr with a basket of fruit overflowing on his head squatted on the apex of a pediment above a double-arched window divided vertically by a thin marble column.

There things stood still for more than two centuries before work began again about 1765, in a style barer of Renaissance grotesques but developing into a high Baroque interpretation of Classical elements. At the fourth stage the tower began to narrow, and it was brought in between four narrow stone pavilions with stepped pyramidal stone roofs, like that on the original Mausoleum at Halicarnassus. These stepped pyramids were used on contemporary towers at Santiago de Compostela, and earlier, in 1731, by Hawksmoor, for the steeple of St George's, Bloomsbury.

At Murcia, these corner pavilions at the beginning of the bell stage have been called 'conjuratories', the idea being that they were used by clergy to repel storms and thunderbolts by prayers and the showing of relics. A notion general in England as much as in Spain was that the ringing of church bells (here directly above the pavilions) warded off thunder, or more importantly lightning, since these blessed instruments repelled devils that had power over meteorological forces.

As at Compostela, the upper parts of the tower were interfered with by the classicising Ventura Rodriguez in the second half of the eighteenth century, though the ribbed octagonal dome here pierced by oculi and topped by a tall lantern did not rob the tower of life.

Sacheverell Sitwell, who said that he had wanted to visit Murcia all his life, wrote in his book *Spain* (1950) that 'the interior of the cathedral is uninteresting'. Nothing could be less true.

It was factually interesting to see that the interior retains the Gothic vaulting of the medieval cathedral begun in the late fourteenth century, unreconstructed by the classicisers of the façade and tower. It was more than interesting to see what had been done in a large chapel completed a decade before the attempt to build a Renaissance tower. This was the chapel of the Vélez family, vaulted with a wonderful star-polygon, which formed a ten-petalled flower at the central apex, and reached out in an organic way to span a geometrically irregular space.

Even more organic was the exuberant carving on the walls of this tall chapel (which emulated that of the Constables of Castile at Burgos cathedral). It was as though the vegetation carved by the sculptor was on some miracle-grow fertiliser. The ribs on the wall rising to the vaulting were as fat as celery; the wall behind a stone-carved crucifix was covered with leaves like a pond with lilies; acanthus capitals seemed about to burst into blossom; bellflowers rose on stalks like giant hollyhocks and coats of arms rested on beds of curley parsley.

Strange naked dancing figures climbed the jungle. Stone was made to do things stone seldom does: stone doughnuts hung on the stone spikes of railings of stone. On the outside wall of the chapel, a stone chain of connected stone links hung from stone rings fastened into the wall. It was the wildest Baroque, achieved in a Gothic language, even before the Renaissance had been attempted.

'Gothic persisted long into the post-medieval era,' observed James Lees-Milne in his long essay *Baroque in Spain and Portugal*. 'That the Renaissance did not thrive in Spain is possibly explained by the absence of materialism in the Spanish character, and by the abundance of deep spiritual faith.'

'I regret you were that man's wife'

ON A STONE BENCH by the river Segura a black man from Africa sat alone. In a green aviary beneath the trees a dozen little parakeets whistled, one of them disgustingly bald. Two girls in jeans, one fat, one thin, walked past talking in Arabic.

Nearby, Calle Cánovas del Castillo was at midday a narrow canyon of shade, wide enough for one car at a time to pass the line of big, wheeled rubbish bins next to a wall of illegible graffiti. The street takes its name from a Spanish prime minister shot dead in 1897 by an Italian Anarchist, Michele Angiolillo.

Antonio Cánovas had been blamed for the torture of prisoners arrested after an Anarchist bomb had been thrown at a Corpus Christi procession in Barcelona. As Emma Goldman, the energetic American propagandist, told the story, in *Anarchism and Other Essays* (1910), Angiolillo had been motivated while in exile in London by seeing at a rally in Trafalgar Square the scars of some of Cánovas' victims. Angiolillo made his way to the spa of Santa Agueda at Mondragón in the Basque Country, where Cánovas was spending the hot August days.

'Cánovas, about to leave his house, stepped on the veranda,' wrote Emma Goldman.

> Suddenly Angiolillo confronted him. A shot rang out, and Canovas was a corpse. The wife of the Prime Minister rushed upon the scene. 'Murderer! Murderer!' she cried, pointing at Angiolillo. The latter bowed. 'Pardon, Madame,' he said, 'I respect you as a lady, but I regret that you were the wife of that man.'

Angiolillo was tried and garotted. The spa of Santa Agueda became a lunatic asylum.

The makings of a tobacconist

IN THE CALLE Cánovas del Castillo, a knot of people taking a pre-lunch drink at the bar Vino Tinto spilled out on to the pavement for a cigarette. One crossed the road to buy a packet of Ducados, the pungent, black-tobacco cigarettes, at Tabacos Exp No 23.

'Exp' stands for *Expendeduría de tabaco y timbre* (Vendor of tobacco and stamps), but the shops are called *estancos*, a reference to the controlled goods that they sell. *Estancar* means 'to block a watercourse', producing an *estanque* or pond, full of *estancado* or stagnant water. *Timbre* is a stamp, even though postage stamps are usually called *sellos*.

A licence to open an *estanco* is granted by the Commissioner for the Sale of Tobacco, an arm of a subsecretariat of the Treasury and Ministry of Finance. There are glorious possibilities for bureaucratic interference in the granting of these licences (for 25 years), which are limited by propinquity to other tobacconists (bad) and distance from places of education (good).

Tobacconists may not be bankrupts or smugglers, nor may they have been condemned (to imprisonment). They must be citizens of a country in the European Union. They do not have to live over the shop, but they must live nearby. The great thing is that they must be physical persons. In other words they are not commercial chains but real people, usually of a quieter disposition than those who have dreamt of ending their days as prosperous bar-owners.

The tobacconist pays a tax when granted a licence, and an annual fee set according to the size of the town: in villages of less than 10,000 people it is set at a 120 euros and 20 *céntimos* a year, and at twice as much in cities of more than 100,000 – or provincial capitals (no matter how small). There is an intermediate rate which we need not bother with.

It doesn't stop there, for there is also an annual tax depending on gross takings, amounting to about 2 per cent. The tobacconist is allowed to make a margin on sales to the public of 9 per cent on cigars and 4 per cent on stamps.

Generally *estancos* are spick and span, with a patch of shiny floor before a counter, which may have a glass vessel like an ashtray for money to be laid down. Stamps are traditionally wrapped for customers in scrap paper taken from the wholesale cartons of cigarettes.

The tobacconist, in the eyes of the Ministry, should also observe the customary hours of attention to the public. At two o'clock the licensee of Exp No 23 pulled down the metal shutters and, as is customary, went home for lunch.

No tomatoes to be had for lunch

HE WAS NOT the only one who wanted lunch. There was a Chinese restaurant, the Bambu Garden, in the Calle de Cánovas del Castillo. Chinese restaurants in Spain are not without their interest – but instead, what about this reticent façade, the Restaurante Salzillo, quietly boasting La Gran Cocina Murciano?

On the menu for the first course were tomatoes, in season. But this was not the season, for they were no ordinary tomato but the celebrated *raf*. Anyone who complains that tomatoes these days do not taste of tomatoes should try a plate of sliced *raf* tomatoes dressed simply with good olive oil and salt.

These tomatoes contain high levels of sugar (glucose and fructose) and of acids (citric and malic), but there's more to it than that. It is like trying a tropical fruit for the first time – which is precisely what tomatoes are. Stout Cortés may not have stared at the Pacific as Keats imagined, but after his conquest of Mexico in 1521 he doubtless looked upon the Aztec *tomatl* when it was yellow and sent back seeds from New Spain to the Old.

It would be nice to think that *raf* was some Arabic word adopted to denote this treasure from America. But it is simply a modern acronym, standing for *resistente a fusarium*, resistant to the *fusarium* fungus, which does to tomatoes what phylloxera did to grapevines. The variety has been introduced only in the last generation, bred from ancestors such as the French Marmande and the Muchamiel, named after a town outside Alicante.

It is a lobed or furrowed fruit and must not be eaten when fully red, when it is over-ripe. It has a dark green pigment in its skin that masks the yellow-red of the maturing fruit. A telling characteristic of the *raf* is its price. This is not just for foolish tourists who like to eat it in restaurants. Go to a market in Almería, or Murcia, and the *raf* tomatoes sell for four times the price of ordinary tomatoes – for €15 a kilo or more at Christmas time.

They are grown near Níjar, south-west of Lorca, between the mountains and the sea. The tomatoes under acres of sheeting form a sea of their own, the Mar de Plástico. The road westward runs parallel to the coast, inland from the endless market gardens. Often the Mar de Plástico shines more brightly in the sun than the Mediterranean itself. Most of these plastic-swaddled tomatoes go for export. *Raf*, with a smaller yield per acre, account for a small percentage of production, and they are harvested only from November to April, 'until people put on their short sleeves'. There were plenty of short sleeves in Murcia that day.

So instead it was *chipirones*, little cuttlefish, with small garlic cloves and parsley; then kid cutlets. Cutlets, either of lamb or kid, tend to be small in Spain: nut-sized ovals of meat on long, thin ribs. The butchery often shatters a bit of bone. They can be over-salted or over-cooked. But here they were just right and came with *patatitas al montón*. These are sautéed potatoes, except that they are cooked with olive oil instead of butter, and often with a little onion. As one cook explained, it is like making a tortilla, except you don't add the egg, just keep the pieces of potato moving gently with a spatula.

For *postre*, pudding, there was *tarta de turrón. Turrón* is lamely translated as 'nougat', but that gives a false impression. It has a definitely Arabian character. It comes in two kinds: hard, with almonds embedded in sugary brittle, which endows it with the resistance of concrete; soft, which has the consistency of putty and is confected of crushed almonds, honey, egg white, lemon zest and a touch of cinnamon. The tart was made with the latter and proved excellent accompanied by a cup of strong, black, bitter coffee.

There is absolutely no point asking for a menu in English anywhere in Spain, for they are invariably erroneously translated, and even where accurate give less than a clue to what the unknown dishes are like. More unhelpfully, they conceal from the diner the Spanish name of whatever is chosen to eat.

Although the Spanish can eat daunting amounts for lunch, as their *comida* or main meal, this three-course lunch at the Restaurante Salzillo was not heavy, and in any case there was a walk ahead, across the city to see the high point of peculiarly Murcian art.

The Last Supper, with pineapples

THERE WAS, on the wall of the restaurant, a troubling photograph. It showed a mock-up of the Last Supper with figures

– one might almost say dummies – seated round a dining-table spread with a lacey cloth and set with stands of fruit: a fat pineapple, melons standing upright exposing their pink or white flesh where the rind had been cut in a serrated pattern like a cartoonist's idea of a hatched bird's egg, and bunches of red or white grapes the size of conkers.

An epergne of apples concealed the head of the Beloved Disciple reclining on the bosom of Jesus at his place at the head of the table. In the narrow spaces between the displays of exotic food, stood candelabra with barley-sugar-twist candles. Each Apostle had a bread roll. If this was meant to advertise the restaurateur's wares, it seemed in very bad taste.

As usual in Spain, a different explanation awaited, in this case at the church of Jesus, on the other side of the old city, north up the agreeable pedestrian shopping street called Trapería (where once they sold old clothes, or at least cloth of some kind, as in London's Cloth Fair) and left at the old church of Santo Domingo, heading west for half a mile, down past the Teatro Romea (burnt down in 1877 and 1899), outside which they once sold esparto grass, past the end of Calle Jabonerías, 'Soapmaker Street', down Calle Santa Teresa, past butchers' shops and cafés, tobacconists' and hardware shops, all beneath five storeys of flats, until the flats grew less tall, the street narrower, the shops less smart, and at last the street ended in the bright sun of the Plaza San Agustín, on the far side of which blue letters on white tiles spelled out Iglesia de Jesús.

The tiled roof above a whitewashed drum high above the stone portico hinted at what was to be found within: a tall rotunda, like a cardboard roll on end, decked within with marble, opening out into eight chapels joined by an ambulatory and covered by a cupola punctuated with square-headed windows between its eight ribs, and painted with a certain amount of trompe l'oeil work of architectural supererogation.

In each of the chapels leading off the central space stood a different group of statuary – each one a *paso* or processional float, for this building is the chapel of the Real y Muy Ilustre Cofradía de Nuestro Padre Jesús Nazareno – the Royal and Most Illustrious Confraternity of Our Father Jesus of Nazareth. To call Jesus 'Our Father' sounds very strange to non-Hispanic ears. *Padre* has different connotations in Spanish; in Mexico it is widely used as an adjective, meaning 'fantastic, nice' and *muy padre* is a term of universal approval.

In any case this chapel was built by one of the fraternities that carry floats in Holy Week in Murcia, and it was finished in 1692. In the centuries before that, the fraternity had as an object of devotion the Eleven Thousand Virgins reputed to have suffered martyrdom with St Ursula. The Passion of Christ gradually supplanted them as a focus.

For visitors to the chapel, as for the crowds seeing the floats carried through the streets, the polychromatic tableaux told the story. The Agony in the Garden showed an angel comforting Jesus in the Garden of Gethsemane while his three disciples sleep. The Arrest of Jesus depicted a red-headed Judas kissing his Master, at whom a helmeted man-at-arms holding a halberd makes a grab, while hot-headed Peter strikes off with his sword the ear of the High Priest's servant, who tumbles over, his dark-lantern crashing to earth and his legs in striped yellow hose flailing in the air.

So it continued from chapel to chapel: St Veronica rewarded for her pity to Jesus in wiping his face, as he carried his cross, by finding his image imprinted on her handkerchief. (The posture of the saint as she displays the handkerchief – a real cloth here at Murcia – was the inspiration for the common bullfighting term, *una veronica*, signifying a movement typical of the first *tercio*, in which the matador swings the cape in a slow circle round himself in order to persuade the charging bull to follow its movements.)

The figure of St Veronica in her side chapel is carved with drapery that displays the sculptor's virtuosity in representing layers of billowing textiles, coloured in rose and blue and ochre. This sculpture of St Veronica is said to show off the style favoured by the well-dressed courtesan of the mid-eighteenth century.

And here, in a dim, cool space, was the dining-table of the Last Supper seen in the photograph at the restaurant, only now the table was bare, so that the tableau looked less theatrical, if also less like a supper. All these figures were the work of Francisco Salzillo (1707–83), born in Murcia and taken to its heart, for he brought the art of the *paso* to its highest emotional point. A stranger would not realise, unless he had been fortunate in his reading beforehand, that this was the man after whom the restaurant was named. Had it been called Restaurante Cánovas the food would have tasted as good.

The sculptor Salzillo was not ignorant of the sacred scenes he depicted. As a young man he had tried his vocation as a Dominican friar, but returned to the busy world on his father's death, following his trade as a sculptor and painter. While Castile was in decline in the eighteenth century, Murcia was growing in population and wealth.

On each side of the city in the valley of the Segura mulberry trees were planted, 7,000 acres at their greatest extent, and the money-spinning energy of the silkworm was recognised in 1770 by the establishment of a silk-spinning factory under royal patronage, the Real Fábrica de Hilar Seda a la Piamontesa.

Prosperity did not obviously lessen religious fervour, rather the dogmas of religion were embraced and expressed in increasingly flamboyant ways: in painting, music, architecture and mass exercises of corporate piety. The *torcedores* (in English, silk-throwsters), who reeled the fibres from the cocoons, formed a guild which claimed its own place in the Holy Week processions.

Salzillo's Last Supper tableau at the Iglesia de Jesús replaced one made by his father, some figures of which were acquired by the confraternity of the Paso Morado in Lorca. Here at Murcia, the confraternity of Nuestro Padre Jesús Nazareno could not bring itself to replace the figure of its patron, adapted in 1600 to serve as a processional image, its arms articulated, its robe one of many precious silk creations in purple or gold, its face deathly white, its hair real hair, the cross it shoulders of deliberately unreal elaboration, in tortoiseshell with silver mounts. It was the only figure saved from the violent flood of 1651 when 1,500 were drowned when the Segura burst its banks. It now stands in the place of greatest honour under a canopy or *templete* of marble and gold.

Around the church is wrapped the Salzillo museum, amplified at the end of the twentieth century, explaining the sculptor's life, times and techniques. It is the best compromise possible between museum and church for objects made to foster devotion but deserving the attention of lovers of art.

As for Salzillo's Last Supper, it challenged even Sacheverell Sitwell's Baroque soul. 'A minor horror attaches to his carved figures because they are two-thirds life-size,' he observed, 'so that they are not much taller than dwarfs or pygmies.' But he did not have to carry a solid float through the hot candlelit night in Holy Week.

Chinchilla: an appointment with death

THE WORLD CHANGED between Murcia and Chinchilla. In an hour and a half, the train ran past rows of fruit trees on bare white earth, serrated mountains and unexpected fields of rice, pale rocky ridges gripped by the roots of pine trees, past almonds, vines and olives to the dry-stone walls of Hellín.

Heading north, it went straight through the ruined station of Tobarra, then through gaps in a series of sierras 3,000 or 4,000 feet high and over field after unfenced little field of wheat stubble. This was no longer the wind-blown desert of the south-east, nor the citrus-groved seaboard of the Levante but the beginning of the wide tableland of La Mancha.

At the old station of Chinchilla, the tiles were gone from the roof. To the right, atop its rocky hill, the silhouette of the round towers and crenellations of Chinchilla castle cut into the sky. The train did not stop.

In Spain there is a different attitude to risk. Chinchilla seemed safe enough. It was a backwater, not even having colonial connections to chinchillas, the furry rodents of the Andes. The town's name derives from a Latin word for 'thorn bush'; the rodent's name comes either from *chinche*, 'a bug', or from the pre-Columbian people who first turned them into fur coats. But Chinchilla is a pleasant little town and the castle worth visiting. A bus goes from Albacete or Almansa.

The visitor can, or could, walk freely up and over the castle keep, to look out over the wide landscape under the sun. The shadows of the broken stonework were black. From the walkway by the parapet it was possible to jump down on to the white dusty stone roof of the keep, where scrubby briars grew.

From there it was easy to hop down into that patch of black shade by the ruined wall in the blinding sun. The jump was almost made. But wait. That was not shade. It was a void. The black shade was an opening into a space 30 feet, or 60 feet deep. Perhaps down there was where Cesare Borgia, Lucrezia's father, was once imprisoned. If that little jump had been made, it would have been death.

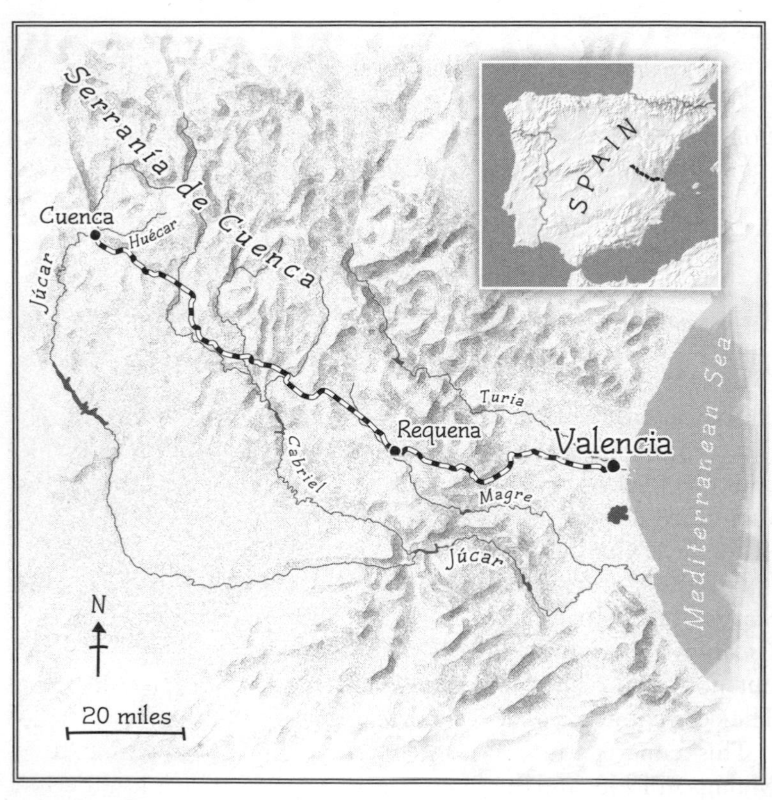
Serranía de Cuenca
Cuenca
Huécar
Júcar
SPAIN
Mediterranean Sea
Turia
Requena
Valencia
Cabriel
Magre
Júcar
N
20 miles

7

Horchata – Orgeat

CUENCA TO VALENCIA

The veiled Slaves – Cuenca: city on a spine – Crashing into ruin – Painter of light – The price of fish – A faithful bohemian – Sweet and chalky – Finding the Holy Grail – Two hundred and seven steps – Valencia's chocolate challenge – Oranges and roses

The veiled Slaves

ONE OF THE SLAVES was kneeling on the floor of the church in front of the Blessed Sacrament that was exposed in the form of bread in a star-like monstrance of silver. All that could be seen of her from behind was a white veil falling to the vacuumed turquoise carpet behind the railings of the front half of the little church off the Plaza Mayor of Cuenca.

For these are the Esclavas del Santísimo Sacramento – the Slaves of the Most Blessed Sacrament and of Mary Immaculate. *Esclavas* may sound a little less strange in Spanish than 'Slaves', but not much. The Slaves have convents in 11 Spanish cities. The convent at Castellón de la Plana was set up only in 2012.

This congregation of contemplative nuns was founded in Malaga in 1943, and their foundress died in 1960, her foundation receiving pontifical approval in 1989. Each Slave spends two hours kneeling in prayer before the Blessed Sacrament: once during the day, once at night.

There must be quite a few annoyances in the Slave's daily horarium of disciplined adoration. There is the physical kneeling to attention; the heat of summer and cold of winter nights; the clock that strikes the quarters with the Westminster chimes, as if it were in an Edwardian parlour; the people coming and going clumsily in the church, invisible behind her back; the noise of the children shouting on the doorstep only separated from the church by the wooden panels of the door; the traffic roaring beneath the archway of the road outside; the drunks outside at night and the disco beat from the nearby nightclub.

At 7.50 p.m. a nun came in silently in her white shoes, her cream habit overhung by her ankle-length veil. There was a changing of the guard. One prie-dieu, with its dented, upholstered kneeler, was vacated while the one next to it was filled by a worshipper facing her unseen God. It is a practice curiously out of step with the times.

The architecture of the church was what might be expected for a building from the 1950s. It bore some resemblance to a fireplace of the time. Above the altar, where white gladioli curled, a little bruised at the edges, the seven gifts of the Holy Spirit were represented in stained glass, with the name of each in Latin spelled out in idiosyncratic script, like spray-can graffiti-lettering before its time. On the P of Pietas, roosted the dove of the Holy Spirit, with the hand of God, the Digitus Dei, descending from the top of the letter. The overall effect was weird.

Who knows whether the Slaves have not found freedom and peace in their distracting confinement? This house at Cuenca was the noviciate, it appeared, and 18 nuns looked out from a group photo in the church porch, five of them black.

Cuenca: city on a spine

THE OBVIOUSLY remarkable thing about the ancient cathedral city of Cuenca is its position on a thin ridge high up between the two deep ravines of the rivers Júcar and Huécar. Cuenca is not so much a name as a description, the word deriving from the Latin *concha*, 'a shell', and meaning 'a river basin', 'a deep valley' (or in the human context 'an eye-socket').

Although the city of Cuenca traditionally insists that it was founded on the same day as Rome, it was finally wrested from its true founders the Moors only under Alfonso VIII in 1177 – 21 September, the feast of St Matthew, it says (in Gothic letters as vertical as railings) in an old inscription in the cathedral. Its old streets rise steeply up the ridge till there is width enough for only one thoroughfare, which narrows to a drawbridge as it passes under a castellated gateway.

The literally breathtaking approach to the cathedral was across the footbridge above the gorge of the Huécar from the old monastery of St Paul, now a Parador. In the early heat of May, thermals drove the poplar seed-fluff upwards in a snow storm around the planks of the bridge 144 Castilian feet (132 imperial feet of the English or American size) above the watercourse.

A visitor might be forgiven for thinking that this iron-framed bridge, its spindly towers of girders fitted over stumps of ancient stonework, was built to replace a masonry bridge destroyed in the Civil War. Certainly, during the Civil War, the cathedral was sacked, the relics of St Julian, the city's patron, were burnt and the bishop was shot. He was beatified in 2007.

But the Puente de San Pablo, built in five fine arches in the sixteenth century, fell long before that. The two arches nearest the cathedral collapsed in 1786, another fell in 1895, and the city council ordered the demolition of the remains with dynamite. After that nothing happened for years, so the Bishop of Cuenca built the present iron bridge with its rickety wooden planks, which was opened in 1903.

Eastward, upriver, the floor of the Huécar ravine lay parcelled into kitchen gardens, where a man in blue overalls and a flat hat was planting out seedling vegetables from a tray of expanded polystyrene. The fine tilth was moulded into corrugated channels and little ramparts for irrigation. Some lettuces planted out earlier in the day lay floppily on the surface. A bed of potatoes flourished in its own embankment. A bed of unruly onions bordered a row of peonies, with rosemary between. Poppies and roses bloomed next to the stone field walls. A smallholder's dog barked, setting off a dozen others. A donkey brayed and a distant car engine echoed from the rocky walls of the gorge.

From the walkway of the bridge, the cathedral was straight ahead, the walls of its chapter-house edging on to the sheer drop. Pleasing enough as the stonework of the backside of the cathedral complex looked, the *casas colgadas* were more eye-catching – the hanging houses of which tourists love to take pictures.

On the side of a house to the left hung a three-storey wooden balcony, diminishing in size as it went down, and beneath the lowest floor, nothing but space, for the walls of the house turned into the perpendicular rock side of the gorge. This house is said to date from the fifteenth century. Certainly by the end of the nineteenth century it was in a poor state, and others like it had been demolished (just as at Tortosa the houses on the side of the more modest rock walls by the bishop's palace above the river Ebro are today ruinous and tottering).

The present-day appearance of the balconies of this hanging house was attributable to the work done in 1927 by the architect Fernando Alcántara, who intended to reconstruct their ancient appearance. Further work was done on the house between 1950 and 1978, and it now housed a museum of abstract art. Other remarkable houses did remain on the edges of the ravines of Cuenca. The five storeys of houses seen from the roadway may have another five storeys or more plunging down the cliff-side. These had the appearance of the more vertiginous parts of the Old Town of Edinburgh.

The ridge on which the old city of Cuenca stood was in part broken into vertical fingers – the texture and colour of sponge fingers for a trifle – of a kind like the Mallos near Jaca. Some houses were built on the finger tips, some on arches of stone bridging two fingertips, and others on high retaining walls of stone filling the gaps between fingers. From the end of the Puente de San Pablo, a path ran down from the city along the wall of rock on which it stands.

The trees on the distant high ridges beyond the city were *encinas*, and above those pines. In the gorge, yellow broom grew, with blue irises between, and, in clumps separated by bare earth, spurges, coarse grass, poppies, roses, small ash trees, mallows, figs, and, on the rockface, mature ivy, with its broad leaves. From the overhanging rock above the path a stick fell – but it wasn't a stick, for it rapidly wound across the path like a serpentine green wave and disappeared into the shrubs.

The heath-like vegetation on the steep slope was dotted with wild flowers of unknown kinds, yellow, pink and blue. A smell of crushed thyme came up from every footstep. The breeze sent grasshoppers sailing many times further than even their elastic spring could take them. Against the high, thin clouds, five vultures moved at great speed across the gorge, higher and more distant every second. The wind in the warm valley sounded in the ears as little birds cheeped and the odd bee made its rounds of the new flowers, for Cuenca is famed for its honey.

Crashing into ruin

BACK PAST THE END of the Puente de San Pablo, through a stone-paved alley, lay the Plaza Mayor, little more than a widening of the street that ran up the spine of the little city. The square was given definition by the eighteenth-century town hall that spanned the street on three narrow arches.

People sat on tubular aluminium chairs outside the Bar San Juan as the engine of a city bus revved while it waited for the traffic lights to allow it through the central arch, past the door of the Slaves of the Most Blessed Sacrament. Swifts whisked overhead.

In the square, opposite the plain-fronted houses painted in pastel colours of ochre, terracotta, grey, blue, beige, mauve, stood the massive façade of another convent of enclosed nuns, known as Las Petras, the Peters, since they were founded in 1509 under the protection of the Apostle Peter. But the building that plainly dominated the little square was the cathedral.

The cathedral had a most strange appearance. At the top of a broad flight of steps (eaten into by the slope of the hill) it boasted three deep doorways beneath Gothic arches, but above this, all that was visible was a Gothic curtain wall with empty window spaces showing the sky on each side of a small, central rose window. Although the cathedral was begun in the twelfth century, its whole appearance was changed in one day in 1902.

At that date, two modest Baroque towers stood each side of the central rose window, above which a bell-tower supported a spire topped by a weather-vane in the form of Alfonso VIII with a shield in one hand and a sword in the other. It gave its name to the bell-tower, the Giraldo, like the tower of the Giralda of Seville.

At 10 o'clock on the morning of Sunday, 13 April 1902, María Antón, the 20-year-old daughter of the cathedral bellringer was in the bellchamber of the tower with six children. All the bells had been rung that morning at daybreak, eight and nine. The children in the bellchamber suddenly noticed that mortar was running from between the joints of the masonry. They tried to escape but were buried in the rubble as the tower fell. One of them, Francisco Requena, aged 15, might have escaped, but he went back because he had forgotten his cloak.

The Bishop of Cuenca was on his way out of the cathedral and had reached the pulpit when the archway to the cloister crashed down in a cloud of dust and a roar. The tower fell to the north, destroying two houses. In one of them, no one was at home, and in the other, the inhabitants miraculously escaped with their lives.

The bishop wept, the governor and the mayor arrived and with them the city architect, who immediately began the rescue attempt, with the help of neighbours from Calle San Pedro and the houses near the castle. Hearing faint cries, one of them set about levering apart two great blocks of stone and pulled out Francisco Requena, the youngster who'd forgotten his cloak.

The corpse of the bellringer's daughter was found later, as were those of three of the children. At half past one in the night of 14 April, the rescuers heard the cries of children and found two young boys still alive.

The bell-tower of Cuenca cathedral fell four months before the great campanile of St Mark's in Venice. Unlike the campanile, the ruins at Cuenca were not faithfully reconstructed. As far as it went, the style chosen by Vicente Lampérez, the architect of the cathedral's reconstruction in 1910, was what he called 'Anglo-Norman', in homage to Queen Eleanor, the wife of Alfonso VIII the reconqueror of Cuenca and the daughter of Henry II of England.

The façade remains unsatisfactory, but the interior is still largely medieval Gothic. Architectural historians debate how far it was influenced by France and how far, if at all by England. It has, if one is interested, an architectural peculiarity unique in Spain of a clerestory possessing internal tracery without glazing, in place of a triforium – a feature partly paralleled at St Seine l'Abbaye in Burgundy.

The attached museum, empty of visitors, had plenty of things of great beauty: a couple of El Grecos, devotional art of strong character and a powerful catafalque-hanging from the seventeenth century of black silk with silver skulls. The cathedral itself also has astonishing Renaissance and Baroque additions, which are not noticed with any enthusiasm by the admirer of the Gothic, John Harvey.

He, though, may be quoted in judgement on the feeling of one of the most satisfying, airy and under-familiar of the five dozen or so splendid ancient cathedrals of Spain. 'It has a clarity of detail and fine finish,' he wrote, 'giving it a jewel-like quality the more appreciated in the almost savage beauty of its natural setting.'

Painter of light

CUENCA'S STATION for fast trains, which opened in December 2010, lay two or three miles from the city, which appeared from that distance like a great rock in a cleft of the scalloped ridge. The new station was named after Fernando Zóbel, who died in 1984, the abstract painter who installed the museum of Spanish abstract art in the hanging house.

The fast line made Cuenca, halfway to Valencia, only 50 minutes from Madrid – plus the taxi ride, which added 11 euros to the 15-euro train fare. The driver to the station, a man from Segovia, was not impressed with Cuenca. It was fine for a visit, but a dead-end place to live. The new town at the foot of the ridge certainly showed signs of poverty.

In 58 minutes the train reached Valencia, travelling too fast to see a bird or a goat, thwacking over a new-laid line that passed through no villages, but among fields of wheat with bare patches the shape of flints where the land was too steep to plough, through flat vineyards, through pine-covered valleys and through tunnels into a wide, flat region of orange groves near the coast of the Levante. By stopping-train it would have taken three hours.

The big, bare, new station at which the train arrived was named after a painter too – Joaquín Sorolla (1863–1923), not an abstract painter, but one hard to categorise, and not widely known in Britain, where little of his work is to be seen. Leeds has some oil studies of beach scenes and Southampton an uncharacteristic landscape of Asturias. Like John Singer Sargent, with whom he is often compared, he followed a line quite different from the Impressionists. Both were captivated by Velázquez.

The Thyssen-Bornemisza Museum in Madrid mounted a joint exhibition of Sargent and Sorolla in 2006, and it is indeed in Madrid that his work is best represented, both at the Prado and in the Museo Sorolla, originally built as his home and studio. Both Sargent and Sorolla have been called Luminists, painters of light. When Sorolla won praise for the exhibition put on by the Hispanic Society of America in 1909, it was as 'the painter of vibrating sunshine without equal' in the words of the New York critic James Huneker. 'Not Turner, not Monet, painted so directly blinding shafts of sunlight as has this Spaniard.' But what does that mean? All painters paint light.

The price of fish

SOROLLA ENJOYED greater international recognition between 1900 and 1910 than Picasso. His first big solo exhibition – of more than 500 works – had been in 1908, at the Grafton Galleries in London (where Roger Fry was to show the Post-Impressionists two years later). It was the 1908 exhibition that enthused Archer Huntington, an American philanthropist and the founder of the Hispanic Society of America, to put on the exhibition of 352 of his works in New York the next year.

The catalogue for the exhibition, which sold 20,000 copies in a month, illustrated some of the works in black and white, which gave an idea of their tone and form, but little of their luminescence. The last item in the catalogue was *Triste Herencia,* 'Sad Inheritance' (1899), which shows crippled boys, their naked bodies exposing their debility, bathing in the sea at Valencia under the care of a dark-habited brother of the order of St John of God. The title undoubtedly refers to the effects of congenital syphilis, not to poliomyelitis as some have said, for Sorolla had thought of calling it *Children of Pleasure.*

The picture exemplifies the thread of social concern that runs through Sorolla's earlier work. Like his friend and Valencian contemporary the novelist Vicente Blasco Ibáñez (the author of *Sangre y Arena*, in English *Blood and Sand*) he felt the influence of Emile Zola. There is discernible in his painting too something of Zola's friend Edouard Manet, who had visited Madrid in 1865 to see the paintings of Velázquez.

A powerful early canvas by Sorolla was given the title *Otra Margarita* (1892). It shows a young woman in handcuffs in a bare railway carriage, the ochre monochrome of which is relieved by the red collars of the Guardia Civil who escort her to prison. The title refers to Gounod's opera *Faust* from a generation earlier, in which the wronged Marguerite is imprisoned for infanticide but, rejecting Faust's offer of freedom, is taken up to heaven from the gallows, to the rage of Mephistopheles. It is a plot worthy of the Spanish Golden Age dramatist Tirso de Molina.

Otra Margarita is in St Louis, Missouri, but a canvas of social concern that connects with Sorolla's fascination with the sea is in the Prado. *¡Aún dicen que el pescado es caro!* ('Still they say the price of fish is too high', 1894), at 6 feet, 8 inches wide, is almost as big as the painting hanging nearby, showing Queen Joan the Mad, by Francisco Pradilla, who had befriended Sorolla during his student days in Rome. But their two canvases belong to different worlds: Pradilla's history painting is academic and contrived; Sorolla's naturalistic by intention, depicting a scene from daily life, lit as it would be in reality.

The picture shows two fishermen below decks in a small vessel. One supports a young man badly injured in some accident aboard, while the other applies a hot, wet cloth to the wound. The light comes from the hatch above, glancing on the bald head of one fisherman and the other's black, floppy beret (or *barretina*, a Valencian variant of the Phrygian cap or French cap of liberty). The weathered hands of the man with the dressing show dark against the pale flesh of the injured young man, who wears round his neck a medal of Our Lady of Mount Carmel, a patron of seafarers.

The title of the painting features in the novel by Blasco Ibáñez about Valencian fisherfolk, *Flor de Mayo*, 'The Mayflower', the name of a fishing boat. It ends with the angry words of the grandmother of Pascualet, the youngster crushed by a water barrel (of the kind seen in Sorolla's picture), whose dead body is washed ashore in the novel: 'They'll come here to the Fish Market, those whores who haggle so much. And still they'll say that the price of fish is too high!'

A faithful bohemian

THE STATE BOUGHT *¡Aún dicen que el pescado es caro!* in 1895 for the Prado. Its painter had started by copying Velázquez (making a full-size copy of the portrait in the Prado of Queen Mariana of Austria) and then imitated him (with *Nun in Prayer*, 1883). He did not forget Velázquez in his remarkable portraits (of the writer Pérez Galdos, 1894, of King Alfonso XIII outdoors, 1907, and notably of himself in 1904 and 1909).

But when people talk of him as a painter of light, they probably think of the brilliant scenes by the sea, either elegant ladies (his wife and daughter walking on the beach, 1909), bathers in sun-dappled robes (*La bata rosa: Despues del baño*, 1916) or men with oxen in the breakers (1903).

Sorolla survives the decades better than his writer friend Blasco Ibáñez, whose mannered prose and melodrama can seem absurd. Something of Sorolla's self-image may be gathered from the house he built himself in the now traffic-filled Paseo Martínez Campos in Madrid (nearest metro station, Rubén Darío). The street would scarcely have seen a motor vehicle in 1910, when the house, with its little formal garden, was built. The biggest space is given over to the studio where he worked (though he painted in the open air, muffled against the winter cold of Granada and standing in the snow of Burgos). It is a double cube of perhaps 50 feet by 25 feet. It might be called bohemian in the sense that George du Maurier used the word in the second half of the nineteenth century.

But Sorolla was not bohemian in his private life, sticking to Clotilde, the wife he married aged 25, and his children, who appear in his paintings in health (*Madre*, 1900, of Clotilde with the new-born Elena lost in a sea of white bedclothes) and sickness (the moving *Maria Convalescent*, 1907, of his elder daughter with suspected tuberculosis wrapped up in the open air). Family life continued in the house undisturbed by his work in the studio.

The rooms of the house combined the traditional and modern. Sorolla ordered doors to be made for each room like those depicted in *Las Meninas* by Velázquez. The *antecomedor* had a dado of tiles in a sixteenth-century pattern made for Sorolla by Juan Ruiz de Luna at Talavera, the traditional ceramic town of Castile. This room is reminiscent of the modest domestic arrangements of Philip II. A photograph from 1916 showed the stone lattice casing, which survives today, designed for the central heating radiators installed in the house. In each of the rooms stood a statue of the Virgin Mary.

Just when Sorolla reached his high point, good fortune dealt his painting a blow. In 1911 he agreed with Huntington to paint, for $150,000, a series for the Hispanic Society of America showing all the regions of Spain. It was a project much of its time, when *tipos*, men and women dressed in their traditional costumes, were being caught in idealised photographs by José Ortiz Echagüe. For Sorolla it meant years of work and travel, which resulted in crowded canvasses 45 feet across. Spontaneity and truthful representation of outdoor light suffered. It was not the end of his genius, for still he produced wonderful work until a stroke stopped him from painting in 1920.

Sweet and chalky

TWO MARVELS can be reached in five minutes' walk from the house in the heart of Valencia where Sorolla was born: *horchata* and the Holy Grail. First *horchata*.

Sorolla was born in Calle Mantas, round the corner from the tall-towered church of Santa Catalina, where he was baptised. Between the two, in the network of little streets, is the Plaza Redonda. The Plaza Redonda is a circle only 120 feet across surrounded by a continuous façade of 15 houses, four storeys high. All around at ground level are little shops and in the middle stands a fountain. It is known locally as El Clot, 'The Hole'.

It was designed in 1837 by the municipal architect Salvador Escrig. By the end of the twentieth century it had fallen into decay, but the restoration of the first decade of the twenty-first, in the opinion of some, has, by imposing clean uniformity, spoilt the whole effect.

Just to the north, the narrow Calle de la Sombrerería opens into the scarcely wider Plaza de Santa Catalina, at the foot of the church tower. Two rivals in the kingdom of *horchata* face each other across the narrow plaza: the Horchatería de Santa Catalina on the south side, and the Horchatería El Siglo on the north side. It was pleasant enough in the morning sun to sit outside El Siglo, 'The Century'.

The tiles on the façade boasted that the shop was founded in 1836, and they displayed an image of a woman in traditional dress, with a high comb in her hair, ladling *horchata* from a churn. *Horchata de chufa* is a milky white drink that tastes like nothing else. It is best drunk in the shimmering heat, but like all good things it improves the place and time.

Horchata de chufa is made from the earth almond, earthnut, rush nut, tiger nut, chufa or tuber of the *Cyperus esculentus*. It was grown by the ancient Egyptians, and the plant is related to the sedge that produces papyrus. In the fields around Valencia the *chufa* plants look like rough-bladed grass, 18 inches tall, growing on ridges of tilled earth.

The *chufas* are little tubers, half an inch across, growing on the roots. They are harvested in winter by machines that look like mechanical road-surfacers, which shoot the tubers into lorries. The area round Valencia produces up to 12,000 tons a year.

Their production has given a golden opportunity to bureaucrats who in the first decade of the twenty-first century drew up laws and regulations empowering the Consejo Regulador to lay down conditions for the true Valencia *chufa*. It must be grown in the municipalities of Albalat dels Sorells, Alboraya, Albuixech, Alfara del Patriarca, Almassera, Bonrepos i Mirambell, Burjassot, Foios, Godella, Meliana, Moncada, Paterna, Rocafort, Tavernes Blanques, Valencia and Vinalesa.

The harvesting of the *chufa* must be made by machinery 'adequate for the purpose'. And the Consejo Regulador decides what's adequate. The fresh *chufa* must be between 0.9 and 1.6 centimetres long and 0.7 and 1.1 centimetres broad. There is such a thing as UHT *horchata de chufa*, sold in little bottles, but it is not to be recommended.

The name *chufa* comes by a roundabout route from the Latin *sibilare*, 'to hiss' or 'whistle'. The Spanish meanings of the word developed from 'whistle', whence 'to play around', and then from 'plaything' to 'sweet'. And how should *horchata* (which the Valencians spell *orxata*) be translated? It comes from the Latin *hordeata* 'made from barley'. The Italians have a word *orzata*, meaning 'barley water' or 'almond-syrup'. There is, in theory, an English word *orgeat* (which Thackeray pronounced 'orjaw' but is usually pronounced with the 't' sounded and an indeterminate final vowel: 'ordge-at'. Yet, since few people would understand what you meant by orgeat, the word for the Spanish thing might as well stay in Spanish, as *horchata*.

None of that is of any help if the drink is unfamiliar. The *horchata* at El Siglo was chalky, sweet and of a creamy colour. Refreshed by a glass, it was time to go to see the Holy Grail.

Finding the Holy Grail

THE HOLY GRAIL was just across the Plaza de la Reina (with its palm trees and cafés) in a chapel of the cathedral. 'Historians all over the world,' says a tourist guide to Valencia, 'point all their evidence to this item as being the authentic Cup used in the Last Supper.'

When Joseph Townsend came here in 1787, he was shown 'many thorns of the Redeemer's crown; the curious cup in which he drank at his last supper; and a wretched picture of the Blessed Virgin, painted by St Luke'.

The cup may well date from the time of Christ. It is made of agate, 3½ inches wide, now set on a gold stem and base, with a looped handle each side.

In the rectangular chapel devoted to the Holy Grail it was dim. The atmosphere was stuffy and a group of tourists settled noisily into the benches to be talked at loudly by a guide. Before them was an ogee arch, let in to a dark stone wall with stark, white mortar joints. There behind thick glass, the Holy

Grail stood, brightly lit from above, hard to discern from the benches.

Since Catholics believe that in a nearby tabernacle Jesus Christ is really present in the Blessed Sacrament, body, blood, soul and divinity, it is hard for the Holy Grail to compete. Yet as a reminder of the Last Supper (if it could be regarded for the sake of the exercise as being the cup from that evening) it might be taken as a devotional tool, like an icon or a relic, pointing to something unseen.

Pope Benedict XVI, visiting Valencia in 2006, used this *Santo Caliz* when he celebrated Mass, as had his predecessor in 1982. In any case, the words of the ancient Roman Canon, the traditional form of the Latin Eucharistic prayer, say that Jesus took '*hunc praeclarum Calicem*' – this noble cup. Whichever chalice is on the altar, it becomes, in the sacred drama of the Mass, for the moment, as it were, the same cup that Jesus used, whatever its provenance.

Two hundred and seven steps

FROM THE TOP of the cathedral bell-tower, as Townsend had noted with interest when he took the trouble to climb it 225 years earlier, the sea was visible. The fifteenth-century tower, known as the Miguelete (or Micalet, in Valencian), is 167 feet high, to the broad platform below the narrow 45-foot bell-gable. Like Big Ben, Miguelete refers to the bell, so everyone uses it as the name for the tower. Miguelete, cast in 1539, is the biggest bell in the old Kingdom of Aragon, 7 tons, 8 hundredweight. It rings the hours.

In the late nineteenth century José Aixa, a sculptor by training (windows to whose design remain in the cathedral), proposed that the stone bell-gable or *espadaña* should be replaced with a fantastical, florid, Gothic ironwork structure, a cross between a bird-cage and a bandstand, to support the hour bell and the quarter bell. It was never built. But it might easily have been.

The 207 steps that reached the platform were of the stone spiral kind in which the stairs extend to form part of the central newel. The steps were steep, but it was possible to put a foot squarely on each, at least at the broad end. Passing was only

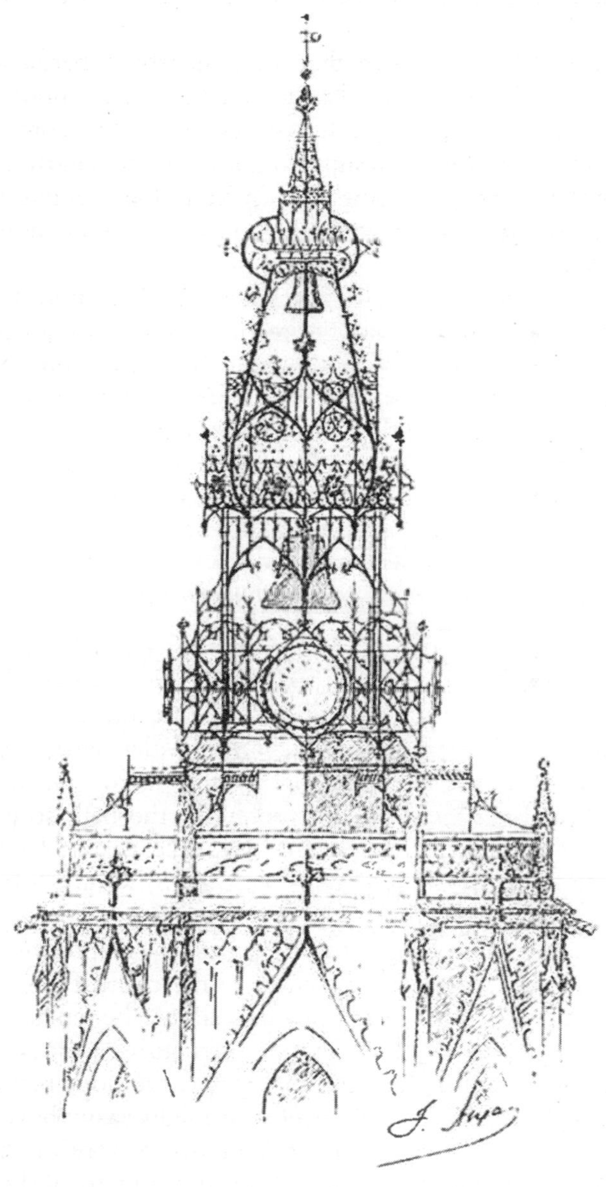

José Aixa's nineteenth-century proposal for an ironwork belfry for the Miguelete, never built.

difficult when the person coming in the opposite direction also preferred not to take the narrow, vertiginous side by the newel. Going down proved more difficult, because it meant staring downwards into space. There was an iron handrail to grasp, and it had come away from its fixings in only one place.

The tower is not immensely high, but it is higher than the buildings in the historic centre of Valencia. In the mid-nineteenth century, great hollow leather balls would be hoisted up on wires above the tower to announce the departure of steam ships in the port. A combination of balls, like beads on an abacus, indicated the number and destination of the ships. Today the city centre does not feel like that of a port, even though Valencia is still the largest in the Mediterranean.

From the Miguelete, the dock cranes were prominent to the east. To the south and west were misty mountains. Endless city flats stretched out to the north. To the south and east, the nineteenth-century Art Nouveau buildings were punctuated by church towers. The nearest was Santa Catalina's, the weather vane of which was level with the platform of the Miguelete.

Over above the central Post Office rose an extraordinary tower, invisible from the street below. It was of iron, its struts enclosing a self-supporting helical staircase, and was topped by a metallic armillary sphere. This seemed a suitable summit for a building constructed in 1915 as the Palace of Communications. Inside the building, 370 stained-glass panels on an elliptical dome depicted the coats of arms of the 48 Spanish provinces.

Southwards, just beyond the ring of the medieval city walls, stood the railway station that Joaquín Sorolla would have known. It is not the station named after him but the old Estación del Norte, an exuberant celebration of the Art Nouveau style, known in Spain as *modernismo*.

Valencia's chocolate challenge

IN THE MORNING, on the way to the station, there was time to drink some breakfast chocolate at the rival to El Siglo, the Horchatería de Santa Catalina. Behind a façade of tiles depicting the towers of the Miguelete and Santa Catalina, and boasting of 'two centuries of tradition', the interior, tiled in black and white squares, was a constant ebb and flow of customers, sitting on light wooden chairs at little stone-topped tables. *Horchata* is sold here, of course, but also the thick hot chocolate that is to cocoa what black Spanish coffee is to instant powder.

The glass display case at the counter was as thick with pastries as a fishmonger's slab with fish: croissants, *ensaimadas* thickly dusted with icing sugar, brioches, *bunuelos* (fritters or doughnuts made with flour, lard and eggs and cooked in hot oil), *bunuelos de calabaza* (which incorporate a purée of the vegetable we call squash, and which, like the ordinary kind of *bunuelo,* are rolled in granulated sugar when they're hot from the oil), *barquillos* (crisp, rolled-up unleavened bread with cinnamon) or *rosquilletas* (thick, unsweetened bread sticks made with olive oil and a touch of *anise*).

The things to eat with *horchata* are said to be *fartones.* These spongy fingers are meant to be dunked. They have been popularised only since the 1960s, by the manufacturer Polo, and are made with sunflower oil rather than lard. The factory is in a light industrial estate at Alboraya, north of Valencia on the plain where *chufas* are grown. The word for one of these absorbent sticks in Valencian is *fartó* (plural *fartons*). It is not a made-up word, but derives from the Latin *fartus*, meaning 'stuffed', from the verb *farcire* (giving us *farce* in English; the word *fart* is unrelated). The Castilian equivalent is *harto*, which means, or used to mean, 'bread'.

Or for breakfast you might prefer *tostadas* (thick batons of bread cut in half and toasted, available here with olive oil and salt, with tomato smeared on, or with home-made jam). Or if you're ready, you could order a prawn and avocado salad or a pork loin roll with tomato and fried onions. Wine is always a possibility, or if you are keeping to the sweet side of things a glass of *leche merengada*, a sort of posset made with milk, eggs, sugar, lemon, cinnamon and a pinch of salt.

But, to go with chocolate, the thing, even here in the Levante, is *churros. Churros* are made with batter extruded from a nozzle that leaves them ridged, and immediately fried in hot oil till crisp on the outside. They are not in themselves sweet, but may be dipped in sugar, which sticks to their greasy sides, or dunked in coffee or chocolate. A fat version is called a *porra* (truncheon), not to be confused with a *porro*, a word for a fat joint of marijuana. Here at the Horchatería de Santa Catalina, the *churros* are slender and elegantly looped round to bite their own tails.

The chocolate, when it came, which it did quickly, was hot, very thick, sweet and strong. In Spanish terms it was *rico*, 'rich', a term of approbation, which is applied in Seville, it is said, even to good water. The *churros* ('four entities' as the menu promised) made a meal of it. It was impossible to finish the rich cup of chocolate, but nothing could provide a more solid foundation for a morning's travel.

Oranges and roses

THE STATION, in walking distance from the old city centre, was alive with Art Nouveau curves, vegetative ornamentation and exotic additions, in metal, ceramics, mosaic, wood and glass. Above the centre of the wide frontage, stood an eagle with outstretched wings, the emblem of the Compañía de los Caminos de Hierro del Norte de España.

Globe lamps hung from pillars covered with mosaics of oranges among dark green leaves. The capitals of the columns were adorned with glazed ceramic oranges and roses. The ceiling they supported was constructed of parallel beams, the narrow space between each of which was covered with shallow-arched, crazy-paving-patterned ceramics. An Art Nouveau motif marked the end of each furrow of ceiling.

The woodwork around the guichets had a touch of John Rennie Mackintosh, and panels of mosaic were let into the woodwork, depicting baskets of roses and a device standing for Norte: a large O with the N, R, T and E overlapping it at the four corners. On the walls of the booking hall, plaques wished passengers *bon voyage* in different languages, picked out in letters of gold: *Buon viaggio*, *Kalon taxeidion* and something in Russian and Chinese.

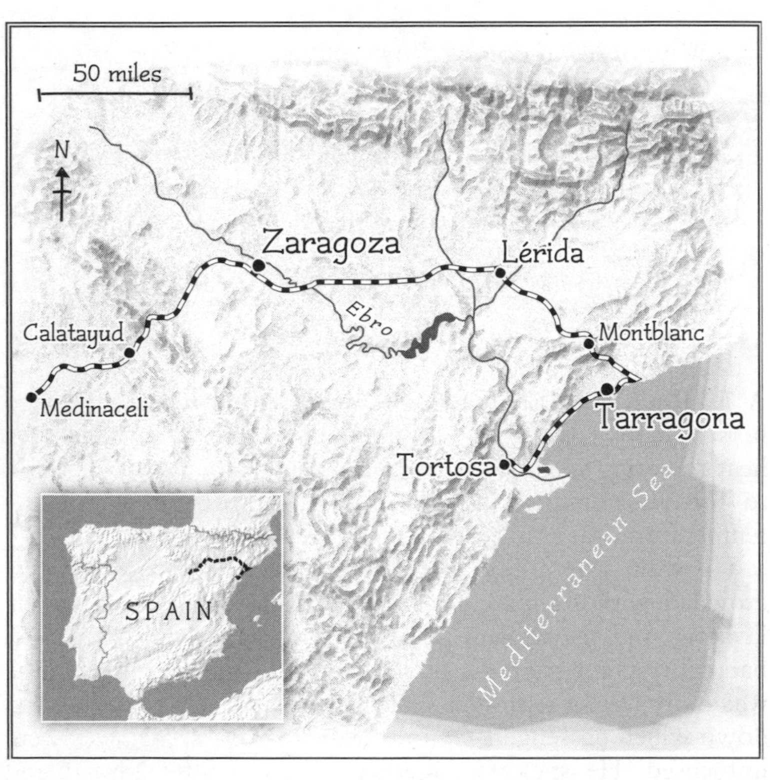
50 miles
N
Zaragoza
Lérida
Ebro
Calatayud
Montblanc
Medinaceli
Tarragona
Tortosa
Mediterranean Sea
SPAIN

8

Ruinas – Ruins

TORTOSA TO MEDINACELI

Ways of being drunk – Tortosa's thin cats – On strike – Chartreuse and fireworks – Traditions newly invented – Tarragona's seaside arena – City on a hill – Don't look down – Montblanc, the Perfect Walled Town – Not open all hours – First peel your garlic – Calatayud, the castle of Job – A ruin with a view

Ways of being drunk

A RAILWAY EMPLOYEE in a high-visibility jacket fanned herself with a traditional folding fan as she stood near the heat-radiating locomotive that was waiting to pull the train to Tortosa. For this journey took place in September, and the temperature was in the upper eighties Fahrenheit.

The train was full. In the lobby at the front of a carriage, crowded with standing passengers and a pram between the lavatory and the driver's door, a young man snuffled with a bad cold. As the train got under way it became clear that there was more wrong with him than that. He sat on the inside step down which passengers climb to leave the train. His eyes were unfocused. He spoke incoherently on a mobile phone and banged on the metallic wall with his fist.

When the guard came round he had no ticket. The guard asked for his identity card, which he showed. He was Romanian. He said he had no money and the guard told him to get off at the next stop. After 45 minutes he did, at nowhere very much.

After another two hours, at the destination of Tortosa, a man standing at the counter of the *cafetería* was drunk. He had difficulty with his words and his limbs moved in unplanned directions. Public drunkenness is taboo in Spain: it is not so much forbidden as despised.

'Rare to see a Spaniard drunk,' Samuel Pepys noted in 1683. 'So that it is enough to take away the credit of a public notary to be proved to have been seen in a tavern.' A century or so later, the same trait was just as noticeable. 'Temperance is, and ever has been, a distinguishing characteristic of the Spaniard,' wrote Alexander Slidell Mackenzie in 1829.

While his friend and fellow-countryman Washington Irving was living in the Alhambra, busy writing his histories, Mackenzie (or Slidell as he was still called before changing his name in 1837) published, at the age of 26, *A Year in Spain* under the pen-name A Young American. Published in Britain by John Murray, it was a bestseller.

When he came to sum up the Spanish character, sobriety struck Slidell forcefully. 'Aversion to drunkenness amounts to destestation,' he wrote. 'Mention is said to be found in Strabo of a Spaniard who threw himself into the fire because someone had called him a drunkard.'

There is drunkenness and drunkenness. It is a question of comportment, of how one behaves when drunk. At a fiesta in a village or in a city, when everyone is together and it is getting late, then people will be drunk. Even so, there is no feeling of being threatened. Parents will go about with little children.

Young people have in the past 20 years acquired the British convention of getting drunk with large amounts of beer, late at night. Drugs are also used to a varying degree. Informal meeting-places in the street can attract large numbers. The word that describes this use of drink is *botellón*, 'a big bottle'. *Prohibido "El Botellón"* say street signs, invoking recently passed laws by name and date.

Anyone who is familiar with formerly quiet back streets, even in genteel places such as El Escorial or Pontevedra, can see the change over a generation. Sometimes local people complain. In 2006 a square near the cathedral in Guadix was hung with sheets painted with slogans in big black letters: BASTA BOTELLON. ESCANDALO – ALCOHOL, DROGAS, 'MIAOS', VOMITAS.

By *miaos*, the protest banner was referring not to the drug mephedrone (sometimes nicknamed *miaow-miaow* in English) but to home-made mixtures of spirits and fruit juice that youngsters bring to the nocturnal gathering. A banner opposite declared: QUEREMOS DORMIR – We want to sleep.

But the drunk man in the station bar belonged to another convention. He was in his fifties, a manual worker, alone, it was Sunday afternoon and he had enough money for a drink. Perhaps he had a wife at home.

There would be plenty of men at home asleep. To be drunk in public is to court shame, *vergüenza*, and *vergüenza* only works where you are known. In a big city, people can behave without shame, *sin vergüenza,* or shamelessly.

Another style of being drunk is followed by men who have some money, dress in a suit, with a clean shirt, perhaps with a golden bracelet on one wrist, smoke cigars, are overweight and have rasping voices from drink, smoke and late nights. They are approved of by their circle of male friends and often argue loudly in a joshing fashion, but are not obviously out of control. They restart the day with brandy.

Tortosa's thin cats

IN THE COSTA del Castell, a street below the castle of Tortosa, now a Parador, an alcove bore the date 1976. Coloured tiles framed a public tap, an improvement for the nearby houses when it was installed. In 2012 it was no longer working.

The broken street was impassable to traffic. A teenage girl, with bare feet had found a way to turn on the hydrant in the middle of the street and had filled two 4-litre plastic containers. The girl was of North African origin by her dress. A thin little cat with bright eyes lapped up spilled water from the ground.

The medieval streets nearby were full of ruinous, empty houses. Some had been demolished, and mallows and jasmine grew amid the rubble and the abandoned plastic bags and excrement. Here too, thin cats crept out warily. Some houses were occupied by people who had nowhere else to go, mostly recent immigrants. In the medieval Carrer dels Capellans, two little children ran down from the waste ground of prickly pears and joined their mother in a cave-like, crumbly stone room while the cock outside crowed. In another deserted house, a bare-chested Spanish man was hanging out his newly washed shirt on the iron balcony.

There are more ruins here than in earthquake-struck Lorca. Tortosa is down at heel. It was once the capital of a Moorish statelet, and a square stone plaque inscribed with Kufic letters is preserved in the outside wall of the cathedral. The city was reconquered in the twelfth century by Ramon Berenguer IV, Count of Barcelona, with the help of the Genoans.

Apart from the castle, the cathedral is splendid. The Rev Joseph Townsend did not think so in 1787, finding that 'the whole edifice is devoid of taste and the interior is loaded with preposterous ornaments'. He did not say what in particular repelled him, but from the dignified Gothic walls project corbels supporting medieval bishops' tomb-chests, like those in Winchester cathedral, or like the money-chest of El Cid in Burgos.

The pitched tile roof of the cathedral has been replaced with flat PVC and aluminium. Next to the exuberant Baroque gateway to the cathedral, with its Solomonic columns, a long-established shoe shop had closed down. The most inescapably prominent building in the city was the hideous modern hospital, built in 1963 on a summit opposite the castle, where a mid-eighteenth century barracks had been. The rest of the town is squashed in the narrow space by the river.

The sun set behind the 4,000-foot mountains to the west. Tortosa stands only 40 feet above sea level. The traditional boats here are called *llaguts* and bear a lateen sail, but there were none to be seen. They are as outmoded as Thames lighters. Weed whirled in roulades in the full Ebro, surprisingly clear here, unlike the clouded waters up-river at Zaragoza. Perhaps here the tides clean the river.

This is a strategic spot, where until 1894 the Ebro was crossed by a bridge of boats. It was the scene of terrible fighting in the Civil War. The historic streets have never really recovered. Moreover, a Catalan historian, Jacobo Vidal, likens the physical degradation suffered by the historic town in the 1980s to the destruction it bore in the Civil War.

On the corner of the Rua Moncado (a trench of tall, decrepit, medieval houses), a *locutorio* offered internet access. These shops enable migrant workers to telephone home at cheap rates. In Tortosa, the black Africans seemed isolated: lone men hanging about the streets sadly for lack of anything else to do. The North Africans and Muslim Asian men more often had women and children with them, or at least other men to drink tulip-glasses of tea with in back-street bars.

The keeper of the *locutorio* was affable and helpful, darting from one telephone booth to another to help customers. The seat in front of the vacant internet screen was smelly. The man at the neighbouring terminal was smelly. But a fan stirred the air as the thermometer reached 32°C. In a room on the other side of the street from the open door, men prostrated themselves in prayer.

On strike

A TRANSPORT STRIKE was announced for the day set for leaving Tortosa. Strikes can bring out unpleasant antipathies among Spaniards. At Tortosa station the television in the *cafetería* was showing footage of frustrated commuters in Madrid, where the buses, metro and railways were on strike. Passengers tussled with pickets.

With delicious bureaucratic flair, which must please both employers and workers, the state railway company Renfe offered a 'minimum service' during the strike. For a leisurely traveller this should mean turning up for the rare train scheduled to run. But the 15.54 did not come. Some people waited patiently, some fumed. It was very hot: 34°C, or 93°F. A man smelling of stale sweat jumped up from the bench and started pacing about.

But after three quarters of an hour a train did arrive from Barcelona, and everyone got off. There were no announcements of its destination. The crowd waiting on Platform One rushed to Platform Two, and boarded. It was cooler in the train. After ten minutes it started, in the direction of Barcelona, as intuition had suggested. Those without tickets saved money that day, as no guards or ticket collectors were to be seen. It would have suited that poor Romanian.

Chartreuse and fireworks

THE LION JUMPED down the steps and the children screamed. These steep, wide steps ran up to the cathedral at Tarragona, and the lion wore a crown, for it was the feast of St Thecla – Santa Tecla – which was to last for ten days, with loud drumming, trumpets, drink, crowds, close-up fireworks and more drink, day and night.

The adopted drink of the fiesta was, surprisingly, Chartreuse, green or yellow, in bottles with special Santa Tecla labels. The emblematic T of Santa Tecla, shaped like a Franciscan Tau-Cross, was everywhere in Tarragona. The Chartreuse was drunk as a *granizado*, with pulverised ice, from litre flasks. In another context this would be a *botellón* or 'doing the litre' as another modern phrase puts it. But as part of the fiesta it was not a story of bored, inebriated youth in opposition to settled customs of behaviour. Everybody was joining in.

On these 19 high steps of Roman masonry (from the ancient Forum), linking the Carrer Major and the little cathedral square, children sat on their fathers' shoulders, or in their mothers' arms, joggling in time to the beat of the drum and the fierce-eyed lion. 'Papa!' called out a woman, not to her father, but to the father of her children, who was manoeuvring the pushchair. Later came the Drac, the dragon breathing fire and covered with spikes, on which fireworks rotated and exploded.

There was another beast too, 10 feet high, called a Vibria, winged, beaked and clawed, with a woman's breasts. The one that was carried here weighs 180 pounds, but danced as lightly as the lion. A toddler standing on the lid of a wheelie bin jumped up and down with over-excitement, wafting out rubbish-flavoured billows, as the simple dance tune was repeated again at greater volume. It was all so happy that it seemed nothing else mattered. The crisis (the economic crisis) was submerged by the fiesta.

A conga of T-shirted young people appeared in front of the cathedral, preceded by the stupendously loud beating of a drum, sending the pigeons up in a wheel of wings. This small cathedral square is beautiful by accident. It fronts the façade of the cathedral, where martins glue their nests of mud to the triple Gothic door-arches. On one side, the old houses rest on ground-floor pillars. On the other, the walls of the houses are variegated with hundreds of years' patching and rendering of stonework, with one beautiful window divided by characteristically thin Catalan columns headed by trefoil tracery. The stone platform of the square is supported by gigantic, ancient Roman blocks, with a street of pointed arches running to one side.

On this dramatic stage, the day before, as at other points throughout the city, the *castellers* had performed. These clubs of young people build human castles, towers, six, seven, eight storeys high. At the bottom they are crushed together by human props squashing them in, in order to resist the outward pressure. The numbers in each storey diminish until, at the top, one small child stands alone. Often the towers fall down on to the delighted crowd.

Not only are the castles built in the crowded squares, but they walk. A local policeman on a motor bike makes way for them as they sway through the street. It is madness – or perhaps co-operation, courage, skill and grace.

Traditions newly invented

DOWN FROM the cathedral, a tobacconist's shop, at the corner of the Carrer Major and the Carrer de les Cuirateries (Skinner Street), offered little models of the Lion, Dragon, Vibria and other festival beasts for sale in the window.

The tobacconist cheerfully explained their parts in the fiesta, and the part of the fiesta in Catalan identity. 'Of course, when I was young I couldn't speak a word of Catalan at school. It was forbidden.' Today, the language may be a proud badge of identity, but 69 per cent of people in Catalonia said that the last book that they read was in Castilian.

The city of Tarragona happily dates the feast of Santa Tecla from a papal bull of 1091, even before the resettlement of the city began under Ramon Berenguer III, in 1118. But the tobacconist's perspective is right too. The present figure of the Vibria for the procession of beasts was made only in 1993. The Dragon, the Drac de Sant Roc, is first mentioned in writing in 1426, but it was lost to festive folklore during the Peninsular Wars, being revived only in 1985.

So it goes for the other beasts: the Cucafera, resembling a fat crocodile, which dances very delicately as the fireworks explode, is mentioned in 1381, but the present figure was made only in 1991. A great gilt, fat-bodied Eagle, the Aliga, looking like the ancient, oil-dispensing Ampulla from the English Coronation, now dances at the Ball de Diables (where devils spray fireworks from their tridents), as it might have done continuously since the fifteenth century, had the tradition not been cut dead by Napoleon's invasion. The Ox (Bou) and giant Mule or Mulassa have similar histories.

The festival features Moorish giants and black giants, too, big-headed dwarfs, dancing horsemen, a dance of the seven deadly sins, bands of men with arquebuses, stick-dancers and round-dancers whose headdresses are like waste-paper baskets. The effect of the fireworks is like strong drink: their noise stuns, their fire delights and they add surprise to a social gathering. Then there is music: too loud and, on one night, never-ending.

During the Civil War, neither side had any time for such things. The Republic had suppressed public religious festivals. The victorious Nationalists hated and feared expressions of Catalan culture. What has been so impressive since the 1980s is not only the enthusiasm with which the customs have been embraced again (an enthusiasm for extremes that drives Tarragona to exhaustion after ten days), but also the strength of the quite erroneous notion that this is how things have always been done.

Tarragona's seaside arena

THE RUINS of the Roman amphitheatre looked all the more striking in the morning sun for being silhouetted against the Mediterranean, from which little white wavelets hissed rhythmically on to the sand. There was just room between its banked stone seats and the sea for the railway line to edge past.

On the land side, a van with a hatch in the side had been selling *churros* and *chocolate* to fiesta-goers into the early hours. By half past three in the morning the esplanade under the palm trees was quiet, and individual sounds punctuated the foamy noise of the sea: a night train squealing round the curve, the tyres of a lone taxi making a swishing *chee-chee* through the water on the road where council workers had been watering the flowerbeds, a persevering cicada.

For centuries, the amphitheatre was more than a curious survival from the Roman era. It was in this arena that the local bishop Fructuosus, with two deacons, Augurius and Eulogius, the founding martyrs of the new Christian polity, were burnt at the stake in AD 259. The *Acta* recounting their martyrdom are the earliest from Hispania that survive. An apparently verbatim extract from the court records includes this exchange between Aemilianus, the procurator, and the prisoner.

Aemilianus: Are you the bishop?
Fructuosus: I am.
Aemilianus: You were.

Like Eulalia of Mérida, Fructuosus was chosen by the Latin writer Prudentius at the beginning of the fifth century as the subject of a poem in the *Peristephanon*. As the historian Guy Halsall points out, in recounting the exchange between Fructuosus and the procurator, Prudentius recognises its grim humour and adds to the reply by Aemilianus the participle *subridens*, 'Smiling, he said: "You were".'

Prudentius also picks up a detail of Christians witnessing the martyrdom and pouring wine on the saints' remains to cool them among the embers so that they could rescue them as relics. The poet then describes the three martyrs, now dressed in shining white clothes, appearing in a vision to command that their relics should be gathered together and enshrined in a sepulchre of marble.

A church was later built in the arena and rebuilt after the Moorish period. In a letter dated 25 May 1915, Emilio Morera, a local archaeologist and historian, wrote, as vice-president of the Tarragona provincial commission for monuments, to the director of the royal academy of history, to tell him that the ancient church (known as St Mary of the Miracle), while awaiting to be declared a national monument, had finally collapsed entirely. The hollow-cross outline of its Romanesque walls and the Visigothic foundations enclosing the martyrs' sepulchre may still be seen.

City on a hill

TARRAGONA IS still shaped by its Roman past. At the bottom of the Carrer Major, there is a sudden bend to negotiate a steep little bit of hillside. This steep slope was once the banking for the seats of the big Roman circus. The houses of the nearby Carrer dels Ferrers can be seen to stand on vast arched caverns of Roman construction, where archaeologists have dug into the hillside below.

The whole of the old city is built on a tilted platter of hillside embraced by a circuit of ancient walls. Before even the Romans secured this hill by the sea, the Carthaginians had built defensive walls of Cyclopean masonry. On the seaward side, outside the eighteenth-century gateway of the Portal de Sant Antoni, vast blocks of stone, keyed into the bedrock, support a terrace of houses with windows cut through the Roman and medieval walls. Green slatted blinds (the kind that roll up when a string is pulled) shelter pot plants and kitchen furniture from the sun, where the legionaries once mustered.

The cathedral occupies the summit, once the site of the forum and the temple of the imperial cult of Augustus. He had lived here, in agreeable Tarraco, rather than by the rainy north coast when he was waging war there against the fiercely resisting Cantabrians.

During the noise and heat of the jollifications for St Thecla, the cathedral proved a soothing refuge for a few minutes' peace. The tranquil nave was in the transitional style between Romanesque and Gothic, built of the beautiful honey-coloured local stone.

G. E. Street, enjoyed this cathedral by the Mediterranean when he visited it in the middle of the 1860s for his influential *Gothic Architecture in Spain*. 'It produces in a very marked degree an extremely impressive internal effect, without being of exaggerated scale,' he wrote, 'and combines in the happiest fashion the greatest solidity of construction with a lavish display of ornament in some parts, to which it is hard to find a parallel.'

Street stayed for some time, contentedly drawing the nave and a carving in the cloister that depicted the fable of the cat and the rats. He made a bare mention of the carved retable, behind the high altar, made up mostly of marble, he said.

This most extraordinary work of art turned out to be made up of 19 subtly coloured panels of alabaster surmounted by three improbably tall Gothic pinnacles. At head-height ran a series of six panels depicting the legend of St Thecla, carved in the early fifteenth century by a craftsman called Pere Joan.

The individuality and expressiveness of the faces of townspeople and clerics that he carved were clearly intended to meet the desire of the dean and chapter to ornament their cathedral church richly and to honour the local martyr. A chubby black man figured among the witnesses in the carved scene of the finding of a relic (the arm) of St Thecla. The historical value of the images is intriguing, too – copes worn in one scene match the cathedral inventory of vestments from 600 years ago.

Everyone agrees that the design and execution of the panels are an artistic tour de force. They demonstrate the subtle possibilities of carving in alabaster (for which Nottingham was celebrated in the Middle Ages, though Tarragona had its own supplies of the stone).

St Thecla, a reputed follower of St Paul, is shown overcoming a burning, fiery furnace, lions that refuse to roar at her and venomous reptiles. The story dates from the second century, but the details are unreliable. In the Prayers for the Dying in the Roman Missal, however, St Thecla is the only figure not mentioned in the Bible whose delivery by God is invoked: 'As thou didst deliver thy holy virgin and martyr Thecla from the threefold ordeal of torture, so now deliver the soul of this thy servant.' And without her, there would be no Chartreuse and fireworks in Tarragona each September.

Don't look down

AN APPOINTMENT with fear, at least for anyone who is frightened of heights, lies two or three miles north of Tarragona. The Puente de Ferreras is a 2,000-year-old aqueduct spanning a valley 240 yards wide on 25 graceful arches of golden stone at a height of 90 feet, only a little lower than the famous aqueduct in the centre of Segovia.

'The view from above is charming,' Richard Ford found when he came here in the early 1830s. 'The lonely rich ochry aqueduct looks truly the work of those times when there were giants on the earth.' It proved a little less lonely now, among the pines on the sandy hills, being too close to the Autopista del Mediterráneo, which formed a formidable barrier on the walk from the city.

The great liberty, though, which would surely not be granted in Britain, was being allowed to walk over its lofty arches, along the dry channel that once brought water from the river Francolí, which rises on the other side of the mountains behind Tarragona, near the great medieval abbey of Poblet.

Walking across the gigantic masonry arches instilled a true respect for its builders. The problem for human frailty was that the sides of the dry channel were only knee-high, and there was nothing to hold on to. Empty air was the outlook in every direction but down, and it was not wise to look down. But success in reaching the other side invited a return journey. There felt a certain virtue in the exercise.

The Perfect Walled Town

THERE WAS A TRAIN from Tarragona westward, inland, to Calatayud, that would take only 1 hour and 34 minutes. It is 200 miles. The stopping train via Flix takes 5 hours. A better route than either, which goes through mountain scenery at a speed slow enough to allow it to be taken in, is via Montblanc, a contender for the title of Perfect Walled Town.

The ideal of the Perfect Walled Town is one that is still filled with its medieval streets but has not overflowed into ugly new suburbs. Nor should it have intrusive multi-storey buildings.

Avila is a contender from the point of view of extant walls, but its new housing now spreads over the adjacent hills. In Extremadura, Coria's old streets within the walls are dead. The mile-and-a-half ring of fat granite walls of Lugo, in Galicia, said to be the only remaining complete Roman circuit in the peninsula, is overlooked by houses on both sides. At Madrigal de las Altas Torres, in Old Castile, the walls seem to have melted, where the ancient rubble and bricks have crumbled away, and within their perimeter, great spaces have appeared where once stood prosperous streets. The circuit of walls at Daroca in Aragon is two miles long, but the town has been declining since 1714. At Zamora or Betanzos or Jaca, the old walls were demolished in the age of progress and steam.

From the railway, Montblanc seemed to have a grassy gap among the streets enclosed by its medieval walls. But a few minutes walk from the station, through the stone gateway, across the Carrer Major, past the great church of St Mary Major, brings the traveller to that grassy gap, which is simply the ancient castle mound, with nothing left at its summit but some foundations of early medieval church buildings and fortifications.

The settlers of Montblanc moved down from this hilltop refuge of St Barbara after the twelfth century, as life became more secure. The rest of the town inside the walls is full of old streets on a modest scale. Montblanc does spill out, with residential streets to the south-west, but it is within the walls that the focus of life remains.

Its tranquil, red-brown rooftops could be seen spread out below the church, from the flat roof running above its side aisles (€2 for entry to the spiral staircase that climbs to it by 54 steep steps). The town walls from there were invisible, for houses had been built against them on the inside. All that could be seen of the walls were the 17 square towers that stood high above the parapets. It was from the outside that they were to be examined.

The peacefulness of the scene was suddenly broken by squawks and shrieks as if a bird's nest was being raided by a savage predator. This alarming outburst proved to be a recording amplified through loudspeakers, meant to repel birds that had been harming the medieval stonework of the church. Some starlings sat on the finials of the buttresses unperturbed.

Outside the extravagant Baroque porch of the church, a forecourt had been paved in an old geometrical pattern of oval white stones and flat black pebbles laid edgeways to mark out zig-zags, diamonds and figures of eight. The workmen had left a date in large, thick letters

ANY 1786

A more recent inscription on a board hung opposite the church door. It might have said 'No fireworks'. Instead it said:

> To preserve the historic patrimony of Montblanc it is forbidden in every case to let off rockets, petards or other fireworks in this square, or in any of the surroundings of the church of Santa María. – Town Council of Montblanc

Not open all hours

THE CARRER MAJOR ran for four or five hundred yards more or less north-south through the centre of Montblanc from St Antony's Gate to the demolished St Francis's Gate. It was a continuous street of mostly five-storey houses with the ground floor taken by shops. Halfway up, a street turned off to the irregular space of the Plaza Mayor, with its shops beneath the shade of projecting storeys supported on columns. The fine, wide Romanesque church of St Michael, with no side-aisles, in the Catalan architectural convention, stood back from the street in the south-eastern quarter, leaving room for a bench where townspeople sat and talked.

At its extremities, the Carrer Major possessed a more domestic character, with garage entrances and frequently half-doors to the houses, over which women might look out for a chat to passers-by. At the St Antony's end, a glazed shrine to St Antony himself was attached to a wall. The old desert monk wore a habit bearing the Tau-shaped capital T. Over an arch where a side-alley led off the street, were printed the words 'San Cristófol', and a few yards down the alley there was a glass-fronted shrine in the wall, with St Christopher bearing the Christ Child, and an electric lamp lighting it from each side.

Packets of seeds hung on strings above the door of No 82, a grocer's with no name. Inside was a large, high room fitted with wooden shelves on each wall, with a family waiting to serve behind the counter at the end. It was the kind of shop that honoured the expertise of the customers in knowing what they wanted: there was no explanation or brand-marketing.

In the window a sign said laconically: 'Carquinyols €2.30 ¼ kg.' These are not snails (*caragols* in Catalan) but almond *biscotti*. It is important to remember the difference. The form *carquinyols* is slightly archaic, like the shop itself, the more frequent if less correct modern form being *carquinyolis* in Catalan. The word derives from an earlier form meaning 'to crunch', so these biscuits might be called *crunchies* in English, were the Italian word *biscotto* not so familiar from coffee shops.

On the shelves of No 82 stood bottles of rich red wine. In a glass-fronted cupboard hung, by their wicks, various sizes of large votive candle. On the door, the opening hours were stated uncompromisingly: 'Dimarts a dissabte: 10–13.15 17.30–20.30. Dilluns tancat.' *Tancat* means 'closed', one of the first words of Catalan to be learnt.

At seven o'clock in the evening, in a pleasant September temperature of 70°F or so, the Carrer Major was at its most social. A little girl swung her violin case from side to side as her mother talked to a friend. A Muslim woman in a headscarf held her little boy's hand as they walked home. A boy on a scooter waited for his mother, blocking the way to a Yorkshire terrier on a lead.

The street was 12 or 15 feet wide here in the middle of the town, and closed to vehicles for most of the day. The few chairs outside the Xinxonenc *horchatería* dammed the flow of pedestrians and thrust them closer together. The scooter-Yorkie entanglement was repeated by a teenager on a mountain bike meeting a recalcitrant bull terrier. A youth with hair brushed up into a ridge, like the fur of an anteater, held hands with a girl in a pelmet skirt. At half past eight, as at No 82, the shops shut for the night.

First peel your garlic

CARLES BLASI, the proprietor of the Fonda Cal Blasi, was a philosopher. 'You are not in a hotel,' he said, 'and we are not in our house – it is a contradiction.' He, in his sixties, and his wife

Carme, spent all their time running their bed-and-breakfast business in their old house in a quiet street in Montblanc. Her speciality was cooking, his logistics, he said.

'You must enjoy every day,' Carles said in carefully articulated English. The key was 'simple pleasures'. His party piece was to show foreigners how to prepare their own toast and tomato for breakfast in the best Catalan manner. The toast came via Carme, a broad crusty slice.

First peel your garlic. The garlic should be compressed at the ends to make it easier to peel off the skin. The peeled clove should then be smeared on the toast, starting with the surface next to the crusts. Then the half tomato was to be smeared. The important trick there was to hold the tomato with the fingers squeezing it from the sides, not from the top. The final step was to pour on oil, good, green, local, organic olive oil, copiously.

Pan, vino, y ajo crudo hacen andar al mozo agudo, goes the proverb that Richard Ford quoted in his *Handbook for Spain* – bread, raw garlic and good red wine make a fellow get on fine. Garlic, if not such a staple of the Spanish diet as it was, is everywhere, but in the raw form can still stick a stiletto into a tender foreign stomach, first thing in the morning.

Carles was a Catalan nationalist, or better, he saw Catalonia as a country hampered, taxed and betrayed by the central powers in Madrid. It was a more than usually hopeful and exasperating time for Catalans, just then, for that very day Artur Mas, the President of the Generalitat of Catalonia, had gone to Madrid to demand financial autonomy. Spain's economy was on the edge of a cliff and in Barcelona more than a million had marched the weekend before to demand a final showdown with the government of Spain.

It looked as though everything would change that week, but everything did not. For Carles, the key that unlocked history was 11 September. Not 11 September 2001 – he didn't even mention it – but 11 September 1714. That was the day that the siege of Barcelona was broken, and with it Catalan liberties. It is now the national day of Catalonia, the anniversary of a defeat.

Calatayud, the castle of Job

'IT LOOKS LIKE a bomb's gone off. A bomb,' declared a woman in the Calle de Baltasar Gracián in Calatayud. 'And there are many more like that.' She was speaking about a site where an old, five-storey house had stood. The demolition men had left a void and removed the side-walls of the rooms next to it, so that they were exposed like those of a doll's house.

The remnants looked pathetic: the broken bannisters of the stairs that led nowhere, the weeds growing on a balcony, the laths lying higgledy-piggledy like a senseless game of spillikins, the dirty distemper on the plastered wall of a bedroom that had been dirty long before it was demolished. A lizard scuttled across a patch of sun. Taking the wall off had uncovered the unsquared tree trunks that had been used as beams, and the floors added from time to time. One floor sagged with a well-established sag, so that the steps of the people who once lived there must have become hurried as they crossed the room.

The name Calatayud was 'Job's Castle' in Arabic (*qal'at Ayub*). The town sits on the river Jalón, but it looks upwards towards the vast, empty castle, 100 yards long, high above it on the bare, barren, terrible, sun-blasted ridges into which dry channels have been eroded over aeons of geological time. Some of the ridge is sheer, some flanked by slopes of sharp shards of stone heaped up like rubbish dumps. The castle is the hub of a series of five (or eight, depending how you count them) fortresses connected by walls over acres of precipitous rock.

Calatayud, a town of 20,000, is the fourth biggest in Aragon, a kingdom where half the population live in Zaragoza, leaving 600,000 to cover thinly an area twice that of Wales. Calatayud is on the western side of Aragon, and Castilian is spoken, yet in one little bar a sign asked hopefully: *Charra me en Aragones* – talk to me in Aragonese. Richard Ford, travelling eastwards from Castile in the 1830s, noticed that at Calatayud, the Aragonese projecting wooden eaves began. The central streets still possess impressive old churches and ancient public buildings of an Aragonese cast. But in this town, buildings tend to lean.

The tower of the church of San Pedro de los Francos leans out by 4 feet over the old street called the Rua. It used to rise higher and even more alarmingly, but the council decided in 1840 to demolish everything above its fourth storey on the grounds that, when she came to stay at the palace on the other side of the street, Queen Isabel II, still only 9 years old, would be frightened by the beetling mass of masonry.

In the old town, houses chose to lean in a particular manner. The wall of the ground floor would lean outwards and the wall of the storeys above would lean inward. This force made the frontage bend at the knees, as it were, at the level of the first floor. That outward thrust is understandable if the houses were built anything like the one exposed by the demolition in the Calle Gracián. Perhaps iron or steel ties might have saved them, but an alternative solution was put into effect, where the streets were narrow enough. Great beams of wood were fitted across the street, so that one bending knee of wall supported the bending knee of the house opposite.

It was not a lasting solution. In the last decade of the twentieth century and the first of the twenty-first, demolition has in many cases resolved the difficulty permanently.

An elderly husband and wife were looking in the window of a hardware and furniture shop in the middle of the town. '*Que mierda*,' she said – what crap. '*Que mierda. Que mierda*.' Calatayud is in some ways a dump. A hundred years ago, its extreme exoticness – of costume, food, climate, manners, architecture – might have distracted the foreign visitor from the painful poverty of most of its people. Today the poverty is less a life-and-death struggle, and the shabbiness of international culture shows on the surface more obviously. '*Igual trabajo, igual salario*,' – equal work, equal pay – said a graffito next to the bus station, and next to it, in baffling isolation and flawed English: 'Nazi rubish.'

A ruin with a view

FROM THE PLATFORM at Medinaceli station, the triple Roman triumphal arch stood out in silhouette high on the ridge 600 feet above. The station was already 1,014.4 metres above sea level (the sea at Alicante, of course), which is to say 3,328 feet. Twenty minutes' walk was all it took to reach a most extraordinary viewing point.

Through the central opening of the first-century AD arch, the landscape stretched far away, an open valley with stands of trees, backed by slopes up to a ridge, and a hazier, more distant hillscape beyond. The juxtaposition of the arch (the details of its pilasters and moulding blasted smooth by centuries of wind, dust, rain and frost) and the wild countryside was startling.

Archaeologists have found that the arch once stood as a gateway to a walled Roman settlement. There was no continuity between the ancient Roman and subsequent Christian township. Medinaceli is an Arabic name, from *Madinat Salim*, 'city of Salim'. Even the surviving medieval town today combines desertion, decay and prettification. The windswept Plaza Mayor, castle, collegiate church and ducal palace are far too grand for a place of 564 inhabitants (many living at the foot of the hill).

But what a location the Romans chose! This is the dividing line of the peninsula, as far as rivers go. To the east, the waters flow into the Jalón, through Calatayud, to join the Ebro and into the Mediterranean near Tortosa. To the west of Medinaceli, the flow is into the river Henares, which joins the Tagus, running through Toledo in its deeply incised channel, and reaching the Atlantic at Lisbon.

Railway lines, which so often follow rivers for the sake of the gentle incline, found it more difficult to join up the Atlantic and the Mediterranean. A grand project for a line from Santander, on the north coast, to Valencia, on the Mediterranean, planned since the beginning of the twentieth century, collapsed in 1985. The line north of Soria was closed in 1996. Now, for the railway passenger on the watershed at Medinaceli wanting to head north to Bilbao, the choice was between going back to Calatayud or joining the confluence of lines to Madrid.

All railroads lead to Madrid, or seem to. The route via Calatayud is more interesting, through out-of-the way little cities like Calahorra, where the heads of Saints Emeterius and Celedonius, after their posthumous voyage in boats of stone, were placed in golden reliquaries ornamented with mustachios beneath the altar of the cathedral. But by that route there will be frustrating waits at uninteresting junctions like Miranda de Ebro.

So first, a good lunch, not on the picturesque hilltop, but down near the station near the junction of the N-11 and the N-111 highways. The huge lorries parked outside the restaurant Carlos-Mary recommended it, and the food did not disappoint. The menu of the day offered artichokes and bacon. The artichokes were whole little tender heads and the bacon not too thin or hard. With fresh crusty bread, here of the elastic kind, they came steaming in a terracotta *cazuela*. What could be better after a ramble over a hilltop?

Bay of Biscay
Bilbao
Mercadillo
Aranguren
Cordillera Cantabrica
Embalse del Ebro
Fuentes Carrionas Nature Reserve
Mataporquera
Cervera
Ebro
Esla
León
Pisuerga
N
50 miles
SPAIN

9

Claro – Of course

BILBAO TO LEÓN

Not the Guggenheim – Alpine outlook – Sunflowers and death – León: occupying the square – Hard street to crack – Isidore arrives from Seville – A bowl for the dog

Not the Guggenheim

THE BULL JUMPED, surprisingly like a cat, on to the barrier round the arena and from there came crashing through a cement block wall and up into the seating. It headed up the tiers towards a back exit and then caught sight of a little girl, aged about four, in the aisle. She, quite rightly, ran, and was sheltered by the angle of a door when the bull went at her with its horns.

The beast then ran along a tier of seats, tossing a child aside as it charged into a crowd of people. A bullfighter pulled its tail, and another tried to distract it with a cape, but had to jump aside. Once the bull was clear of the crowd, a policeman drew his pistol and shot it dead.

This was all on the television news in a bar near the museum of fine art in Bilbao that September Wednesday lunchtime. No one took much notice. Accidents, corpses, war victims and cruelty are commonplace on Spanish television, and in any case television is more an atmospheric accompaniment than a focus of attention.

Bilbao, historically sympathetic to Britain, is proud of its transformation from industrial decay to something of a city of culture. It may not compare to many a Spanish city, but it is more pleasant to walk round than most in Britain.

The silvery sides of the Guggenheim museum, next to the double-highway bridge over the river Nervión, were looking yellow and tarnished in the autumn sun. The Guggenheim advises visitors to take a bus to the Plaza del Museo de Bellas Artes. The museum after which the plaza is named repays attention. Its collection includes great works and curiosities: El Greco, Ribera, Zurbarán, Goya, Gauguin, Sorolla, even Francis Bacon. Then there is Darío de Regoyos (1857–1913).

Several Spanish galleries own paintings by Regoyos, credited with introducing Impressionism into Spain from his sojourns in Brussels. The young Federico García Lorca was a great fan. None of his work is known to hang in a gallery in Britain. His most striking picture in Bilbao is *Viernes Santo en Castilla*.

This canvas, about 30 inches high, was finished in 1896, the year he was excitedly writing to Camille Pissarro about becoming a father. In the same year Pissarro painted the Pont Boieldieu in Rouen, with steam from a dock-crane rising above the iron bridge over the Seine. Regoyos had seen an opportunity to represent steam against sky too, but in his painting, the counterpoint of ancient and modern is bolder.

At an un-named spot in Castile, a religious confraternity, wrapped in sombre robes, walk in procession, each carrying a long candle of unbleached wax. They bear on a float a shrouded and crowned statue, perhaps of Nuestra Señora de los Dolores, Our Lady of Sorrows, on this, the saddest day of the Church calendar, Good Friday. Caught in that moment of time, the dark mass of a steam train, the emblem of modernity, roars over the bridge above them. It would have looked less absurd in 1896.

Alpine outlook

FOR THE TOURIST, the prettiest part of Bilbao is where the city first began: the Seven Streets, the Zazpi Kaleak in Basque, narrow and parallel, between the river and the medieval cathedral.

Under the shade of table umbrellas, smartly dressed ladies pulled apart seafood. The temperature was 86°F. A Neoclassical fountain like a fat gate-pier topped with an urn, and with a spout projecting from each of its four faces, went unremarked.

'Reinando Carlos III la N. Villa de Bilbao por el bien publico,' it was inscribed. 'Ano de MDCCLXXXV. Restaurada en 1915.'

The façade and tower of the ancient cathedral nearby date only from 1885, built in a Gothic revival style by Severino de Achúcarro. He is better remembered for Concordia station, an Art Nouveau extravaganza in coloured ironwork and stone built in 1902, on the opposite bank of the Nervión. Above its gate, ironwork lettering declared: 'FC de Santander a Bilbao' ('Railway from Santander to Bilbao').

'Is this the right station for León?'

'*Claro*,' answered a middle-aged woman in blouse, skirt and sensibly flat shoes. 'Of course.'

Henry Blackburn, travelling through Spain in 1864, soon learnt not to ask strangers the way. 'Travellers who depend upon being told what to do and where to go at the various stations and junctions are continually being left behind,' he wrote. 'This is not thought much of in Spain, and amuses the officials immensely.'

Blackburn was a prickly traveller, mistaking differences of culture for incivility. Most rules of life are unwritten. A

Spaniard visiting Italy is astonished to find that to buy a cup of coffee he must first pay a cashier, then take his receipt to the bar counter. The unspoken procedure in Spain is to order at the bar, eat and drink and then pay on leaving. The barman tenders change on a saucer or plastic disc made for the purpose. The memory and trust involved in all this might make the barman's job more difficult, but those are the rules of the game. Everyone, of course, knows them.

But Concordia was the right station for León, despite appearances, and the daily train for the city was preparing to leave at 14.30. It was kept upstairs (as at the Gare Montparnasse in Paris, where on 22 October 1895 the 08.45 from Granville ran through the buffers, sending the locomotive nosediving like a rogue bull into the street). The afternoon was hot, but the new carriages were air-conditioned. There was a seat free on the right-hand side, which on the journey west would be the northern, shady side. *Sol y sombra*, sun and shade, matter in trains as well as bullrings, though railway tickets cost no more for seats in the shade.

The width of the carriage accommodated only three seats across, for this was the Feve, the narrow-gauge railway. Unlike the wide trains of the standard Iberian gauge of 6 Castilian feet (5 feet 6 inches imperial), this train ran on rails only 3 feet 3⅜ inches apart, or, prosaically, 1 metre. The excitement of the anomalous gauge soon wore off, but the journey to León was spectacular in part, and was timetabled to take 7½ hours for the 208 miles, a speed of just under 28 mph.

As the train pulled out, an old lady crossed herself, not out of fear, but in the familiar custom of the kind of travellers who also say grace before meals. All meals are a gift; all life is a journey.

Piped music flutingly moaned the melody of *Moon River*. In Spain piped music is a curse to those who mind it; most Spaniards do not.

As it approached Aranguren, along meandering track, the gait of the train, despite its leisurely pace, became drunken. Cows in the fields paused in their chewing of the cud and stared as it bounced, bucked, bucketed, rolled, pitched and jolted.

The outlook was Alpine. There were chalets with wide eaves and painted beams and peppers drying on balconies.

The land was green, far different from the desiccated brown or straw-bleached expanses of the meseta further south. Above Balmaseda, 50 minutes from departure, the valley sides rose steep and pine-clad. The guard read *El Mundo*. The piped music played *Fly Me to the Moon*. An hour after departure, the train had made 25 miles.

It stopped below some spectacular sun-beaten crags, nerving itself to enter the station at Mercadillo. There, three people got off, then another, hurrying. He need not have rushed. The train stayed. Beside a plane tree, stood a pebbled pillar, with a tap on one side above a basin. A sunburnt man with earrings turned the tap, but no water came out.

There was a problem. The line was closed, for half an hour, the guard said. He sounded upset, his pride dented. He got out and walked over to a low wall in the shade. After a while, calmed, he got back on the train, with much self-exculpatory gesturing and sat in his seat again, giving *El Mundo* another try. A dozen people got off and stood about, in the shade. Only a man wearing a tie sat down, on a stone bench.

Spanish railway engineers are proud of getting trains to run like clockwork, but there are many enemies of promise: long distances, single-track lines, extremes of heat and cold, steep inclines, savage geology, cows. In 1866, Lady Herbert of Lea, travelling for her health, in mourning and shunned by society (even Gladstone) for having become a Catholic, was enjoying the scenery from her railway carriage when:

> Suddenly the train came to a standstill: an enormous fragment of rock had fallen across the line in the night, burying a luggage train; our party had no alternative but to get out, with our manifold bags and packages, and walk across the débris to another train, which, fortunately, was waiting on the opposite side of the chasm.

She soon learnt 'to expect such incidents half a dozen times in the course of a day's journey'.

Now, at Mercadillo, just as everyone was beginning to wonder about the availability of overnight lodgings in this quiet spot in rural Biscay, a goods train rumbled past in the opposite direction, and off we went. It was only half an hour, as the guard had said.

The train climbed, overlooking a wide valley, burying its head in the dark leafiness of beech, oak and chestnut woods, then out into broad day where grassland ran below sharp crags. We were in high Castile now, and winter ski-slopes were not far away.

A passenger succeeded in stopping the train at the request stop (*parada discrecional*) at Quintana de los Prados. As the westering sun shone in the train-driver's eyes, the Feve line followed the dammed course of the infant Ebro and, at Mataporquera, crossed the standard-gauge line that goes north to Santander, and south to Palencia.

Mataporquera is a name that suggests the killing of pigs, the *matanza* of November. The *porquera* element in the name is porcine, right enough, though the reference would be to wild boar. The *mata-* element does not mean 'kill'. It is an old Iberian word for a 'stretch of forest'. So Mataporquera would be 'Hogwood' in English.

As the train stumbled on, passengers got off, station by station. After three hours, it had been left half full. The effect of the gentle progress was slightly hypnotic. Little by little the landscape changed, from chestnut woods to rough pasture, from boulder-strewn slopes to treeless, scorched grassland. Despite the soothing cradle-rock of the carriage, not many people would want to sit on a train with no buffet (though with a lavatory at least) for seven or eight hours. A good plan for those with time is to get off in the emptiness of the countryside and stay somewhere overnight.

Cervera would do, near the border of Castile and Cantabria. There was a Parador there, a plain modern building among woods by a flooded river valley on the edge of the Fuentes Carrionas nature reserve, where brown bears survived and capercaillie were being reintroduced.

There were more common smaller creatures, lizards and a kind of grasshopper that showed metallic-blue wings when it jumped, and a little dung-beetle pulling a Malteser-sized sphere of dung. Autumn crocuses had sprung up in the grass.

Ten miles to the north was the sierra, cutting off access by road to the Liébana with its mountain-top relic of the True Cross, and, beyond, the Picos de Europa, rising above 8,500 feet.

The fare from Bilbao to Cervera had been only €9.70. It cost that amount for a taxi the four miles to the Parador. The ticket for the rest of the journey next day to León was €7.65. The booking clerk, in a black waistcoat, seemed to open up the ticket office especially to sell it. No one else was about.

As time passed before the train came, a man rode by on a combed and trimmed bay horse. A dog came sniffing along. A fly landed. A slightly drunk man with a moustache and a cold arrived, and settled down to read a grubby copy of *El Norte de Castilla* in the afternoon sun.

The remaining 60 miles to León was scheduled to take 3 hours and 19 minutes. After dark, as the train neared the capital of the Kingdom of Leon, it began to fill up a little. A group of five teenage girls chatted and giggled and sang and ate sunflower seeds.

Sunflowers and death

IT IS NOT EASY to eat sunflower seeds, *pipas*, neatly. The edible kernel lies inside the brittle, stripy shell, which is easily cracked with the teeth. The husk, of course, is blown away from the lips at the same time, on to the floor. So it is not unusual in cinemas, buses and trains to find patches of discarded husks like fallen leaves around an autumn tree. In context it is no more bad manners to do this than to throw the discarded head of a prawn on to the floor of a bar.

On the empty bag that the girls left was a picture of a bull with a sword lodged in its backbone and a boy dressed as a matador. Next to them were printed the words:

Y el toro dijo al morir
Siento dejar este mundo
sin probar pipas Facundo

And the bull said before it died:
'I go with one regret;

I leave the world but haven't tried
Facundo's pipas yet.'

It is a peculiarly Spanish approach: to appeal to young people through the medium of a philosophical bull, mortally wounded in the ring, regretting its lack of experience of sunflower seeds. The bull's plight is a matter of course.

The sunflower-seed company likes to tell its own story through the early commercial struggles of Facundo Blanco and his wife Dolores (Lola, for short) in the shop they opened on their marriage in 1944 at Villada in the province of Palencia. Villada, on the railway from León to Palencia (six trains a day each way) had a population then of well over 2,000, but is now barely 1,000. An annual fiesta is the Day of the Absent Villadan.

The Blancos' shop sold *frutos secos*, not dried fruits like figs and raisins, but peanuts and hazelnuts. The concept *frutos secos* overlaps with *golosinas*, 'sweets', and today a shop usually sells both. In the 1940s most goods were rationed, under state control; *frutos secos* were exempted.

In 1950, Facundo and Lola rigged up a cart (with little wheels fitted with pneumatic tyres), painted with the trade name 'Facundo' and pulled by their donkey, Baldomero, to attract publicity at the local fair. The company expanded, as the century passed, diversifying into cheese balls and potato needles.

Villada named a street after Facundo Blanco after his death in 1990. In 2006, when his widow died, another street was named Calle Facundo y Lola. In the Plaza de Santa María, a hideous monument was erected to the *pipa*, with a leaning column of whitewashed bricks supporting a giant sunflower seed.

In the year of Doña Lola's death, the workers in her factory played an heroic role in helping passengers injured in a train crash. That Monday, 21 August 2006, at six minutes to four in the afternoon, a six-carriage train from Galicia, bound for Bilbao, carrying 426 passengers, was derailed at Villada station, killing seven and injuring more than 100.

The train was called the Diurno Camino de Santiago. The *diurno,* 'daytime', is a type of long-distance stopping train, formerly called, without intended irony, a *rápido*. The journey would have been timetabled to take about 11 hours. Many of the 426 passengers were pilgrims returning from Santiago de Compostela.

The train was supposed to negotiate points at the station in order to pass a local service. The official hypothesis later found that it was travelling too fast. The first and second carriages left the track and smashed into the pillars of the bridge over the line.

Workers from the nearby Facundo factory climbed over the fence to help the injured, and a makeshift field-hospital was set up until ambulances arrived. The only chemist in the town helped with first aid and dressings. Afterwards it emerged that the Facundo company, with neighbourly tact, had quietly reimbursed the generous pharmacist for the stock he'd lost.

León: occupying the square

AN HOUR BEFORE midnight a lorry drew up in the deserted Plaza Mayor in León and men jumped out from the tailgate as if members of an occupying army. That day, there had been news on television of the Indignados, protesters against the economic crisis, loosely allied with the 15-M and Occupy movements, with their slogan *Toma la Plaza* – Take the Squares.

The men in the square, dressed in T-shirts and combat trousers, began assembling tents. It was done with precision. Four steel struts were laid out on the marble paving and connected into a rectangle, with four diagonal struts making a pyramidal roof, to be covered with canvas and then raised on legs.

The process was practised. This was no sudden occupation, but the regular preparation for the weekly market. Tented canopy after tented canopy was set up, in rows across the wide space. The men were still at it at 1.30 a.m. It is impossible to erect a steel-framed stall on a stone pavement quietly, and those with bedrooms around the square either get used to it or stay awake. A moon sharp as a nail-paring hung among the television aerials on the roofs.

By 9.30 next morning the market was in full swing in the bright sun, with fat onions so white and smooth they looked like china, blotchy pears, perky lettuces, mushrooms with compost still on their fungal roots, piles of peppers fat and folded or long and twisted, glossy aubergines and white-flowered herbs labelled *azar*. Oranges for juice were going for 65 *céntimos* a kilo, big new potatoes slightly dearer at 70 *céntimos* a kilo.

The market brought people and movement to the great square, bounded by three-storey stone houses with continuous wrought-iron balconies on the first floor, and individual balconies outside each window on the second. The square was built in the 1670s, when Charles II was on the throne in England, and with it the old Casa Consistorial, in the Herreran style, with a nod to the town hall in Toledo, encrusted with iron balconies and sporting finials on its twin towers.

By the last decade of the twentieth century the square was in a sorry state. In 1989, one house was shored up with timbers, and another, next to the police station, quite ruinous. In a street off the square, a butcher sold horsemeat for food. Now, it had disappeared, and, with a chain hotel on the side opposite the Casa Consistorial, the square looked spruce, for all the national economic crisis.

On a stone bench running along its wall, public functionaries took a break from their recondite duties and an old lady sat tranquilly, her handbag on her lap, as the market swung on. In an old-fashioned bar in one corner the proprietress walked with an arthritic gait over to the machine to make cups of *café cortado* and pour little glasses of the colourless spirit *orujo* (made, like *marc*, from the leftovers of grape-pressings). As for the crisis, she shared a joke about it with the customers. What else could she do?

Hard street to crack

OFF THE PLAZA MAYOR in León, the Calle Cascalería ran towards the Calle Azabachería. *Azabache* simply means 'jet', and this is where it was sold. Between the ends of the two streets ran a line of shops with their backs against the old walls of the city, which date from Roman times. The stone ramparts were visible above a single-storey haberdasher's called Mar y

Mar, where stickers in the window announced a final sale, long past, which had marked the end of the business.

Cascalería is a harder name to crack. Roberto Cubillo in his book on food in León in the eighteenth century, says that it may come from *casca* meaning 'the bark of a tree', as used by tanners. Or, he suggests, it comes from *casca* as meaning the remnants of pressed grapes, from which *orujo* is made (as sold in the bar nearby). According to the journalist and historian Máximo Cayón Waldaliso (1921–87, after whom another street in León is named), Cascalería refers to *casquería*, which in English is 'offal'.

Someone who would have been very interested in finding out which was the right answer lay just round the corner. Isidore of Seville did more than most people to make Spain what it is. He was also one of the most influential writers in the history of European civilisation. He lived a hundred years before England's St Bede, dying in 636, and is buried, not in Seville, where he reigned as bishop, but in the church in León now dedicated to his name.

Isidore's fame in Europe spread through his book called the *Etymologies*, found in every monastic library that preserved ancient learning through thin times. (The oldest book in the library that Samuel Pepys proudly built up was a twelfth-century manuscript of the *Etymologies*.) It can too easily be dismissed as a book that foolishly confuses the origins of words with their current meanings. But Isidore intended to wield four grammatical weapons to anatomise meaning, and thus the world where meaning finds its place.

The four weapons were: difference, gloss, analogy and etymology. Claudia Di Sciacca, in her study of Isidore's earlier book *Synonyma*, as used in Anglo-Saxon England (and it is worth noting that learning travelled great distances in the supposedly Dark Ages), quotes his own explanation of the function of difference in arriving at the property of the object of investigation. Thus, 'man (*homo*) is an animal – rational, mortal, terrestrial, two-footed and able to laugh'.

The notion of differences that Isidore explored was not shallow. Ludwig Wittgenstein once said that he had been disappointed that 'Hegel seems to me to be always wanting to say that things which look different are really the same. Whereas my interest is in showing that things which look the same are really different.' Isidore, if not doing the same thing as Wittgenstein, was interested in things and what could be said of them with words. His work could be characterised by the motto that the twentieth-century thinker had considered using for his book that became known as *Philosophical Investigations*, a sentence from *King Lear*: 'I'll teach you differences.'

Isidore arrives from Seville

SO LEON IS the place to come to do homage to Isidore. The way that he got here was accidental in the extreme, or so it seemed. King Ferdinand I of Leon (who died in the year before the Battle of Hastings), once he had stopped waging war against the King of Navarre, found some success in exerting pressure on the Arab half of the peninsula, which since the collapse of the Caliphate of Cordoba, 30 years earlier, had been divided into a patchwork of kingdoms, or taifas as modern historians like to call them.

In 1063 he despatched two bishops to Seville to collect the relics of St Justa. Santa Justa is now the name of the main railway station in Seville, but she meant more to Spanish Christians of the Middle Ages. With her sister Rufina she was identified with the so-called Mozarabic liturgy – the Latin Mass and church services used by Christians under Arabic rule.

These two martyrs of the third century, so their legend said, died for refusing to give money towards a feast in honour of the goddess Venus. This story appealed to Christians living under a form of Muslim rule that was often abrasive at least. Indeed a more recent martyr, St Pelagius (San Pelayo in Spanish) had been put to death as a prisoner of Abd al-Rahman in 925, for refusing his advances. To him, together with St John the Baptist, the royal church in León was dedicated. It was sacked in 988 by the Moorish general known as Almanzor.

So King Ferdinand, in amplifying the royal church, wanted the relics of St Justa to be honoured there, not left to the vicissitudes of Muslim rule. The fact that, about this time, al-Mu'tadid Ibn Abbad, the King of Seville, had thought it wise to pay tribute to Ferdinand, may have eased negotiations.

The anonymous contemporary chronicler of these events, a monk from Santo Domingo de Silos, gave the Arab ruler's name as Benahabet, a Latinisation of Ibn Abbad. When Ferdinand's envoys, Bishop Alvito of León and Bishop Ordoño of Astorga, arrived in Seville, Benahabet told them he was terribly sorry but he couldn't find the remains of St Justa anywhere.

Bishop Alvito, not to be discouraged, set about praying, and while at prayer fell asleep, and in a dream St Isidore himself appeared, banging on the floor with his staff where, he said, his body was buried. Sure enough, at the spot indicated they found a coffin, inside which, from the remains of a man, came a most sweet smell. But no sooner was the coffin opened, says the chronicler, than Bishop Alvito was struck down by sickness, and died within a week.

Undeterred, his brother bishop brought back to León the body of St Isidore, as a substitute for that of St Justa, wrapped in a piece of tapestry given by al-Mu'tadid. The church of St John and St Pelagius was renamed after St Isidore, San Isidoro. (Still preserved there, are a couple of liturgical stoles, a curious link with England, prettily woven for this church by Queen Eleanor – Leonor in Spanish – the daughter of Eleanor of Aquitaine and Henry II of England, and the wife of Alfonso VIII of Castile, whom she came over the sea to marry aged 10, living as his consort for 44 years, until his death in 1214, which hers closely followed.)

The relics of St Isidore were later given an ornate sarcophagus, and so the eleventh-century casket in which they had been laid in 1063 was put on display in the treasury. It is lined with a beautiful silk textile, with stylised birds and animals embroidered within squares. This, say some archaeologists, could be the tapestry that al-Mu'tadid gave. And why not?

A bowl for the dog

THERE WAS SOMETHING more striking at the church of San Isidoro than the last resting place of the saint. He now lies in an unremarkable nineteenth-century silver coffer, the reliquary that replaced al-Mu'tadid's box having been stolen by the French in 1808, when they took the trouble to dig up the graves of ancient monarchs of Leon too.

Most tourists to León head straight for the stained-glass windows of the cathedral. They do not disappoint. But the wall paintings in the church of San Isidoro are a wonder of a rarer kind. They cover the roof of the narthex, the lower, arched chamber before the entrance to the church proper, as at St Mark's Venice. So they can be examined not too far away from the head of the visitor, unlike the cathedral windows, the details of which, even with binoculars, are difficult to make out.

In the six vaults of the narthex the murals look like large-sized illuminations from a manuscript. They date from the mid-twelfth century. The most majestic is the central figure of Christ enthroned within an almond-shaped frame known as a mandorla, holding his right hand up in blessing, and an open book in his left hand with pages inscribed *Ego sum lux mundi* – I am the light of the world. His feet are to the east, his head to the west, making him seem to face towards the altar of the church, where Isidore lies.

In the four corners of the vault with Christ in majesty stand robed figures with wings. Each holds a book, and their heads are those of a man, an ox, a lion and an eagle. Beside each, in sinuous Romanesque capitals, are helpful captions in a language not quite classical Latin nor yet modern Spanish – *Mateus Omo*; *Lucas Vitulo*; *Marcus Leo; Johannes Aquila* – for the four beasts, as mentioned in the book of Daniel and the Apocalypse, represent the four Evangelists.

Some of the vaults are in less good condition, but one that impresses with its colours and poise shows an angel appearing to the shepherds at the birth of Jesus: *Angelus a pastores,* its caption says. One shepherd sits on his cloak playing pan-pipes, holding his crook with the curved end downwards, like a hockey-stick. Next to him, another seated shepherd holds out a bowl from which his mastiff laps. Two sharp-horned goats rear up fighting in a corner and three pigs look up to acorns falling from an oak. Next to the angel, sheep graze, one with a bell attached to a sort of halter round its ears and nose.

On an arch of the narthex 12 roundels depict the labours of the months: grapes picked and put into a heavy-looking bucket for September; a pig fed on acorns for October and a fatter-looking pig held by the ear to be slaughtered in November. Everything is composed, mannered, emblematic and framed.

In a section devoted to the Passion of Christ, Peter is shown cutting off the ear of the High Priest's servant. Pilate washes his hands under a small shower of water from a vessel like a sugar-sifter, held by a boy above a basin. Peter is also shown later, after his denial of Jesus, weeping. *Petrus flevi*, says the caption, and in a frame on a pendentive opposite him a cock crows.

SPAIN
Burgos
Palencia
Lerma
Pisuerga
Valladolid
Duero
Aranda de Duero
Duero
Medina del Campo
Adaja
Somosierra Tunnel
Sierra de Guadarrama
Gascones
Buitrago de Lozoya
N
Arévalo
25 miles
Avila
El Escorial
Colmenar
Chamartín
Ramón y Cajal
Recoletos
Sierra de Gredos
MADRID

10

Esperar – Waiting

BURGOS TO MADRID

A bar from 'Casablanca' – No lamb at Lerma – The Fitzrovia factor – Last stop before the end

A bar from 'Casablanca'

ON THE WINDOW-SILL of the booking hall at Aranda de Duero station lay a dead bee and a dead moth. The ticket-window was closed. The idea was to catch the 12.44 to Madrid, the only train to run that day, except for the one train that ran in the other direction. There were no passengers waiting, no departure signs, no evidence that a train would ever come. Donkeys grazed the waste land outside.

But the train did at least arrive at Aranda, only 25 minutes late on its long haul from the Atlantic coast. It was a Talgo, one of those low-slung, silver-bodied expresses first built when the film *Casablanca* was newly released.

The old-fashioned bar of chrome and wood served drinks as the landscape changed, quite quickly, from rolling fields to deep valleys filled with mist and pine trees. At 3.20 p.m., announcements, one in Basque for those who'd joined the train at Bilbao and might be feeling homesick, told us we were at Chamartín, the northern terminus of Madrid.

That was in 2007. Now it is impossible to catch that train from Bilbao via Burgos. The route had been planned as part of a direct trajectory due north from the capital to the French frontier, instead of going on a westward diversion via Avila and Valladolid.

Spanish railways had always tended to join up cities like stars in constellations, sending passengers by very indirect routes.

The mechanism of government backing for railway companies in the nineteenth century positively encouraged wandering lines, as subsidies were calculated by kilometres covered.

The direct route from Burgos to Madrid was included in the Priority Plan for the Urgent Construction of Railways drawn up in 1926 by the Count of Guadalhorce, the minister of development during the dictatorship of Miguel Primo de Rivera. What with one thing and another – the Civil War, the hungry forties, the difficulty of the terrain, which included the mountains of the central Cordillera – it was not completed until 1968.

A plaque was unveiled at Burgos declaring: 'Francisco Franco, Caudillo of Spain, inaugurated the Madrid-Burgos railway, 4 July 1968. Kilometre 282.149.' It was either the last thread connecting dictatorship with modernity or a wave on the tide of technocracy that would sweep away the sandcastle.

The physical barriers to construction made the line spectacular to travel on. Among its many viaducts, the 270-yard stretch over the river Riaza arched 190 feet above the canyon. The longest of its 44 tunnels bored through the Guadarrama mountains for 4,260 yards at the Somosierra pass (where the road reaches an altitude of 4,724 feet).

Then, in 2008, a collapse inside the Somosierra tunnel led to the closure of the line, although, north of the tunnel, it is still used for freight from Aranda to Burgos. The 15 miles from Madrid to Colmenar serve too for commuter trains.

Even shorter-lived than the international link to France through the tunnel at Canfranc (which lasted from 1928 to 1970, 42 years), the Madrid-Burgos direct line, 1968–2008, expired at the age of 40.

No lamb at Lerma

SO THE OLD indirect route from Burgos to Madrid has triumphed. It goes through some remarkable places: Arévalo and Avila, Palencia and El Escorial. It was on this route that the English traveller Henry Blackburn noticed in 1864 that the sunrise over the Guadarrama mountains gave 'just that effect that Holman Hunt strove to render in his picture *The*

Scapegoat. Warmth of colour and cold photographic hardness – almost harshness – of form and outline, with a background of the most delicate blue.'

That you may still see, but there is no way now to take a train to Lerma, that astonishing Baroque toy-set of monumental architecture built in the middle of empty countryside by the 1st Duke of Lerma when Shakespeare was alive – or then to eat the excellent local lamb cooked in a wood-fired oven at the *asador* in the great square.

The mountainside stations on the direct route are falling into ruin – San Mamés, on the road to nowhere, or Gascones, the stop for Buitrago de Lozoya, a walled town encircled by rivers and named after the vultures that wheel above it.

Now, the 'Intercity' train from Burgos at 8.32 a.m. takes 4 hours and 36 minutes to reach Madrid. There isn't another until 11.36, so in the meantime the timetable suggests going in the opposite direction to Zaragoza and changing there. That means travelling 400 miles instead of 200, but it only takes five hours, because the new high speed train from Zaragoza to Madrid is so quick.

The high-speed trains have cut travel time astonishingly, at least on paper. It is now only half an hour from Madrid to Segovia, where the train used to take two hours. But the high-speed train drops you in a field full of storks miles outside Segovia, and at the Madrid ends stops short at Chamartín, on the northern side of the city, instead of carrying on as before, under the centre and stopping at Recoletos, conveniently near the Prado.

The high-speed lines, built with money from the European Union as well as from the central government, seemed to save the railways of Spain, which towards the end of the twentieth century were seeing their own version of Britain's Beeching axe, lopping off branch lines and leaving even provincial capitals like Soria out on a limb.

But investment in fast lines, built to the international gauge, incompatible with the Iberian gauge of the existing lines, left the little stations to decay. The implicit idea was that business users of fast city-to-city trains would drive to the station or be taken by taxi. Villagers, even townspeople, with their own station, would in future have to travel into a city – Zaragoza, say – and then perhaps back again on the fast train to Madrid.

The Fitzrovia factor

THE BRIGHT YELLOW dustjacket of *A Train to Tarragona* by Anthony Carson shows a uniformed Guardia Civil smoking a cigarette. The jacket was designed by Charles Mozley (1914–91), a book illustrator in much demand, and if, in 1957, Methuen paid him what he got from Norah Smallwood at Chatto, he'd have received a cheque for 15 guineas.

Anthony Carson's real name was Peter Brooke (1907–73), and he was a regular at the Wheatsheaf public house in Fitrovia, which is to say, Soho north of Oxford Street. His humorous book was about Tarragona, of course, not trains, and the people with whom he became friends there hardly knew what to make of this single Englishman in his late forties much given to drink and the life of a writer.

One insight of Carson's book was that Spanish people are always waiting. There is something in this, as in all the other stereotypes, about their solipsism, fascination with death, hospitality, cruelty, politeness, endurance, mysticism and pride.

They wait. Everything else – talking, eating, drinking, dancing, working, reading, singing, sleeping, even love and marriage – is just something to do while they are waiting.

Certainly the Spanish are very good at waiting for trains, and always arrive in plenty of time, to get stuck into the waiting before the train is due. The waiting-room and *cafetería* are often busy even when no more trains are expected that day, and there is nothing specifically left to wait for. 'Oh! the misery of those wayside stations in Spain,' wrote Lady Herbert in 1866, stranded at one in the small hours of the morning. 'One long low room filled with smokers and passengers of every class, struggling for chocolate, served in dirty cups by uncivil waiters, with insufficient seats.' Civility, of a cheerful kind, has generally returned, but the smoke has gone.

Last stop before the end

THE LAST STOP before the terminus at Chamartín is called Ramón y Cajal. It serves the big teaching hospital next to it of that name, but every city in Spain has its Calle Ramón y Cajal. He was a hero who stood for the modernity of Spain, his instrument the microscope, the prime emblem of scientific discovery.

This was the intelligent new world portrayed by Joaquín Sorolla in his painting *Una Investigación* (1897). The painting portrays not Cajal, but Luis Simarro, who ten years earlier had shown Cajal the staining technique with silver chromate that made his microscopic researches possible.

Sorolla's canvas depicts just the scene of exciting empirical discovery that caught the imagination of a young generation liberated in its own eyes from the Church and traditional society. It was a sort of Spanish enlightenment. Light is Sorolla's medium and metaphor.

The lighting and coloration have been compared to those of Sorolla's hero Velázquez. The oil lamp with its swathed chimney throws light on to the laboratory bench crowded with glass-stoppered bottles of chemicals, where the bearded scientist in his white coat delicately manipulates his sample, while, craning over their stiff shirt collars, his colleagues and students focus on the research, deep into the night, lit by the reflected light.

Santiago Ramón y Cajal (1852–1934) was awarded the Nobel Prize for his work in histology, the microscopic study of organic tissue. But it is a wonder that he survived to win it. As a boy be built a cannon that exploded. He fell through the ice one winter. A bolt of lightning struck his schoolroom. A horse smashed its hoof into his skull. He engaged in knife-fights and was knocked down by stone slingshots. He was prostrated by dysentery and malaria.

Once he had survived into adulthood, he came to stand for the best of nineteenth-century scientific rationalism. As a child he represented the irrepressible vitality of the Spanish picaresque hero.

Ramón y Cajal, as a scientist, made his leading discoveries in the last quarter of the nineteenth century, and they represented everything at odds with the image of Spain as backward, isolated, obscurantist, credulous and incapable of progress. In his memoirs he often quotes Herbert Spencer, but he never mentions going to church.

His sought the secrets of the mind in the minute structures of the brain. Cajal, as he called himself, choosing to go by his second, his mother's, surname, wrote many scientific papers, which by force of their brilliant observation slowly penetrated the non-Hispanic world. He wrote scientistic short stories too and collections of aperçus, but nothing he wrote is as vivid as his memoir *My Infancy and Youth* (1901).

Cajal claimed to have inherited from his father

> traits of character to which I owe everything that I am: a profound belief in the sovereign will; faith in work; the conviction that a persevering and deliberate effort is capable of moulding and organising everything, from the muscles to the brain.

But the first 17 years of his life saw unrelenting warfare between himself and his father, and with the world. He recounted it all without recrimination and with quiet irony. He looked back without affection on the poor part of rural Aragon (technically an enclave of Navarre within Aragon) where he was born, and the villages of Larrés, near Sabiñánigo, and Luna, near nowhere, which today boast a population even smaller than the one he knew as a boy.

To present-day travellers this countryside towards the foothills of the Pyrenees appears charming and impressive by turns; to him it was 'characteristically desolate and dismal', deforested and prone to flash flooding. It was in Luna that the horse kicked him in the head, when he was three or four. He had tried to hit it. 'The wound was very serious, but I recovered.'

The young Santiago, however, did not torture animals, like some of his playmates, as he noted in his memoir. He was drawn to study nature, he recalled, by his habitual shyness. 'How often we go to the café,' he wrote of later life, 'and come away with a dejection of the spirit.'

His father, a barber-surgeon, was driven by a desire for self-improvement, and saved up to go to Madrid to qualify as a doctor of medicine. Before he left, he taught the boy French, holding the classes in an abandoned shepherd's cave. It was a period of tranquillity seldom to be repeated in the subsequent decade.

For all his shyness, the young Santiago became a gang leader, adept at fashioning bows and arrows. His father, on his return, responded to his naughtiness with beatings, beginning with a whip and ending with cudgels. Schools were chosen with the object of knocking his rebellion out of him.

He did not mind, he insists in retrospect, being locked in an empty room. He became accustomed to missing meals while in disgrace, simply growing thinner as the term progressed. Nothing could cure his inattentiveness at school and his doodling in the margins of his books (since he dreamt of being an artist). 'The furious blows of the strap sounded in my head like a doorknocker in an empty house.'

Cajal's ingenious nature led him at the age of 11 to fashion a cannon out of an old beam. It worked so well that its charge smashed the gate of a neighbouring smallholder, whose complaint to the mayor of the town landed the boy in a damp and infested jail cell, where he was left without food for three or four days until his mother had some smuggled in.

This did not deter the young Santiago, whose improved home-made cannon blew up, sending a splinter of metal into his eye, permanently scarring his iris. Sent to board at Huesca, he encountered bullying and fought back with determination, by building up his muscles in the school holidays.

His father's next move was to apprentice him (aged 14, when he still saw himself as an artist and a romantic hero from Dumas) to a barber. There he listened avidly to revolutionary talk, learnt to play the guitar poorly and studied the art of the knife-fight. With a gold coin found in the street he bought a pistol.

Pursued by police armed with swords (which they generally used in order to given delinquents a pasting with the flat of the blade), he held them off through his expertise with the sling-shot, wounding one policeman badly enough to send him to bed for several days. In their battle of wills, his father then apprenticed him to a shoemaker.

In the attempted revolution of 1867, Cajal saw defeated and dying soldiers after skirmishes at Linás de Marcuello and Ayerbe, in rural Aragon. He was struck by the transformation wrought by death: 'How distressing is the indifference with which Nature casts away, like vile dross, the masterpiece of creation, the sublime cerebral mirror in which it gains consciousness of itself.'

Allowed to return to school the next year, he was violently expelled from the classroom by a clerically inclined master whose caricature he had painted on a wall. 'I was not disheartened,' he declared in true picaresque spirit, 'in spite of everything.'

The turning-point came at the age of 16, when he began to learn from his father the anatomy of human bones. To gather material for study they raided a local cemetery together by night. When the young Cajal aired his osteological knowledge in front of his father's medical friends, 'I remember how great were his pride and pleasure.'

Despite one last engagement in gang warfare at the age of 17, Cajal had at last turned his mind to practical research, abetted by his artistic skill in recording what the microscope showed. This was his road to eminence as a neurologist.

The Nobel Prize that he shared with Camillo Golgi was for their work on the structure of the nervous system. Strangely, they contradicted each other in the Nobel lectures that they delivered on being given the prize. Golgi, an Italian psychiatrist who sought the causes of mental illnesses in the anatomy of the brain, was convinced the nervous system was not made up of independent cells or neurons but functioned as a continuous network.

Cajal saw neurons (which he had drawn so carefully through the microscope) as entities transmitting nerve currents from one to another by 'a sort of induction or influence at a distance'. Cajal was, among all his contemporaries, the most persevering and accurate in his observations.

His last quarter century was as a grand old man of science, never forsaking the microscope, but often called upon to receive honours and deliver lectures. Patriotism, liberalism and science had met and thriven in one man's life.

From middle age, Cajal complained of weak health, but he lived to 82. A lined pocket-notebook, in which he entered daily observations in a small, neat hand, went on show at the popular exhibition called 'Brains', at the Wellcome Collection, London, in 2012. On 16 October 1934, on a right-hand page, he noted: 'I cannot keep down coffee.' At the bottom of the page, in a different hand, his son noted that in the early hours of the next day he breathed his last. Beyond the grave lay the street-signs in his honour, and the last station before the terminus. '*Chamartín,*' the announcement says, '*fin de trayecto*.'

Bibliography

Albareda, Anselm M. (1974), *Historia de Montserrat* (Montserrat: Publicacions de L'Abadia de Montserrat).

Alemán, Mateo (1924), *The Rogue or the Life of Guzmán de Alfarache,* translated by James Mabbe (London: Constable).

Arnaldo, Javier ed. (2006), *Sargent/Sorolla* (Madrid: Turner).

Beevor, Antony (2004), *The Spanish Civil War* (London: Cassell).

Biarge, Fernando (2004), *Mallos: Un Relieve Emblemático* (Huesca: Iniciativas sobre Espacios Naturales de Huesca).

Blackburn, Henry (1866), *Travelling in Spain in the Present Day* (London: Sampson Low, Son & Marston). Available free online through Google Books.

Bozal, Valeriano and others (2002), *Darío de Regoyos* (Madrid, Fundación Cultural Mapfre Vida).

Brenan, Gerald (2010), *The Face of Spain* (London: Serif).

Byron, George Gordon, Lord (1981), *Childe Harold's Pilgrimage*, Jerome J. McGann ed. (Oxford: Clarendon Press).

Cajal, Santiago Ramón y (1989), *Recollections of My Life* (Cambridge, MA: MIT Press).

Calatrava, Juan and others (2011), *Owen Jones y la Alhambra* (Granada: Patronato de la Alhambra).

Carson, Anthony (1957), *A Train to Tarragona* (London: Methuen).

Cayón Waldaliso, Máximo (1986), *Tradiciones Leonesas* (León: Everest).

Celdrán, Pancracio (2002), *Diccionario de Topónimos Españoles* (Madrid: Espasa).

Cervantes, Miguel de (1881), 'Rinconete y Cortadillo' in *Exemplary Novels*, translated by Walter K. Kelly (London:

George Bell and Sons). Available free online through Project Gutenberg.

Clifford, Henry (1887), *The Life of Jane Dormer, Duchess of Feria,* Joseph Stevenson ed. (London: Burns and Oates).

Corominas, Joan (1980), *Diccionario Crítico Etimológico Castellano e Hispánico* (Madrid: Editorial Gredos).

Courtauld, Simon (1996), *Spanish Hours* (London: Libri Mundi Publishing).

Cubillo, Roberto (2009), *Comer en León. Un siglo de Historia: 1700–1800* (León: University of León).

Cuevas, Pedro José (2000), *Cuenca* (Cuenca: Editorial Alfonsípolis).

Davidson, Alan (1992), *The Tio Pepe Guide to the Seafood of Spain and Portugal* (London: Gonzalez Byass).

Di Sciacca, Claudia (2008), *Finding the Right Words: Isidore's 'Synonyma' in Anglo-Saxon England* (Toronto: University of Toronto Press).

Duffy, Eamon (1992), *The Stripping of the Altars* (London: Yale Universtiy Press).

Emery, Gilles and Matthew Levering (2011), *The Oxford Handbook of the Trinity* (Oxford: Oxford University Press).

Enciclopedia del Románico en Castilla y León (2002), (Aguilar de Campoo: Fundación Santa María la Real).

Espín Rael, Joaquín (1999), 'La Piedra Miliaria Augustal y la Lápida Sepulcral de L. Rubellius, de Lorca' in *Miscelánea in Memoriam Joaquín Espín Rael* (Lorca, Asociación de Amigos del Museo Arqueológico de Lorca).

Fernández Gracia, Ricardo and Francisco Javier Roldán Marrodán (2006), *La Capilla del Espíritu Santo de la Catedral de Tudela* (Pamplona: Gobierno de Navarra).

Ferry, Kathryn (2007), 'Owen Jones and the Alhambra Court at the Crystal Palace' in *Revisiting Al-Andalus*, Glaire D. Anderson and Mariam Rosser-Owen (eds) (Leiden: Brill).

Fisher, Tyler (2011), 'Giants on Parade, Tyrants Aflame in Quevedo's Sonnet, "Desengaño de la exterior apariencia"' in *On Wolves and Sheep: Exploring the Expression of Political Thought in Golden Age Spain*, Aaron Kahn ed. (Newcastle: Cambridge Scholars).

Floro, Lázaro (pseudonym of José Sanchís) (1909), *Descripción é Historia del Miguelete y sus Campanas* (Valencia: Manuel Pan).

Ford, Richard (1966), *A Handbook for Travellers in Spain, 1845* (London: Centaur Press).

—(2010), *Gatherings from Spain* (London: Pallas Athene).

Halsall, Guy (2010), *Humour, History and Politics in Late Antiquity and the Early Middle Ages* (Cambridge: Cambridge University Press).

Harvey, John (1957), *The Cathedrals of Spain* (London: Batsford).

Herbert, Lady (1867) *Impressions of Spain* (London: Richard Bentley).

Howse, Christopher (2011), *A Pilgrim in Spain* (London: Continuum).

Irving, Washington (1951), *Tales of the Alhambra* (Granada: Padre Suarez).

Isidore (2006), *The Etymologies of Isidore of Seville* trans Stephen A. Barney, W. J. Lewis, J. A. Beach, Oliver Berghof, with the collaboration of Muriel Hall (Cambridge: Cambridge University Press).

—(1989), *Isidori Hispalensis Episcopi Etymologiarum sive Originum*, W. M. Lindsay ed. (Oxford: Clarendon Press).

—(2004), *Etimologías*, José Oroz Reta and Manuel-A. Marcos Casquero ed. (Madrid: BAC).

James, M. R. (1930), *Suffolk and Norfolk* (London: J. M. Dent).

Jones, Owen (1856), *The Grammar of Ornament* (London: Day & Son).

Kavanagh, P. J. (1995), *The Perfect Stranger* (Manchester: Carcanet).

Lees-Milne, James (1960) *Baroque in Spain and Portugal* (London: Batsford).

Lockhart, J. G. (1856), *Ancient Spanish Ballads* (London: John Murray).

Lo Ré, Anthony G. (2002), *A Facsimile Edition of the First English Translations of Miguel de Cervantes Saavedra's 'El Ingenioso Hidalgo Don Quixote de la Mancha'* (Chapel Hill: University of North Carolina).

Mackenzie, Alexander Slidell (1831), *A Year in Spain* (London: John Murray).

Melero Moneo, María Luisa (1997), *Escultura Románica y del Primer Gótico de Tudela* (Tudela: Centro Cultural Castel Ruiz).

Menéndez Roblés, María Luisa et al. (2009), 'Sorolla and Velázquez' in *Dialogues: Sorolla & Velázquez* (Madrid: Ministerio de Cultura).

Morris, Jan (2008), *Spain* (London: Faber).

Morton, H. V. (1983), *A Stranger in Spain* (London: Methuen).

Norris, Margaret van Antwerp (1970–1), 'The Rejection of Desengaño', *Revista Hispánica Moderna* 36, Nos 1–2.

Ortega y Gasset, José (1991), *Cartas de un Joven Español* Soledad de Ortega ed. (Madrid: Ediciones El Arquero).

Pepys, Samuel (1935) *The Tangier Papers of Samuel Pepys* Edwin Chappell ed. (London: Navy Records Society).

Pritchett, V. S. (1954) *The Spanish Temper* (London: Chatto & Windus).

Rodero, Cristina García (1994) *Festivals and Rituals of Spain* (New York, NY: Harry N. Abrams).

Rowe, D. Trevor (1966), *Railway Holiday in Spain* (Newton Abbott: David and Charles).

Rubio Masa, Juan Carlos (2001), *El Mecenazgo Artístico de la Casa Ducal de Feria* (Mérida: Editora Regional de Extremadura).

Serlio, Sebastiano (1982) *The Five Books of Architecture: An Unabridged Reprint of the English Edition of 1611* (New York: Dover Publications).

Sitwell, Sacheverell (1950), *Spain* (London: Batsford).

SMC [Sister Mary Catherine] ed. (1954), *A Christology from the Sermons of St Vincent Ferrer* (London: Blackfriars).

Street, G. E. (1865), *Gothic Architecture in Spain* (London: John Murray).

Swinburne, Henry (1787), *Travels through Spain, in the Years 1775 and 1776* (London: Paul Elmsly). Available free online through Google Books.

Torres González, Begoña (2009), *Sorolla: Vida & Obra* (Madrid: Libsa).

Townsend, Joseph (1791), *A Journey through Spain in the*

Years 1786 and 1787 (London: C Dilly). Available free online through Google Books.

Tremlett, Giles (2006), *Ghosts of Spain: Travels through a Country's Hidden Past* (London: Faber).

Tudela (2006), *La Catedral de Tudela* (Pamplona: Gobierno de Navarra).

Vasari, Giorgio (1998), *The Lives of the Artists* trans. Julia Conway Bondanella and Peter Bondanella (Oxford: Oxford World's Classics).

Verner, Willoughby (1909), *My Life among the Wild Birds of Spain* (London: John Bale Sons and Danielson).

Vidal, Jacobo (2008), *Tortosa, El Patrimoni* (Benicarlo: Onada).

Acknowledgements

Robin Baird-Smith of Bloomsbury Continuum deserves more than thanks for his unfailing encouragement, and Joel Simons of Bloomsbury Continuum for his unflagging patience.

John Plumer, who drew the maps, never faltered.

Maurice Lipsedge kindly read the text and made only useful suggestions.

Tony Gallagher, the editor of *The Daily Telegraph*, looked benignly on my endeavours.

Rupert Shrive long ago introduced me to Valencia.

Juan José Insa Sánchez took the cover photograph of the little train from Jaca passing the big rocks of the Mallos at Riglos in the province of Huesca.

Index

Index